STUDY GUIDE

STUDY GUIDE

Richard O. Straub

University of Michigan, Dearborn

to accompany

The Developing Person
Through Childhood and Adolescence

EIGHTH EDITION

Kathleen Stassen Berger

WORTH PUBLISHERS

Study Guide
by Richard O. Straub
to accompany
Berger: **The Developing Person Through Childhood and Adolescence**, Eighth Edition

© 2009, 2006, 2002, 1999, 1995, 1989, 1984 by Worth Publishers

ISBN 10: 1-4292-1782-0
ISBN 13: 978-1-4292-1782-8

First printing

Worth Publishers
41 Madison Avenue
New York, NY 10010
www.worthpublishers.com

Contents

Preface

This Study Guide is designed for use with *The Developing Person Through Childhood and Adolescence*, Eighth Edition, by Kathleen Stassen Berger. It is intended to help you to evaluate your understanding of that material, and then to review any problem areas. "How to Manage Your Time Efficiently, Study More Effectively, and Think Critically" provides detailed instructions on how to use the textbook and this Study Guide for maximum benefit. It also offers additional study suggestions based on principles of time management, effective note-taking, evaluation of exam performance, and an effective program for improving your comprehension while studying from textbooks.

Each chapter of the Study Guide includes a Chapter Overview, a Chapter Review section to be completed after you have read the text chapter, and two review tests. Most sections of the Chapter Review also include several Application questions that evaluate your understanding of the text chapter's broader conceptual material and its application to real-world situations. Many sections also include one or more Study Tips and Think About It questions designed to engage your critical thinking skills and promote deeper reasoning about the material. In addition, one chapter in each section of the text includes a crossword puzzle that provides an alternative way of testing your understanding of the terms and concepts. For the two review tests, the correct answers are given, followed by textbook page references (so you can easily go back and reread the material), and complete explanations not only of why the answer is correct but also of why the other choices are incorrect.

I would like to thank Betty and Don Probert of The Special Projects Group for their exceptional work in all phases of this project. My thanks also to Sharon Prevost, Jenny Chiu, and Stacey Alexander for their skillful assistance in the preparation of this Study Guide. Finally, heartfelt thanks to Pam for sticking with me on this wonderful journey that has now lasted more than 30 years. We hope that our work will help you to achieve your highest level of academic performance in this course and to acquire a keen appreciation of human development.

Richard O. Straub
October 2008

How to Manage Your Time Efficiently, Study More Effectively, and Think Critically

How effectively do you study? Good study habits make the job of being a college student much easier. Many students, who *could* succeed in college, fail or drop out because they have never learned to manage their time efficiently. Even the best students can usually benefit from an in-depth evaluation of their current study habits.

There are many ways to achieve academic success, of course, but your approach may not be the most effective or efficient. Are you sacrificing your social life or your physical or mental health in order to get A's on your exams? Good study habits result in better grades *and* more time for other activities.

Evaluate Your Current Study Habits

To improve your study habits, you must first have an accurate picture of how you currently spend your time. Begin by putting together a profile of your present living and studying habits. Answer the following questions by writing *yes* or *no* on each line.

_____ 1. Do you usually set up a schedule to budget your time for studying, recreation, and other activities?

_____ 2. Do you often put off studying until time pressures force you to cram?

_____ 3. Do other students seem to study less than you do, but get better grades?

_____ 4. Do you usually spend hours at a time studying one subject, rather than dividing that time between several subjects?

_____ 5. Do you often have trouble remembering what you have just read in a textbook?

_____ 6. Before reading a chapter in a textbook, do you skim through it and read the section headings?

_____ 7. Do you try to predict exam questions from your lecture notes and reading?

_____ 8. Do you usually attempt to paraphrase or summarize what you have just finished reading?

_____ 9. Do you find it difficult to concentrate very long when you study?

_____ 10. Do you often feel that you studied the wrong material for an exam?

Thousands of college students have participated in similar surveys. Students who are fully realizing their academic potential usually respond as follows: (1) yes, (2) no, (3) no, (4) no, (5) no, (6) yes, (7) yes, (8) yes, (9) no, (10) no.

Compare your responses to those of successful students. The greater the discrepancy, the more you could benefit from a program to improve your study habits. The questions are designed to identify areas of weakness. Once you have identified your weaknesses, you will be able to set specific goals for improvement and implement a program for reaching them.

Manage Your Time

Do you often feel frustrated because there isn't enough time to do all the things you must and want to do? Take heart. Even the most productive and successful people feel this way at times. But they establish priorities for their activities and they learn to budget time for each of them. There's much in the saying "If you want something done, ask a busy person to do it." A busy person knows how to get things done.

If you don't now have a system for budgeting your time, develop one. Not only will your academic accomplishments increase, but you will actually find more time in your schedule for other activities. And you won't have to feel guilty about "taking time off," because all your obligations will be covered.

Establish a Baseline

As a first step in preparing to budget your time, keep a diary for a few days to establish a summary, or baseline, of the time you spend in studying, socializing, working, and so on. If you are like many students, much of your "study" time is nonproductive; you may sit at your desk and leaf through a book, but the time is actually wasted. Or you may procrastinate. You are always getting ready to study, but you rarely do.

Besides revealing where you waste time, your time-management diary will give you a realistic picture of how much time you need to allot for meals, commuting, and other fixed activities. In addition, careful records should indicate the times of the day when you are consistently most productive. Table 1 shows a sample time-management diary.

Plan the Term

Having established and evaluated your baseline, you are ready to devise a more efficient schedule. Buy a calendar that covers the entire school term and has ample space for each day. Using the course outlines provided by your instructors, enter the dates of all exams, term paper deadlines, and other important academic obligations. If you have any long-range personal plans (concerts, weekend trips, etc.), enter the dates on the calendar as well. Keep your calendar up to date and refer to it often. I recommend carrying it with you at all times.

Develop a Weekly Calendar

Now that you have a general picture of the school term, develop a weekly schedule that includes all of your activities. Aim for a schedule that you can live with for the entire school term. A sample weekly schedule, incorporating the following guidelines, is shown in Table 2.

1. Enter your class times, work hours, and any other fixed obligations first. *Be thorough.* Using information from your time-management diary, allow plenty of time for such things as commuting, meals, laundry, and the like.

Table 1   Sample Time-Management Diary

Activity	Time Completed	Duration Hours: Minutes
Monday		
Sleep	7:00	7:30
Dressing	7:25	:25
Breakfast	7:45	:20
Commute	8:20	:35
Coffee	9:00	:40
French	10:00	1:00
Socialize	10:15	:15
Videogame	10:35	:20
Coffee	11:00	:25
Psychology	12:00	1:00
Lunch	12:25	:25
Study Lab	1:00	:35
Psych. Lab	4:00	3:00
Work	5:30	1:30
Commute	6:10	:40
Dinner	6:45	:35
TV	7:30	:45
Study Psych.	10:00	2:30
Socialize	11:30	1:30
Sleep		

Prepare a similar chart for each day of the week. When you finish an activity, note it on the chart and write down the time it was completed. Then determine its duration by subtracting the time the previous activity was finished from the newly entered time.

2. Set up a study schedule for each of your courses. The study habits survey and your time-management diary will direct you. The following guidelines should also be useful.

(a) Establish regular study times for each course. The 4 hours needed to study one subject, for example, are most profitable when divided into shorter periods spaced over several days. If you cram your studying into one 4-hour block, what you attempt to learn in the third or fourth hour will interfere with what you studied in the first 2 hours. Newly acquired knowledge is like wet cement. It needs some time to "harden" to become memory.

(b) Alternate subjects. The type of interference just mentioned is greatest between similar topics. Set up a schedule in which you spend time on several *different* courses during each study session. Besides reducing the potential for interference, alternating subjects will help to prevent mental fatigue with one topic.

(c) Set weekly goals to determine the amount of study time you need to do well in each course. This will

Table 2   Sample Weekly Schedule

Time	Mon.	Tues.	Wed.	Thurs.	Fri.	Sat.
7–8	Dress Eat	Dress Eat	Dress Eat	Dress Eat	Dress Eat	
8–9	Psych.	Study Psych.	Psych.	Study Psych.	Psych.	Dress Eat
9–10	Eng.	Study Eng.	Eng.	Study Eng.	Eng.	Study Eng.
10–11	Study French	Free	Study French	Open Study	Study French	Study Stats.
11–12	French	Study Psych. Lab	French	Open Study	French	Study Stats.
12–1	Lunch	Lunch	Lunch	Lunch	Lunch	Lunch
1–2	Stats.	Psych. Lab	Stats.	Study or Free	Stats.	Free
2–3	Bio.	Psych. Lab	Bio.	Free	Bio.	Free
3–4	Free	Psych.	Free	Free	Free	Free
4–5	Job	Job	Job	Job	Job	Free
5–6	Job	Job	Job	Job	Job	Free
6–7	Dinner	Dinner	Dinner	Dinner	Dinner	Dinner
7–8	Study Bio.	Study Bio.	Study Bio.	Study Bio.	Free	Free
8–9	Study Eng.	Study Stats.	Study Psych.	Open Study	Open Study	Free
9–10	Open Study	Open Study	Open Study	Open Study	Free	Free

This is a sample schedule for a student with a 16-credit load and a 10-hour-per-week part-time job. Using this chart as an illustration, make up a weekly schedule, following the guidelines outlined here.

depend on, among other things, the difficulty of your courses and the effectiveness of your methods. Many professors recommend studying at least 1 to 2 hours for each hour in class. If your time-management diary indicates that you presently study less time than that, do not plan to jump immediately to a much higher level. Increase study time from your baseline by setting weekly goals [see (4)] that will gradually bring you up to the desired level. As an initial schedule, for example, you might set aside an amount of study time for each course that matches class time.

(d) Schedule for maximum effectiveness. Tailor your schedule to meet the demands of each course. For the course that emphasizes lecture notes, schedule time for a daily review soon after the class. This will give you a chance to revise your notes and clean up any hard-to-decipher shorthand while the material is still fresh in your mind. If you are evaluated for class participation (for example, in a language course), allow time for a review just before the class meets. Schedule study time for your most difficult (or least motivat-

ing) courses during hours when you are the most alert and distractions are fewest.

(e) Schedule open study time. Emergencies, additional obligations, and the like could throw off your schedule. And you may simply need some extra time periodically for a project or for review in one of your courses. Schedule several hours each week for such purposes.

3. After you have budgeted time for studying, fill in slots for recreation, hobbies, relaxation, household errands, and the like.

4. Set specific goals. Before each study session, make a list of specific goals. The simple note "7–8 PM: study psychology" is too broad to ensure the most effective use of the time. Formulate your daily goals according to what you know you must accomplish during the term. If you have course outlines with advance assignments, set systematic daily goals that will allow you, for example, to cover fifteen chapters before the exam. And be realistic: Can you actually

expect to cover a 78-page chapter in one session? Divide large tasks into smaller units; stop at the most logical resting points. When you complete a specific goal, take a 5- or 10-minute break before tackling the next goal.

5. Evaluate how successful or unsuccessful your studying has been on a daily or weekly basis. Did you reach most of your goals? If so, reward yourself immediately. You might even make a list of five to ten rewards to choose from. If you have trouble studying regularly, you may be able to motivate yourself by making such rewards contingent on completing specific goals.

6. Finally, until you have lived with your schedule for several weeks, don't hesitate to revise it. You may need to allow more time for chemistry, for example, and less for some other course. If you are trying to study regularly for the first time and are feeling burned out, you probably have set your initial goals too high. Don't let failure cause you to despair and abandon the program. Accept your limitations and revise your schedule so that you are studying only 15 to 20 minutes more each evening than you are used to. The point is to identify a regular schedule with which you can achieve some success. Time management, like any skill, must be practiced to become effective.

Techniques for Effective Study

Knowing how to put study time to best use is, of course, as important as finding a place for it in your schedule. Here are some suggestions that should enable you to increase your reading comprehension and improve your note-taking. A few study tips are included as well.

Using SQ3R to Increase Reading Comprehension

How do you study from a textbook? If you are like many students, you simply read and reread in a *passive* manner. Studies have shown, however, that most students who simply read a textbook cannot remember more than half the material ten minutes after they have finished. Often, what is retained is the unessential material rather than the important points upon which exam questions will be based.

This *Study Guide* employs a program known as SQ3R (*Survey, Question, Read, Recite,* and *Review*) to facilitate, and allow you to assess, your comprehension of the important facts and concepts in *The Developing Person Through Childhood and Adolescence*, Eighth Edition, by Kathleen Stassen Berger.

Research has shown that students using SQ3R achieve significantly greater comprehension of textbooks than students reading in the more traditional passive manner. Once you have learned this program, you can improve your comprehension of any textbook.

Survey Before reading a chapter, determine whether the text or the study guide has an outline or list of objectives. Read this material and the summary at the end of the chapter. Next, read the textbook chapter fairly quickly, paying special attention to the major headings and subheadings. This survey will give you an idea of the chapter's contents and organization. You will then be able to divide the chapter into logical sections in order to formulate specific goals for a more careful reading of the chapter.

In this Study Guide, the *Chapter Overview* summarizes the major topics of the textbook chapter. This section also provides a few suggestions for approaching topics you may find difficult.

Question You will retain material longer when you have a use for it. If you look up a word's definition in order to solve a crossword puzzle, for example, you will remember it longer than if you merely fill in the letters as a result of putting other words in. Surveying the chapter will allow you to generate important questions that the chapter will proceed to answer. These question correspond to "mental files" into which knowledge will be sorted for easy access.

As you survey, jot down several questions for each chapter section. One simple technique is to generate questions by rephrasing a section heading. For example, the "Preoperational Thought" head could be turned into "What is preoperational thought?" Good questions will allow you to focus on the important points in the text. Examples of good questions are those that begin as follows: "List two examples of . . .." "What is the function of . . .?" "What is the significance of . . .?" Such questions give a purpose to your reading. Similarly, you can formulate questions based on the chapter outline.

Read When you have established "files" for each section of the chapter, review your first question, begin reading, and continue until you have discovered its answer. If you come to material that seems to answer an important question you don't have a file for, stop and write down the question.

Using this Study Guide, read the chapter one section at a time. First, preview the section by skimming it, noting headings and boldface items. Next, as you read the chapter section, search for the answer to each of your questions.

Be sure to read everything. Don't skip photo or art captions, graphs, marginal notes. In some cases, what may seem vague in reading will be made clear by a simple graph. Keep in mind that test questions are sometimes drawn from illustrations and charts.

Recite When you have found the answer to a question, close your eyes and mentally recite the question and its answer. Then *write* the answer next to the question. It is important that you recite an answer in your own words rather than the author's. Don't rely on your short-term memory to repeat the author's words verbatim.

Recitation is an extremely effective study technique, recommended by many learning experts. In addition to increasing reading comprehension, it is useful for review. Trying to explain something in your own words clarifies your knowledge, often by revealing aspects of your answer that are vague or incomplete. If you repeatedly rely upon "I know" in recitation, you really may not know.

Recitation has the additional advantage of simulating an exam, especially an essay exam; the same skills are required in both cases. Too often students study without ever putting the book and notes aside, which makes it easy for them to develop false confidence in their knowledge. When the material is in front of you, you may be able to recognize an answer, but will you be able to recall it later, when you take an exam that does not provide these retrieval cues?

After you have recited and written your answer, continue with your next question. Read, recite, and so on.

Review When you have answered the last question on the material you have designated as a study goal, go back and review. Read over each question and your written answer to it. Your review might also include a brief written summary that integrates all of your questions and answers. This review need not take longer than a few minutes, but it is important. It will help you retain the material longer and will greatly facilitate a final review of each chapter before the exam.

In this Study Guide, the *Chapter Review* section contains fill-in and one- or two-sentence essay questions for you to complete after you have finished reading the text and have written answers to your questions. The correct answers are given at the end of the chapter. Generally, your answer to a fill-in question should match exactly (as in the case of important terms, theories, or people). In some cases, the answer is not a term or name, so a word close in meaning will suffice. You should go through the Chapter Review several times before taking an exam, so it is a good idea to mentally fill in the answers until you are

ready for a final pretest review. Textbook page references are provided with each section title, in case you need to reread any of the material.

At the end of most Chapter Review sections you will find one or more Applications, Think About It questions, and Study Tips. Application questions evaluate your ability to apply text material to real-life situations. Many students find questions of this type difficult on exams, and you should make certain you understand the correct answers to any questions you miss. Think About It questions are intended to promoter deeper thinking about the material. Although questions of this type often do not have a single "correct" answer, they promote critical thinking skills and the kind of deep processing of material that many instructors prefer to evaluate on exams. Finally, the Study Tips focus on practical suggestions for facilitating your mastery of the material by making meaningful connections between it and your own life experiences.

Also provided to facilitate your review are two *Progress Tests* that include multiple-choice questions and, where appropriate, matching or true–false questions. These tests are not to be taken until you have read the chapter, written answers to your questions, and completed the *Chapter Review*. Correct answers, along with explanations of why each alternative is correct or incorrect, are provided at the end of the chapter. The relevant text page numbers for each question are also given. If you miss a question, read these explanations and, if necessary, review the text pages to further understand why. The *Progress Tests* do not test every aspect of a concept, so you should treat an incorrect answer as an indication that you need to review the concept.

The chapter concludes with *Key Terms*, either in list form only or also in a crossword puzzle. In either form, it is important that the answers be written from memory, and in list form, in your own words. The *Answers* section at the end of the chapter gives a definition of each term, sometimes along with an example of its usage and/or a tip to help you remember its meaning.

One final suggestion: Incorporate SQ3R into your time-management calendar. Set specific goals for completing SQ3R with each assigned chapter. Keep a record of chapters completed, and reward yourself for being conscientious. Initially, it takes more time and effort to "read" using SQ3R, but with practice, the steps will become automatic. More importantly, you will comprehend significantly more material and retain what you have learned longer than passive readers do.

Taking Lecture Notes

Are your class notes as useful as they might be? One way to determine their worth is to compare them with those taken by other good students. Are yours as thorough? Do they provide you with a comprehensible outline of each lecture? If not, then the following suggestions might increase the effectiveness of your note-taking.

1. Keep a separate notebook for each course. Use standard notebook pages. Consider using a ring binder, which would allow you to revise and insert notes while still preserving lecture order.

2. Take notes in the format of a lecture outline. Use roman numerals for major points, letters for supporting arguments, and so on. Some instructors will make this easy by delivering organized lectures and, in some cases, by outlining their lectures on the board. If a lecture is disorganized, you will probably want to reorganize your notes soon after the class.

3. As you take notes in class, leave a wide margin on one side of each page. After the lecture, expand or clarify any shorthand notes while the material is fresh in your mind. Use this time to write important questions in the margin next to notes that answer them. This will facilitate later review and will allow you to anticipate similar exam questions.

Evaluate Your Exam Performance

How often have you received a grade on an exam that did not do justice to the effort you spent preparing for the exam? This is a common experience that can leave one feeling bewildered and abused. "What do I have to do to get an A?" "The test was unfair!" "I studied the wrong material!"

The chances of this happening are greatly reduced if you have an effective time-management schedule and use the study techniques described here. But it can happen to the best-prepared student and is most likely to occur on your first exam with a new professor.

Remember that there are two main reasons for studying. One is to learn for your own general academic development. Many people believe that such knowledge is all that really matters. Of course, it is possible, though unlikely, to be an expert on a topic without achieving commensurate grades, just as one can, occasionally, earn an excellent grade without truly mastering the course material. During a job interview or in the workplace, however, your A in Cobol won't mean much if you can't actually program a computer.

In order to keep career options open after you graduate, you must know the material and maintain competitive grades. In the short run, this means performing well on exams, which is the second main objective in studying.

Probably the single best piece of advice to keep in mind when studying for exams is to *try to predict exam questions.* This means ignoring the trivia and focusing on the important questions and their answers (with your instructor's emphasis in mind).

A second point is obvious. How well you do on exams is determined by your mastery of both lecture and textbook material. Many students (partly because of poor time management) concentrate too much on one at the expense of the other.

To evaluate how well you are learning lecture and textbook material, analyze the questions you missed on the first exam. If your instructor does not review exams during class, you can easily do it yourself. Divide the questions into two categories: those drawn primarily from lectures and those drawn primarily from the text. Determine the percentage of questions you missed in each category. If your errors are evenly distributed and you are satisfied with your grade, you have no problem. If you are weaker in one area, you will need to set future goals for increasing and/or improving your study of that area.

Similarly, note the percentage of test questions drawn from each category. Although exams in most courses cover both lecture notes and the textbook, the relative emphasis of each may vary from instructor to instructor. While your instructors may not be entirely consistent in making up future exams, you may be able to tailor your studying for each course by placing additional emphasis on the appropriate area.

Exam evaluation will also point out the types of questions your instructor prefers. Does the exam consist primarily of multiple-choice, true–false, or essay questions? You may also discover that an instructor is fond of wording questions in certain ways. For example, an instructor may rely heavily on questions that require you to draw an analogy between a theory or concept and a real-world example. Evaluate both your instructor's style and how well you do with each format. Use this information to guide your future exam preparation.

Important aids, not only in studying for exams but also in determining how well prepared you are, are the Progress Tests provided in this Study Guide. If these tests don't include all of the types of questions your instructor typically writes, make up your own practice exam questions. Spend extra time testing yourself with question formats that are most difficult for you. There is no better way to evaluate your preparation for an upcoming exam than by testing yourself under the conditions most likely to be in effect during the actual test.

A Few Practical Tips

Even the best intentions for studying sometimes fail. Some of these failures occur because students attempt to work under conditions that are simply not conducive to concentrated study. To help ensure the success of your time-management program, here are a few suggestions that should assist you in reducing the possibility of procrastination or distraction.

1. If you have set up a schedule for studying, make your roommate, family, and friends aware of this commitment, and ask them to honor your quiet study time. Close your door and post a "Do Not Disturb" sign.

2. Set up a place to study that minimizes potential distractions. Use a desk or table, not your bed or an extremely comfortable chair. Keep your desk and the walls around it free from clutter. If you need a place other than your room, find one that meets as many of the above requirements as possible—for example, in the library stacks.

3. Do nothing but study in this place. It should become associated with studying so that it "triggers" this activity, just as a mouth-watering aroma elicits an appetite.

4. Never study with the television on or with other distracting noises present. If you must have music in the background in order to mask outside noise, for example, play soft instrumental music. Don't pick vocal selections; your mind will be drawn to the lyrics.

5. Study by yourself. Other students can be distracting or can break the pace at which your learning is most efficient. In addition, there is always the possibility that group studying will become a social gathering. Reserve that for its own place in your schedule.

If you continue to have difficulty concentrating for very long, try the following suggestions.

6. Study your most difficult or most challenging subjects first, when you are most alert.

7. Start with relatively short periods of concentrated study, with breaks in between. If your attention starts to wander, get up immediately and take a break. It is better to study effectively for 15 minutes and then take a break than to fritter away 45 minutes

out of an hour. Gradually increase the length of study periods, using your attention span as an indicator of successful pacing.

Critical Thinking

Having discussed a number of specific techniques for managing your time efficiently and studying effectively, let us now turn to a much broader topic: What exactly should you expect to learn as a student of developmental psychology?

Most developmental psychology courses have two major goals: (1) to help you acquire a basic understanding of the discipline's knowledge base, and (2) to help you learn to think like a psychologist. Many students devote all of their efforts to the first of these goals, concentrating on memorizing as much of the course's material as possible.

The second goal—learning to think like a psychologist—has to do with critical thinking. Critical thinking has many meanings. On one level, it refers to an attitude of healthy skepticism that should guide your study of psychology. As a critical thinker, you learn not to accept any explanation or conclusion about behavior as true until you have evaluated the evidence. On another level, critical thinking refers to a systematic process for examining the conclusions and arguments presented by others. In this regard, many of the features of the SQ3R technique for improving reading comprehension can be incorporated into an effective critical thinking system.

To learn to think critically, you must first recognize that psychological information is transmitted through the construction of persuasive arguments. An argument consists of three parts: an assertion, evidence, and an explanation (Mayer and Goodchild, 1990).

An assertion is a statement of relationship between some aspect of behavior, such as intelligence, and another factor, such as age. Learn to identify and evaluate the assertions about behavior and mental processes that you encounter as you read your textbook, listen to lectures, and engage in discussions with classmates. A good test of your understanding of an assertion is to try to restate it in your own words. As you do so, pay close attention to how important terms and concepts are defined. When a researcher asserts that "intelligence declines with age," for example, what does he or she mean by "intelligence"? Assertions such as this one may be true when a critical term ("intelligence") is defined one way (for example, "speed of thinking"), but not when defined in another way (for example, "general knowledge"). One of the strengths of psychology is the use of *operational* definitions that specify how key terms and concepts are measured, thus eliminating any ambiguity about their meaning. "Intelligence," for example, is often operationally defined as performance on a test measuring various cognitive skills. Whenever you encounter an assertion that is ambiguous, be skeptical of its accuracy.

When you have a clear understanding of an argument's assertion, evaluate its supporting evidence, the second component of an argument. Is it *empirical*? Does it, in fact, support the assertion? Psychologists accept only *empirical (observable) evidence* that is based on direct measurement of behavior. Hearsay, intuition, and personal experiences are not acceptable evidence. Chapter 1 discusses the various research methods used by developmental psychologists to gather empirical evidence. Some examples include surveys, observations of behavior in natural settings, and experiments.

As you study developmental psychology, you will become aware of another important issue in evaluating evidence—determining whether or not the research on which it is based is faulty. Research can be faulty for many reasons, including the use of an unrepresentative sample of subjects, experimenter bias, and inadequate control of unanticipated factors that might influence results. Evidence based on faulty research should be discounted.

The third component of an argument is the explanation provided for an assertion, which is based on the evidence that has been presented. While the argument's assertion merely *describes* how two things (such as intelligence and age) are related, the explanation tells *why*, often by proposing some theoretical mechanism that causes the relationship. Empirical evidence that thinking speed slows with age (the assertion), for example, may be explained as being caused by age-related changes in the activity of brain cells (a physiological explanation).

Be cautious in accepting explanations. In order to think critically about an argument's explanation, ask yourself three questions: (1) Can I restate the explanation in my own words?; (2) Does the explanation make sense based on the stated evidence?; and (3) Are there alternative explanations that adequately explain the assertion? Consider this last point in relation to our sample assertion: It is possible that the

slower thinking speed of older adults is due to their having less recent experience than younger people with tasks that require quick thinking (a disuse explanation).

Because psychology is a relatively young science, its theoretical explanations are still emerging, and often change. For this reason, not all psychological arguments will offer explanations. Many arguments will only raise additional questions for further research to address.

Some Suggestions for Becoming a Critical Thinker

1. Adopt an attitude of healthy skepticism in evaluating psychological arguments.

2. Insist on unambiguous operational definitions of an argument's important concepts and terms.

3. Be cautious in accepting supporting evidence for an argument's assertion.

4. Refuse to accept evidence for an argument if it is based on faulty research.

5. Ask yourself if the theoretical explanation provided for an argument "makes sense" based on the empirical evidence.

6. Determine whether there are alternative explanations that adequately explain an assertion.

7. Use critical thinking to construct your own effective arguments when writing term papers, answering essay questions, and speaking.

8. Polish your critical-thinking skills by applying them to each of your college courses, and to other areas of life as well. Learn to think critically about advertising, political speeches, and the material presented in popular periodicals.

Some Closing Thoughts

I hope that these suggestions help make you more successful academically, and that they enhance the quality of your college life in general. Having the necessary skills makes any job a lot easier and more pleasant. Let me repeat my warning not to attempt to make too drastic a change in your life-style immediately. Good habits require time and self-discipline to develop. Once established they can last a lifetime.

STUDY GUIDE

4

Prenatal Development and Birth

Chapter Overview

Prenatal development is the most dramatic and extensive transformation of the entire life span. During prenatal development, the individual changes from a one-celled zygote to a complex human baby. This development is outlined in Chapter 4, along with some of the problems that can occur—among them prenatal exposure to disease, drugs, and other hazards—and the factors that moderate the risks of teratogenic exposure.

For the developing person, birth marks the most radical transition of the entire life span. No longer sheltered from the outside world, the fetus becomes a separate human being who begins life almost completely dependent upon his or her caregivers. Chapter 4 also examines the birth process and its possible variations and problems.

The chapter concludes with a brief discussion of the parent–infant bond.

NOTE: Answer guidelines for all Chapter 4 questions begin on page 56.

Chapter Review

When you have finished reading the chapter, work through the material that follows to review it. Complete the sentences and answer the questions. In some cases, Study Tips explain how best to learn a difficult concept, while Think About It and Applications help you to know how well you understand the material. As you proceed, evaluate your performance for each section by consulting the answers beginning on page 56. Do not continue with the next section until you understand each answer. If you need to, review or reread the appropriate section in the textbook before continuing.

From Zygote to Newborn (pp. 97–103)

1. Prenatal development is divided into
_____ main periods. The first two weeks of development are called the _____ period; from the _____ week through the _____ week is known as the _____ period; and from this point until birth is the _____ period.

2. Once clusters of cells begin to take on distinct characteristics, the cell mass is called a _____ . About one week after conception, the multiplying cells separate into outer cells that will become the _____ and inner cells form the nucleus that will become the _____ .

3. The next significant event is the burrowing of the zygote into the lining of the uterus, a process called _____ . This process _____ (is/is not) automatic.

4. At the beginning of the period of the embryo, a thin line down the middle of the developing individual forms a structure that will become the _____ _____ , which becomes the _____ _____ and eventually will develop into the _____ _____ .

Briefly describe the major features of development during the second month.

5. Eight weeks after conception, the embryo weighs about _____ and is about _____ in length. From the start of the ninth week after conception until birth, the organism is called the _____ .

6. The genital organs are fully formed by week _____ . If the fetus has a(n) _____ chromosome, the _____ gene on this chromosome sends a signal that triggers development of the _____ (male/female) sex organs. Without that gene, no signal is sent and the fetus begins to develop _____ (male/female) sex organs.

7. By the end of the _____ month, the fetus is fully formed, weighs approximately _____ , and is about _____ long. These figures _____ (vary/do not vary) from fetus to fetus.

8. During the fourth, fifth, and sixth months, the brain increases in size by a factor of _____ . The brain develops new neurons in a process called _____ and new connections between them (synapses) in a process called _____ . This neurological maturation is essential to the regulation of such basic body functions as _____ and _____ .

9. The age at which a fetus has at least some chance of surviving outside the uterus is called the _____ _____ _____ , which occurs about _____ weeks after conception. This barrier _____ (has/has not) been reduced by advances in neonatal care, probably because maintaining life depends on some _____ response.

10. At about _____ weeks after conception, brain-wave patterns begin to resemble the _____ – _____ cycles of a newborn.

11. A 28-week-old fetus typically weighs about _____ and has about a _____ percent chance of survival.

12. Three crucial aspects of development in the last months of prenatal life are maturation of the _____ , _____ , and _____ systems.

13. By full term, brain growth is so extensive that the brain's advanced outer layer, called the _____ , forms several folds in order to fit into the skull.

14. In the final _____ (how many?) months, the fetus hears many sounds, including the mother's _____ and _____ , as well as her _____ .

THINK ABOUT IT: Compared to the gestation periods of other mammals, the nine-month gestation period in humans is relatively long. Compared to how slowly human development proceeds in other aspects of the life span, however, nine months seems a little on the short side. In fact, some evolutionary biologists have suggested that humans ought to be *in utero* 15 or 16 months! What sorts of evolutionary pressures might have contributed to this "compromise" in the time allotted for prenatal development?

APPLICATIONS:

15. I weigh about 3 pounds (1.3 kilograms) and my brain is developing well as a result of the processes of _____ and _____ . I am a _____ .

16. Karen and Brad report to their neighbors that, 6 weeks after conception, a sonogram of their child-to-be revealed female sex organs. The neighbors are skeptical of their statement because
   a. sonograms are never administered before the ninth week.
   b. sonograms only reveal the presence or absence of male sex organs.
   c. the fetus does not begin to develop female sex organs until about the eighth week.
   d. it is impossible to determine that a woman is pregnant until seven weeks after conception.

Risk Reduction (pp. 104–113)

17. Harmful agents and conditions that can result in birth defects, called _____ , include _____ .

18. Substances that impair the child's action and intellect by harming the brain are called _____ _____ .

Approximately _____ percent of all children are born with behavioral difficulties that could be connected to damage done during the prenatal period.

19. The study of birth defects is called _____ ; it is a science of _____ _____ . As such, it attempts to evaluate the factors that can make prenatal harm more or less likely to occur.

20. Three crucial factors that determine whether a specific teratogen will cause harm, and of what nature, are the _____ of exposure, the _____ of exposure, and the developing organism's _____ _____ to damage from the substance.

21. The time when a particular part of the body is most susceptible to teratogenic damage is called its _____ _____ . For physical structure and form, this is the entire period of the _____ . However, for _____ teratogens, the entire prenatal period is critical.

22. Some teratogens have a _____ effect—that is, the substances are harmless until exposure reaches a certain level. Others have an _____ effect, which occurs when some teratogens taken together make them more harmful than when taken separately.

23. Fraternal twins, who share half their genes, _____ (will/will not) have the same abnormalities if exposed to the same teratogens. This suggests the existence of both _____ and _____ genes.

24. Genes are also known to affect the likelihood of neural-tube defects such as _____ or _____ .

These defects occur more commonly in certain groups. However, if a pregnant woman consumes extra _____ _____ , her embryo would get enough vitamin B to develop normally.

25. Genetic vulnerability is also related to the sex of the developing organism. Generally, _____ (male/female) embryos and fetuses are more vulnerable to teratogens. This sex also has more frequent _____ _____ and a higher rate of birth defects, _____ _____ , and other behavioral problems.

26. Women are advised to avoid all _____ before becoming pregnant. Prenatal development can also be impaired by _____ _____ .

27. (A View from Science) High doses of alcohol during pregnancy may cause _____ _____ _____ . A milder condition that involves emotional and cognitive problems in older children is _____ _____ _____ .

28. One advantage of early prenatal care is protection against _____ . An image of the fetus, called a _____ , allows doctors to see if the fetus is developing normally.

29. (Table 4.5) A number of tests are performed routinely to determine whether a pregnancy is problematic. Among them are the _____-_____ _____ , which tests for neural-tube defects, and _____ , which shows chromosomal abnormalities and other genetic and prenatal problems.

30. Although pediatric AIDS has almost disappeared from _____ _____ and _____ , it is still on the rise in _____ .

STUDY TIP: To emphasize the variety of teratogens to which pregnant women may be exposed every day, imagine that you have decided to become a parent. If you are a male, some teratogens to which you are exposed may affect your unborn child. Make a list of all the teratogens you have experienced recently that you would want to avoid to ensure that your body is teratogen-free for the year during which fertilization and gestation occur. If you are stumped, check the Internet for ideas.

APPLICATIONS:

31. Five-year-old Benjamin can't sit quietly and concentrate on a task for more than a minute at a time. Dr. Simmons, who is a teratologist, suspects that Benjamin may have been exposed to _____ during prenatal development.
    a. human immunodeficiency virus
    b. a behavioral teratogen
    c. rubella
    d. lead

32. Which of the following is an example of an interaction effect?
    a. Some teratogens are virtually harmless until exposure reaches a certain level.
    b. Maternal use of alcohol and tobacco together does more harm to the developing fetus than either teratogen would do alone.
    c. Some teratogens cause damage only on specific days during prenatal development.
    d. All of these are examples of interaction effects.

33. Suppose a woman drinks heavily during pregnancy, and her baby is born with fetal alcohol syndrome. Another mother-to-be drinks only moderately, and her child suffers fetal alcohol effects. This finding shows that to assess and understand risk we must know
    a. the kind of alcoholic beverage (for example, beer, wine, or whiskey).
    b. the level of exposure to the teratogen.
    c. whether the substance really is teratogenic.
    d. the timing of exposure to the teratogen.

34. Sylvia and Stan, who are of British descent, are hoping to have a child. Dr. Caruthers asks for a complete nutritional history and is particularly concerned when she discovers that Sylvia may have a deficiency of folic acid in her diet. Dr. Caruthers is probably worried about the risk of _____ in the couple's offspring.

Birth (pp. 113–126)

35. Most fetuses _____ (change/do not change) position during the last month of pregnancy. About 1 in 20 babies is born "_____ ," with buttocks or, rarely, feet first. Worse is a _____ _____ , in which the fetus turns sideways.

36. About _____ (how many?) weeks after conception, the fetal brain signals the release of certain _____ into the mother's bloodstream, which trigger her _____ _____ to contract and relax. The normal birth process begins when these contractions become regular. The average length of labor is _____ hours for first births and _____ hours for subsequent births.

37. In developed nations, the newborn is usually rated on the _____ _____ , which assigns a score of 0, 1, or 2 to each of the following five characteristics: _____ _____ . A score below _____ indicates that the newborn is in critical condition and requires immediate attention; if the score is _____ or better, all is well. This rating is made twice, at _____ minute(s) after birth and again at _____ minutes.

38. The birth experience is influenced by several factors, including _____ _____ .

39. In about 31 percent of U.S. births, a surgical procedure called a _____ _____ is performed.

40. A growing number of North American mothers today use a professional birth coach, or _____ , to assist them.

41. The disorder _____ _____ , which affects motor centers in the brain, often results from _____ vulnerability, worsened by exposure to _____ and a preterm birth that involves _____ , a temporary lack of _____ during birth.

42. Newborns who weigh less than _____ are classified as _____-_____ babies. Below 3 pounds, 5 ounces, they are called _____-_____- _____ babies; at less than 2 pounds, 3 ounces, they are _____- _____-_____ babies. Worldwide, rates of this condition _____ (vary/do not vary) from nation to nation.

43. Babies who are born 3 or more weeks before the standard 38 weeks have elapsed are called _____ .

44. Infants who weigh substantially less than they should, given how much time has passed since conception, are called _____ _____ _____ _____ .

45. Causes of SGA include problems with the _____ or _____ _____ , as well as maternal illness. However, maternal _____ use is a more common reason. About 25 percent of all LBW births are linked to maternal use of _____ . Prescription drugs can also cause low birthweight.

46. Another other common reason for low birthweight is maternal _____ . In addition, _____ births are more likely to result in LBW. Consequently, the rate of LBW has increased dramatically with the use of _____ _____ _____ .

47. Several factors affect the developing person before birth, via their impact on the pregnant woman. They are _____ _____ .

48. LBW babies are more likely to become adults who are _____ and have health problems, especially affecting the _____ .

49. For vulnerable infants, parents are encouraged to help with early caregiving in the hospital. This _____ stress in both infant and parents. One example of early caregiving is _____ _____ , in which mothers of low-birthweight infants spend extra time holding their infants between their breasts.

50. Parents can also help their newborn by administering _____ therapy. Especially important is the role played by a supportive _____-_____-_____ , who can help _____ _____ .

51. A crucial factor in the birth experience is the formation of a strong _____ _____ between the prospective parents.

52. Some new mothers experience a profound feeling of sadness called _____ _____ .

53. The term used to describe the close relationship that begins within the first hours after birth is the _____-_____ _____ . Research on monkeys using the strategy of _____- _____ suggests that bonding need not occur immediately.

STUDY TIP: "Going metric" will help you remember the differences among low birthweight (LBW), very low birthweight (VLBW), and extremely low birthweight (ELBW) babies. Remember two numbers: 2,500 (grams) and 500 (grams). The LBW threshold is a weight below 2,500 grams. Two decreases of 500 grams each are the criteria for VLBW (2,500 grams minus [2 × 500] equals 1,500 grams). For ELBW, it's three decreases of 500 grams each (2,500 grams minus (3 × 500 grams) equals 1,000 grams). To remember the criterion for a preterm birth, think of "3 (weeks)," which rhymes with "pre." Thus, a preterm birth is one that occurs 3 or more weeks early. Small for gestational age

(SGA) is self-defining. An SGA baby is one who gained weight too slowly during gestation (pregnancy).

THINK ABOUT IT: Thanks to recent medical break-throughs, even extremely-low-birthweight infants have a decent chance of surviving. As a result, ethical and social dilemmas often arise regarding the rights of the fetus as a separate individual. For example, judges have ordered pregnant women who were close to term to have blood transfusions and surgical births, even when those procedures were unwanted by the women. How do you feel about this? Who should have the authority to decide in such cases?

APPLICATIONS:

54. Three-year-old Kenny was born underweight and premature. Today, he is small for his age. What would be the most likely reason for Kenny's small size? _____

55. Your sister and brother-in-law, who are about to adopt a 6-month-old, are worried that the child will never bond with them. What advice should you offer?
   a. Tell them that, unfortunately, this is true; they would be better off waiting for a younger child who has not yet bonded.
   b. Tell them that, although the first year is a bio-logically determined critical period for attach-ment, there is a 50/50 chance that the child will bond with them.
   c. Tell them that bonding is a long-term process between parent and child that is determined by the nature of interaction throughout infan-cy, childhood, and beyond.
   d. Tell them that if the child is female, there is a good chance that she will bond with them, even at this late stage.

56. Which of the following newborns would be most likely to have problems in body structure and functioning?
   a. Anton, whose Apgar score is 6
   b. Debora, whose Apgar score is 7
   c. Sheila, whose Apgar score is 3
   d. Simon, whose Apgar score is 5

57. At birth, Clarence was classified as small for ges-tational age. It is likely that Clarence
   a. was born in a rural hospital.
   b. suffered several months of prenatal malnutri-tion.
   c. was born in a large city hospital.
   d. comes from a family with a history of such births.

58. Of the following, who is most likely to give birth to a low-birthweight child?
   a. 21-year-old Janice, who was herself a low-birthweight baby
   b. 25-year-old May Ling, who gained 25 pounds during her pregnancy
   c. 16-year-old Donna, who diets frequently despite being underweight
   d. 30-year-old Maria, who has already given birth to four children

59. An infant is born 38 weeks after conception, weighing 4 pounds. How would that infant be classified in terms of weight and timing?

_____

60. An infant who was born at 35 weeks, weighing 6 pounds, would be called a _____ infant.

61. One minute and five minutes after he was born, Malcolm was tested using the Apgar scale. The characteristics of a newborn tested by the scale are _____

_____ .

Progress Test 1

Multiple-Choice Questions

Circle your answers to the following questions and check them with the answers beginning on page 57. If your answer is incorrect, read the explanation for why it is incorrect and then consult the appropriate pages of the text (in parentheses following the correct answer).

1. The third through the eighth week after concep-tion is called the
   a. embryonic period.
   b. ovum period.
   c. fetal period.
   d. germinal period.

2. The primitive streak develops into the
   a. respiratory system.
   b. umbilical cord.
   c. brain and spinal column.
   d. circulatory system.

3. To say that a teratogen has a "threshold effect" means that it is
   a. virtually harmless until exposure reaches a certain level.
   b. harmful only to low-birthweight infants.
   c. harmful to certain developing organs during periods when these organs are developing most rapidly.
   d. harmful only if the pregnant woman's weight does not increase by a certain minimum amount during her pregnancy.

4. By the eighth week after conception, the embryo has almost all the basic organs EXCEPT the
   a. skeleton.
   b. elbows and knees.
   c. male and female sex organs.
   d. fingers and toes.

5. The most critical factor in attaining the age of viability is development of the
   a. placenta.   c. brain.
   b. eyes.   d. skeleton.

6. An important nutrient that many women do not get in adequate amounts from the typical diet is
   a. vitamin A.   c. guanine.
   b. zinc.   d. folic acid.

7. An embryo begins to develop male sex organs if _____ , and female sex organs if _____ .
   a. genes on the Y chromosome send a signal; no signal is sent from an X chromosome
   b. genes on the Y chromosome send a signal; genes on the X chromosome send a signal
   c. genes on the X chromosome send a signal; no signal is sent from an X chromosome
   d. genes on the X chromosome send a signal; genes on the Y chromosome send a signal

8. A teratogen
   a. cannot cross the placenta during the period of the embryo.
   b. is usually inherited from the mother.
   c. can be counteracted by good nutrition most of the time.
   d. may be a virus, a drug, a chemical, or environmental pollutants.

9. (A View from Science) Among the characteristics of babies born with fetal alcohol syndrome are
   a. slowed physical growth and behavior problems.
   b. addiction to alcohol and methadone.
   c. deformed arms and legs.
   d. blindness.

10. The birth process begins
    a. when the fetus moves into the right position.
    b. when the uterus begins to contract at regular intervals to push the fetus out.
    c. about eight hours (for firstborns) after the uterus begins to contract at regular intervals.
    d. when the baby's head appears at the opening of the vagina.

11. The Apgar scale is administered
    a. only if the newborn is in obvious distress.
    b. once, just after birth.
    c. twice, one minute and five minutes after birth.
    d. repeatedly during the newborn's first hours.

12. Most newborns weigh about
    a. 5 pounds.   c. $7\frac{1}{2}$ pounds.
    b. 6 pounds.   d. $8\frac{1}{2}$ pounds.

13. Low-birthweight babies born near the due date but weighing substantially less than they should
    a. are classified as preterm.
    b. are called small for gestational age.
    c. usually have no sex organs.
    d. show many signs of immaturity.

14. Approximately one out of every four low-birthweight births in the United States is caused by maternal use of
    a. alcohol.   c. crack cocaine.
    b. tobacco.   d. household chemicals.

15. A newborn is classified as preterm if he or she is born
    a. one or more weeks early.
    b. two or more weeks early
    c. three or more weeks early.
    d. four or more weeks early.

Matching Items

Match each definition or description with its corresponding term.

Terms

_____ 1. embryonic period
_____ 2. fetal period
_____ 3. placenta
_____ 4. preterm
_____ 5. teratogens
_____ 6. anoxia
_____ 7. doula
_____ 8. critical period
_____ 9. primitive streak
_____ 10. fetal alcohol syndrome
_____ 11. germinal period

Definitions or Descriptions

a. term for the period during which a developing baby's body parts are most susceptible to damage
b. agents and conditions that can damage the developing organism
c. the age when viability is attained
d. the precursor of the central nervous system
e. lack of oxygen, which, if prolonged during the birth process, may lead to brain damage
f. characterized by abnormal facial characteristics, slowed growth, behavior problems, and mental retardation
g. a woman who helps with the birth process
h. the life-giving organ that nourishes the embryo and fetus
i. when implantation occurs
j. the prenatal period when all major body structures begin to form
k. a baby born 3 or more weeks early

Progress Test 2

Progress Test 2 should be completed during a final chapter review. Answer the following questions after you thoroughly understand the correct answers for the Chapter Review and Progress Test 1.

Multiple-Choice Questions

1. (Table 4.5) A 35-year-old woman who is pregnant is most likely to undergo which type of test for the detection of prenatal chromosomal or genetic abnormalities?
   a. pre-implantation testing
   b. ultrasound
   c. amniocentesis
   d. alpha-fetoprotein assay

2. In order, the correct sequence of prenatal stages of development is
   a. embryo; germinal; fetus
   b. germinal; fetus; embryo
   c. germinal; embryo; fetus
   d. ovum; fetus; embryo

3. Monika is preparing for the birth of her first child. If all proceeds normally, she can expect that her labor will last about
   a. 7 hours.   c. 10 hours.
   b. 8 hours.   d. 12 hours.

4. (Table 4.4) Tetracycline and retinoic acid
   a. can be harmful to the human fetus.
   b. have been proven safe for pregnant women after the embryonic period.
   c. will prevent spontaneous abortions.
   d. are safe when used before the fetal period.

5. (Table 4.4) The teratogen that, if not prevented by immunization, could cause deafness, blindness, and brain damage in the fetus is
   a. rubella (German measles).
   b. anoxia.
   c. acquired immune deficiency syndrome (AIDS).
   d. neural-tube defect.

6. Kangaroo care refers to
   a. the rigid attachment formed between mothers and offspring in the animal kingdom
   b. the fragmented care that the children of single parents often receive.
   c. a program of increased involvement by mothers of low-birthweight infants.
   d. none of these.

7. Among the characteristics rated on the Apgar scale are
   a. shape of the newborn's head and nose.
   b. presence of body hair.
   c. interactive behaviors.
   d. muscle tone and color.

8. A newborn is classified as low birthweight if he or she weighs less than
   a. 7 pounds.
   c. $5^{1}/_{2}$ pounds.
   b. 6 pounds.
   d. 4 pounds.

9. A critical problem for preterm babies is
   a. the immaturity of the sex organs—for example, undescended testicles.
   b. spitting up or hiccupping.
   c. infection from intravenous feeding.
   d. breathing difficulties.

10. (A View from Science) Which of the following is NOT true regarding alcohol use and pregnancy?
    a. Alcohol in high doses is a proven teratogen.
    b. Not every pregnant woman who drinks heavily has a newborn with fetal alcohol syndrome.
    c. Most doctors in the United States advise pregnant women to use alcohol in moderation during pregnancy.
    d. Only after a fetus is born does fetal alcohol syndrome become apparent.

11. Neurogenesis refers to the process by which
    a. the fetal brain develops new neurons.
    b. new connections between neurons develop.
    c. the neural tube forms during the middle trimester.
    d. the cortex folds into layers in order to fit into the skull.

12. Which Apgar score indicates that a newborn is in normal health?
    a. 4
    c. 6
    b. 5
    d. 7

13. Synaptogenesis refers to the process by which
    a. the fetal brain develops new neurons.
    b. new connections between neurons develop.
    c. the neural tube forms during the middle trimester.
    d. the cortex folds into layers in order to fit into the skull.

14. When there is a strong parental alliance
    a. mother and father cooperate because of their mutual commitment to their children.
    b. the parents agree to support each other in their shared parental roles.
    c. children are likely to thrive.
    d. all of these answers are true.

15. The critical period for preventing physical defects appears to be the
    a. zygote period.
    b. embryonic period.
    c. fetal period.
    d. entire pregnancy.

True or False Items

Write T (*true*) or F (*false*) on the line in front of each statement.

_____ 1. The fetus becomes aware of the mother's voice and smell.

_____ 2. Eight weeks after conception, the embryo has formed almost all the basic organs.

_____ 3. Only 1 percent of births in the United States take place in the home.

_____ 4. In general, behavioral teratogens have the greatest effect during the embryonic period.

_____ 5. The effects of cigarette smoking during pregnancy remain highly controversial.

_____ 6. The Apgar scale is used to measure vital signs such as heart rate, breathing, and reflexes.

_____ 7. Newborns usually breathe on their own, moments after birth.

_____ 8. Research has shown that immediate mother–infant contact at birth is necessary for the normal emotional development of the child.

_____ 9. Low birthweight is often correlated with maternal malnutrition.

_____ 10. Cesarean sections are rarely performed in the United States today because of the resulting danger to the fetus.

Key Terms

Using your own words, write a brief definition or explanation of each of the following terms on a separate piece of paper.

1. germinal period
2. embryonic period
3. fetal period
4. blastocyst
5. placenta
6. implantation
7. embryo
8. fetus
9. age of viability

10. teratogens
11. behavioral teratogens
12. teratology
13. risk analysis
14. threshold effect
15. interaction effect
16. fetal alcohol syndrome (FAS)
17. fetal alcohol effects (FAS)
18. sonogram
19. Apgar scale
20. cesarean section
21. doula
22. anoxia
23. cerebral palsy
24. low birthweight (LBW)
25. very low birthweight (VLBW)
26. extremely low birthweight (ELBW)
27. preterm birth
28. small for gestational age (SGA)
29. kangaroo care
30. parental alliance
31. postpartum depression
32. parent–infant bond

Answers

CHAPTER REVIEW

1. three; germinal; third; eighth; embryonic; fetal

2. blastocyst; placenta; embryo

3. implantation; is not

4. primitive streak; neural tube; central nervous system

The head begins to take shape as eyes, ears, nose, and mouth start to form. A tiny blood vessel that will become the heart begins to pulsate. The upper arms, then the forearms, palms, and webbed fingers appear. Legs, feet, and webbed toes follow. At eight weeks, the embryo's head is more rounded, and the facial features are formed. The embryo has all the basic organs and body parts, including a unisex structure called the indifferent gonad.

5. ⅟₃₀ ounce (1 gram); 1 inch (2.5 centimeters); fetus

6. 12; Y; SRY; male; female

7. third; 3 ounces (87 grams); 3 inches (7.5 centimeters); vary

8. six; neurogenesis; synaptogenesis; breathing; sucking

9. age of viability; 22; has not; brain

10. 28; sleep–wake

11. 3 pounds (1.3 kilograms); 95

12. neurological; respiratory; cardiovascular

13. cortex

14. three; heartbeat; voice; smells

15. neurogenesis; synaptogenesis; fetus. Brain maturity is the key to reaching the age of viability.

16. **c.** is the answer. Before that time, the embryo has only an undifferentiated indifferent gonad.

17. teratogens; viruses, drugs, chemicals, pollutants, extreme stress, and malnutrition

18. behavioral teratogens; 20

19. teratology; risk analysis

20. timing; amount; genetic vulnerability

21. critical period; embryo; behavioral

22. threshold; interaction

23. will not; protective; vulnerable

24. spina bifida; microcephaly; ethnic; folic acid

25. male; spontaneous abortions; learning disabilities

26. drugs, chemicals in pesticides, construction materials, and cosmetics; prescription drugs

27. fetal alcohol syndrome; fetal alcohol effects

28. teratogens; sonogram

29. alpha-fetoprotein assay; amniocentesis

30. North America; Europe; Africa

31. **b.** is the answer. HIV is the virus that causes AIDS. Rubella may cause blindness, deafness, and brain damage. In small doses, lead may be harmless; large doses may produce brain damage in the fetus.

32. **b.** is the answer. An interaction effect occurs when one teratogen intensifies the harmful effects of another. Alcohol and tobacco are both teratogens that separately harm the fetus but together do even more harm.

33. **b.** is the answer. Although researchers do not yet know exactly how much alcohol harms the fetus and to what degree, the general theory is that different amounts of exposure will affect the developing child differently.

34. neural-tube defects. Folic acid is needed for the responsible allele to get enough vitamin B for the fetus to develop normally.

35. change; breech; transverse lie

36. 38; hormones; uterine muscles; 12; 7

37. Apgar scale; heart rate, breathing, muscle tone, color, and reflexes; 4; 7; one; five

38. the parents' preparation for birth, the physical and emotional support provided by birth attendants, the position and size of the fetus, the customs of the culture

39. cesarean section

40. doula

41. cerebral palsy; genetic; teratogens; anoxia; oxygen

42. 2,500 grams (5½ pounds); low-birthweight; very-low-birthweight; extremely-low-birthweight; vary

43. preterm

44. small for gestational age

45. placenta; umbilical cord; drug; tobacco

46. malnutrition; multiple; assisted reproductive technology

47. quality of medical care, education, culture, and social support

48. overweight; heart

49. reduces; kangaroo care

50. massage; father-to-be; the mother-to-be stay healthy, well nourished, and drug-free

51. parental alliance

52. postpartum depression

53. parent–infant bond; cross-fostering

54. Kenny's mother smoked heavily during her pregnancy. Although every psychoactive drug slows prenatal growth, tobacco is the worst and most prevalent cause of SGA.

55. c. is the answer.

56. c. is the answer. If a newborn's Apgar score is below 4, the infant is in critical condition and needs immediate medical attention.

57. b. is the answer. Where a baby is born generally will not affect its size at birth. And certainly size is not hereditary.

58. c. is the answer. Donna's risk factor for having an LBW baby is her weight (teens tend not to eat well and can be undernourished).

59. low-birthweight; small-for-gestational age. Thirty-eight weeks is full term, so a baby at 4 pounds would be small-for-gestational age and, of course, low birthweight.

60. preterm. Any birth before 38 weeks is preterm.

61. reflexes, breathing, muscle tone, heart rate, and color

PROGRESS TEST 1

Multiple-Choice Questions

1. a. is the answer. (p. 99)

    b. This term, which refers to the germinal period, is not used in the text.

    c. The fetal period is from the ninth week until birth.

    d. The germinal period covers the first two weeks.

2. c. is the answer. (p. 99)

3. a. is the answer. (p. 106)

    b., c., & d. Although low birthweight (b.), critical periods of organ development (c.), and maternal malnutrition (d.) are all hazardous to the developing person during prenatal development, none is an example of a threshold effect.

4. c. is the answer. The sex organs do not begin to take shape until the fetal period. (p. 100)

5. c. is the answer. (p. 101)

6. d. is the answer. (p. 107)

7. a. is the answer. (p. 100)

8. d. is the answer. (p. 104)

    a. In general, teratogens can cross the placenta at any time.

    b. Teratogens are agents in the environment, not heritable genes (although *susceptibility* to individual teratogens has a genetic component).

    c. Although nutrition is an important factor in healthy prenatal development, the text does not suggest that nutrition alone can usually counteract the harmful effects of teratogens.

9. a. is the answer. (p. 110)

10. b. is the answer. (p. 114)

11. c. is the answer. (p. 115)

12. c. is the answer. (p. 100)

13. b. is the answer. (p. 119)

14. b. is the answer. (p. 121)

15. c. is the answer. (p. 125)

Matching Items

1. j (p. 99)	**5.** b (p. 104)	**9.** d (p. 99)
2. c (p. 100)	**6.** e (p. 118)	**10.** f (p. 110)
3. h (p. 98)	**7.** g (p. 118)	**11.** i (p. 97)
4. k (p. 119)	**8.** a (p. 104)	

PROGRESS TEST 2

Multiple-Choice Questions

1. c. is the answer. (p. 111)

2. c. is the answer. (p. 97)

3. d. is the answer. (p. 114)

    a. The average length of labor for subsequent births is 7 hours.

4. a. is the answer. (p. 108)

5. a. is the answer. (p. 108)

6. c. is the answer. (p. 123)

7. d. is the answer. (p. 115)

8. c. is the answer. (p. 119)

9. d. is the answer. (p. 102)

10. c. is the answer. Most doctors in the United States advise pregnant women to abstain completely from alcohol. (p. 110)

11. a. is the answer. (p. 101)

12. d. is the answer. (p. 115)

13. b. is the answer. (p. 101)

14. d. is the answer. (p. 125)

15. c. is the answer. (p. 119)

True or False Items

1. T (p. 103)

2. T (p. 100)

3. T (p. 116)

4. F Behavioral teratogens can affect the fetus at any time during the prenatal period. (p. 104)

5. F There is no controversy about the damaging effects of smoking during pregnancy. (p. 121)

6. T (p. 115)

7. T (p. 114)

8. F Though highly desirable, mother–infant contact at birth is not necessary for the child's normal development or for a good parent–child relationship. Many opportunities for bonding occur throughout childhood. (p. 125)

9. T (p. 121)

10. F About 28 percent of births in the United States are now cesarean. (p. 115)

KEY TERMS

1. The first two weeks of development after conception, characterized by rapid cell division and the beginning of cell differentiation, are called the **germinal period.** (p. 97)

    Memory aid: A *germ cell* is one from which a new organism can develop. The *germ*inal **period** is the first stage in the development of the new organism.

2. The **embryonic period** is approximately the third through the eighth week of prenatal development, when the basic forms of all body structures develop. (p. 97)

3. From the ninth week after conception until birth is the **fetal period,** when the organs grow in size and mature in functioning. (p. 97)

4. During the germinal period, once the developing cell mass begins to take on distinct characteristics it is called a **blastocyst**. (p. 97)

5. The **placenta** is the organ that develops in the uterus to protect and nourish the developing person. (p. 98)

6. **Implantation** is the process by which the zygote burrows into the placenta that lines the uterus, where it can be nourished and protected during growth. (p. 98)

7. **Embryo** is the name given to the developing human organism from about the third through the eighth week after conception. (p. 99)

8. **Fetus** is the name for the developing human organism from the start of the ninth week after conception until birth. (p. 99)

9. About 22 weeks after conception, the fetus attains the **age of viability,** at which point it has at least some slight chance of survival outside the uterus if specialized medical care is available. (p. 101)

10. **Teratogens** are agents and conditions, such as viruses, drugs, chemicals, extreme stress, and malnutrition, that can impair prenatal development and lead to birth defects or even death. (p. 104)

11. **Behavioral teratogens** are agents and conditions that can damage the brain, impairing the future child's intellectual and emotional functioning. (p. 104)

12. **Teratology** is the study of birth defects. (p. 104)

13. Teratology is a science of **risk analysis**, meaning that it attempts to evaluate what factors make prenatal harm more or less likely to occur. (p. 104)

14. A **threshold effect** is the harmful effect of a substance that occurs when exposure to it reaches a certain level. (p. 106)

15. An **interaction effect** occurs when one teratogen intensifies the harmful effects of another. (p. 106)

16. Prenatal alcohol exposure may cause **fetal alcohol syndrome (FAS)**, a cluster of birth defects that includes abnormal facial characteristics, slow physical growth, behavior problems, and retarded mental development. (p. 110)

17. Caused by prenatal exposure to alcohol, **fetal alcohol effects (FAE)** is diagnosed when a newborn has some signs of fetal alcohol syndrome, but not enough to be diagnosed with that disorder. (p. 110)

18. A **sonogram** is an image on an unborn fetus produced with high-frequency sound waves. (p. 110)

19. Newborns are rated at one and then at five minutes after birth according to the **Apgar scale.** This scale assigns a score of 0, 1, or 2 to each of five characteristics: heart rate, breathing, muscle tone, color, and reflexes. A score of 7 or better indicates that all is well. (p. 115)

20. In a **cesarean section**, the fetus is removed from the mother surgically. (p. 115)

21. A **doula** is a woman who works alongside medical staff to assist a woman through labor and delivery. (118)

22. **Anoxia** is a temporary lack of oxygen during the birth process that, if prolonged, can cause brain damage or death to the baby. (p. 118)

23. **Cerebral palsy** is a muscular control disorder caused by damage to the brain's motor centers during or before birth. (p. 118)

24. A birthweight of less than $5^1/2$ pounds (2,500 grams) is called **low birthweight (LBW).** Low-birthweight infants are at risk for many immediate and long-term problems. (p. 119)

25. A birthweight of less than 3 pounds 5 ounces (1,500 grams) is called **very low birthweight (VLBW).** (p. 119)

26. A birthweight of less than 2 pounds (1,000 grams) is called **extremely low birthweight (ELBW).** (p. 119)

27. When an infant is born 3 or more weeks before the due date, it is said to be a **preterm birth.** (p. 119)

28. Infants who weigh substantially less than they should, given how much time has passed since conception, are called **small for gestational age (SGA),** or small for dates. (p. 121)

29. **Kangaroo care** occurs when the mother of a low-birthweight infant spends at least one hour a day holding her infant between her breasts. (p. 123)

30. **Parental alliance** refers to the cooperation and mutual support between mother and father because of their mutual commitment to their children. (p. 125)

31. **Postpartum depression** is a new mother's feeling of sadness and inadequacy in the days and weeks after giving birth. (p. 123)

32. The term **parent–infant bond** describes the strong feelings of attachment between parent and child in the early moments of their relationship together. (p. 125)

5

The First Two Years: Biosocial Development

Chapter Overview

Chapter 5 is the first of a three-chapter unit that describes the developing person from birth to age 2 in terms of biosocial, cognitive, and psychosocial development.

The chapter begins with observations on the overall growth of infants, including information on infant sleep patterns. Following is a discussion of brain growth and development and the importance of experience in brain development. The chapter then turns to a discussion of sensory, perceptual, and motor abilities and the ages at which the average infant acquires them. Preventive medicine, the importance of immunizations during the first two years, and the possible causes of sudden infant death syndrome (SIDS) are discussed next. The final section explains the importance of nutrition during the first two years and the consequences of severe malnutrition.

NOTE: Answer guidelines for all Chapter 5 questions begin on page 70.

Chapter Review

When you have finished reading the chapter, work through the material that follows to review it. Complete the sentences and answer the questions. In some cases, Study Tips explain how best to learn a difficult concept, while Think About It and Applications help you to know how well you understand the material. As you proceed, evaluate your performance for each section by consulting the answers beginning on page 70. Do not continue with the next section until you understand each answer. If you need to, review or reread the appropriate section in the textbook before continuing.

Body Changes (pp. 131–135)

1. The average North American newborn measures _____ and weighs about _____ .

2. By age 2, the typical child weighs about _____ and measures _____ . The typical 2-year-old is almost _____ percent of his or her adult weight and _____ percent of his or her adult height.

3. When nutrition is temporarily inadequate, the body stops growing but the brain does not. This is called _____-_____ .

4. A standard, or average, measurement that is calculated for a specific group or population is a _____ .

5. To compare a child's growth to that of other children, we determine a _____ , a point on a ranking scale of _____ (what number?) to _____ (what number?).

6. Throughout childhood, regular and ample _____ correlates with _____ maturation, _____ , _____ regulation, and _____ adjustment in school and within the family.

7. Over the first months of life, the relative amount of time spent in the different _____ of sleep changes. The stage of sleep characterized by flickering eyes behind closed lids and _____ is called _____ _____ . During this stage of sleep, brain waves are fairly _____ (slow/ rapid). This stage of sleep _____ (increases/decreases) over the first months, as does the dozing stage called _____ _____ . Slow-wave sleep, also called _____ _____ , increases markedly at about _____ months of age.

8. In most Western cultures, children _____ (do/do not) sleep with their parents. In contrast, parents in _____ , _____ , and _____ _____ traditionally practice _____ with their infants. This practice _____ (does/does not) seem to be harmful unless the adult is _____ .

THINK ABOUT IT: Growth in early infancy is astoundingly rapid. You can begin to appreciate just how rapid this growth is by projecting the growth patterns of the infant onto an adult, such as yourself. If you were gaining weight at the rate of an infant, your weight would be tripled one year from today. How much would you weigh? If you were growing at the rate of an infant during the first year, you would add an inch each month. What would your height be a year from today?

_____

APPLICATIONS:

9. Two-year-old Rafael weighs 30 pounds and is 34 inches tall. He is considered average because his height and weight are in the _____ percentile for 2-year-olds.

10. The Farbers, who are first-time parents, are wondering whether they should be concerned because their 12-month-old daughter, who weighs 22 pounds and measures 30 inches, is not growing quite as fast as she did during her first year. You should tell them that
   a. any slowdown in growth during the second year is a cause for immediate concern.
   b. their daughter's weight and height are well below average for her age.
   c. growth patterns for a first child are often erratic.
   d. physical growth is somewhat slower in the second year.

11. Concluding her presentation on sleep, Lakshmi notes each of the following EXCEPT
   a. dreaming occurs during REM sleep.
   b. quiet sleep increases markedly at about 3 or 4 months.
   c. the dreaming brain is characterized by slow brain waves.
   d. regular and ample sleep is an important factor in a child's emotional regulation.

Brain Development (pp. 135–142)

12. At birth, the brain has attained about _____ percent of its adult weight; by age 2, the brain is about _____ percent of its adult weight. In comparison, body weight at age 2 is about _____ percent of what it will be in adulthood.

13. The brain's communication system consists primarily of nerve cells called _____ , which are connected by intricate networks of nerve fibers, called _____ and _____ . Some nerve cells are in the area that controls automatic responses, called the _____ _____ . About _____ percent of these cells are in the brain's outer layer called the _____ . This area takes up about _____ percent of human brain material and is the site of _____ , _____ , and _____ .

14. Each neuron has many _____ but only a single _____ .

15. Neurons communicate with one another at intersections called _____ . After traveling down the length of the _____ , electrical impulses excite chemicals called _____ that carry information across the _____ _____ to the _____ of a "receiving" neuron, which is speeded up by a process called _____ . Most of the nerve cells _____ (are/are not) present at birth, whereas there are _____ (as many/far fewer) fiber networks.

16. During the first months of life, brain development is most noticeable in the _____ .

17. From birth until age 2, the density of dendrites in the cortex _____ (increases/decreases) by a factor of _____ . The phenomenal increase in neural connections over the first two years has been called _____ _____ .

Following this growth process, some neurons wither in the process called _____ because _____ does not activate those brain areas. The importance of early experience is seen in the brain's production of stress hormones such as _____ .

18. Brain functions that require basic common experiences in order to develop normally are called _____-_____ brain functions; those that depend on particular, and variable, experiences in order to develop are called _____-_____ brain functions. Between 6 and 24 months, the _____ areas of the brain develop most rapidly. The last part of the brain to mature is the _____ _____ , which is the area for _____ , _____ , and _____ _____ .

19. A life-threatening condition that occurs when an infant is held by the shoulders and quickly shaken back and forth is _____ _____ _____ . Crying stops because of ruptured _____ _____ in the brain and broken _____ connections.

20. An important implication of brain development for caregivers is that early brain growth is _____ and reflects _____ . Another is that each part of the brain has its own _____ for _____ , _____ , and _____ . The inborn drive to remedy any deficit that may occur in development is called _____ .

21. (text and A View from Science) Neuroscientists once believed that brains were entirely formed by _____ and _____ ; today, most believe in _____ , which is the concept that personality, intellect, habits, and emotions change throughout life for _____ (one/a combination of) reason(s). Specific times when particular kinds of development are primed to occur are called _____ _____ . Marion Diamond, William

Greenough, and colleagues discovered that the brains of rats who were raised in stimulating environments were better developed, with more _____ , than the brains of rats raised in barren environments. Orphaned Romanian children who were isolated and deprived of stimulation showed signs of _____ damage. Placed in healthier environments, these children _____ (improved/did not improve); years later, persistent deficits in some of these children _____ (were/were not) found.

THINK ABOUT IT: The text cites several lines of research evidence that environmental events after birth can shape the development of a child's brain and affect overall cognitive functioning in the years beyond infancy. In the face of this evidence, many parents wonder how far they should go in providing their babies with enriched environmental experiences. Based on your reading of this section of the text chapter, what practical advice would you offer to prospective parents?

STUDY TIP: As you can see from the list of Key Terms, this chapter introduces many important new words for you to remember. You will need to spend extra time committing these terms to memory. Many students find flash cards and quizzing a study partner helpful for learning new terminology. To help remember the key parts of a neuron, you might find it useful to practice drawing and labeling dendrites, axons, myelin, and synapses.

APPLICATIONS:

22. I am a chemical that carries information between nerve cells in the brain. What am I?

_____

23. Sharetta's pediatrician informs her parents that Sharetta's 1-year-old brain is exhibiting transient exuberance. In response to this news, Sharetta's parents
   a. smile, because they know their daughter's brain is developing new neural connections.
   b. worry, because this may indicate increased vulnerability to a later learning disability.
   c. know that this process, in which axons become coated, is normal.
   d. are alarmed, because this news indicates that the frontal area of Sharetta's cortex is immature.

24. Trying to impress his professor, Erik explains that we know humans have a critical period for learning certain skills because the brain cannot form new synapses after age 13. Should the professor be impressed with Erik's knowledge of biosocial development?
    a. Yes, although each neuron may have already formed as many as 15,000 connections with other neurons.
    b. Yes, although the branching of dendrites and axons does continue through young adulthood.
    c. No. Although Erik is correct about neural development, the brain attains adult size by about age 7.
    d. No. Synapses form throughout life.

Sensation and Movement (pp. 142–149)

25. The process by which the visual, auditory, and other sensory systems detect stimuli is called _____ ; _____ occurs when the brain tries to make sense out of a stimulus so that the individual becomes aware of it. At birth, only _____ is apparent; _____ requires experience. In the process called _____ , a person thinks about and interprets what he or she has perceived. This process _____ (can/cannot) occur without sensation.

26. Generally speaking, newborns' hearing _____ (is/is not) very acute at birth. Newborns _____ (can/cannot) perceive differences in voices, rhythms, and cadences long before they achieve comprehension of _____ . Infants also become accustomed to the rules of their _____ .

27. The least mature of the senses at birth is _____ . Newborns' visual focusing is best for objects between _____ and _____ inches away.

28. Experience and increasing maturation of the visual cortex accounts for improvements in other visual abilities, such as the infant's ability to see _____ and then notice _____ . By 2 months, they look more intently at a human _____ . The ability to use both eyes in a coordinated manner to focus on one object, which is called _____ _____ , develops at about _____ of age.

29. Taste, smell, and touch _____ (function/do not function) at birth. The ability to be comforted by the human _____ is a skill tested in the _____ Neonatal Assessment Scale.

30. The infant's early sensory abilities seem organized for two goals: _____ _____ and _____ .

31. The most visible and dramatic advances of infancy involve _____ _____ .

32. An involuntary response to a stimulus is called a _____ .

33. The involuntary response that causes the newborn to take the first breath even before the umbilical cord is cut is called the _____ _____ . Other reflexive behaviors that maintain oxygen are _____ , _____ , and _____ .

34. Shivering, crying, and tucking the legs close to the body are examples of reflexes that help to maintain _____ _____ .

35. A third set of reflexes manages _____ . One of these is the tendency of the newborn to suck anything that touches the lips; this is the _____ reflex. Another is the tendency of newborns to turn their heads and start to suck when something brushes against their cheek; this is the _____ reflex. Other important reflexes that facilitate this behavior are _____ , _____ , and _____ _____ .

36. Large movements such as walking and running are called _____ _____ skills.

37. Most infants are able to crawl on all fours (sometimes called creeping) between _____ and _____ months of age. Three factors in the development of walking are

_____ _____ , _____ , and _____

_____ .

List the major hallmarks in children's mastery of walking.

38. Abilities that require more precise, small movements, such as picking up a coin, are called _____ _____ skills. By _____ months of age, most babies can reach for, grab, and hold onto almost any object of the right size.

39. Although the _____ in which motor skills are mastered is the same in all healthy infants, the _____ of acquisition of skills varies greatly.

40. Motor skill norms vary from one _____ group to another.

41. Motor skill acquisition in identical twins _____ (is/is not) more similar than in fraternal twins, suggesting that genes _____ (do/do not) play an important role. Another influential factor is the _____ _____ of infant care.

STUDY TIP: Infants have a number of reflexes that are critical for survival and others that indicate normal body and brain functioning. Filling in the missing information in the table below will provide you with a handy summary of those reflexes. In some cases, the description is provided; in other cases, reflex name is given. First, try to complete the table from memory; then check text page 145.

42. Reflex(es)	Description
a.	breathing, hiccupping, sneezing, and thrashing
b. Maintaining constant body temperature	
c.	Sucking, rooting, swallowing
d. Babinski	
e.	Infants move their legs as if to walk when they are held upright and their feet touch a flat surface
f. Swimming	
g.	Infants grip things that touch their palms
h. Moro	

APPLICATIONS:

43. Sensation is to perception as _____ is to
    _____ .
    a. hearing; seeing
    b. detecting a stimulus; making sense of a stim-
       ulus
    c. making sense of a stimulus; detecting a stim-
       ulus
    d. tasting; smelling

44. Like all newborns, Serena is able to:
    a. differentiate one sound from another.
    b. see objects more than 30 inches from her
       face quite clearly.
    c. use her mouth to recognize objects by taste
       and touch.
    d. do all of these things.

45. Three-week-old Nathan should have the least
    difficulty focusing on the sight of:
    a. stuffed animals on a bookshelf across the
       room from his crib.
    b. his mother's face as she holds him in her
       arms.
    c. the checkerboard pattern in the wallpaper
       covering the ceiling of his room.
    d. the family dog as it dashes into the nursery.

Public Health Measures (pp. 149–158)

46. Without public health practices, the number of
    children who die would be _____
    (how much?) the number who did die between
    1950 and 2008. One method, _____
    _____ _____ (giving
    restorative liquids to children who are sick and
    have diarrhea), saves 3 million children a year.

47. Globally, today most children _____
    (do/do not) live to adulthood. A key factor in
    reducing the childhood death rate was the devel-
    opment of _____—a process that
    stimulates the body's _____ system
    to defend against contagious diseases. This
    process has met with stunning success in eradi-
    cating or reducing diseases such as
    _____ , _____ ,
    _____ , and _____ .
    Other reasons for a decrease in infant mortality
    are _____ .

48. Yet another reason for lower infant mortality
    worldwide is a decrease in _____
    _____ _____
    _____ , in which seemingly healthy
    infants die unexpectedly in their
    _____ .

49. A key factor in SIDS is _____ back-
    ground. In ethnically diverse nations, babies of
    _____ descent are less likely to suc-
    cumb to SIDS than are babies of _____
    or _____ descent.
    Identify several practices that may explain why cer-
    tain ethnic groups have a low incidence of SIDS.

50. The ideal infant food is _____
    _____ , beginning with the thick,
    high-calorie fluid called _____ . The
    only situations in which formula may be healthier
    for the infant than breast milk are when _____
    _____ .
    State several advantages of breast milk over cow's
    milk for the developing infant.

51. Most doctors recommend exclusive breast-
    feeding for the first _____ (how
    many?) months.

52. The most serious nutritional problem of infancy
    is _____-_____
    _____ .

53. Chronically malnourished infants suffer in three
    ways: Their _____ may not develop

normally, they may have no _____
_____ to protect them against disease, and they may develop the diseases
_____ or _____ .

54. Severe protein-calorie deficiency in early infancy
causes _____ . If malnutrition
begins after age 1, protein-calorie deficiency is
more likely to cause the disease called
_____ , which involves swelling or
bloating of the face, legs, and abdomen.

APPLICATIONS:

55. To promote optimal nutrition for her new baby,
Emma's pediatrician recommends exclusive
breast-feeding for the first _____
(how many months?).

56. Before she became pregnant, Nell had a bout of
the measles. After the baby was born, her pediatrician recommended breast-feeding because
_____
_____ .

Progress Test 1

Multiple-Choice Questions

Circle your answers to the following questions and
check them with the answers on page 72. If your
answer is incorrect, read the explanation for why it is
incorrect and then consult the appropriate pages of
the text (in parentheses following the correct answer).

1. The average North American newborn
   a. weighs approximately 6 pounds.
   b. weighs approximately 7½ pounds.
   c. is "overweight" because of the diet of the
      mother.
   d. weighs 10 percent less than what is desirable.

2. Compared to the first year, growth during the
   second year
   a. proceeds at a slower rate.
   b. continues at about the same rate.
   c. includes more insulating fat.
   d. includes more bone and muscle.

3. The major motor skill most likely to be mastered
   by an infant by 4 months is
   a. sitting without support.
   b. sitting with head steady.

   c. turning the head in search of a nipple.
   d. grabbing an object with thumb and forefinger.

4. Norms suggest that the earliest walkers in the
   world are infants from
   a. Western Europe.   c. Uganda.
   b. the United States.   d. Denver.

5. Head-sparing is the phenomenon in which
   a. the brain continues to grow even though the
      body stops growing as a result of malnutri-
      tion.
   b. the infant's body grows more rapidly during
      the second year.
   c. axons develop more rapidly than dendrites.
   d. dendrites develop more rapidly than axons.

6. Dreaming is characteristic of
   a. slow-wave sleep.   c. REM sleep.
   b. transitional sleep. d. quiet sleep.

7. For a pediatrician, the most important factor in
   assessing a child's healthy growth is
   a. height in inches.
   b. weight in pounds.
   c. body fat percentage.
   d. the percentile rank of a child's height or
      weight.

8. Brain functions that depend on babies' having
   things to see and hear, and people to feed and
   carry them, are called
   a. experience-dependent.
   b. experience-expectant.
   c. pruning functions.
   d. transient exuberance.

9. Compared with formula-fed infants, breast-fed
   infants tend to have
   a. greater weight gain.
   b. fewer allergies and stomach upsets.
   c. less frequent feedings during the first few
      months.
   d. more social approval.

10. Marasmus and kwashiorkor are caused by
    a. bloating.
    b. protein-calorie deficiency.
    c. living in a developing country.
    d. poor family food habits.

11. The infant's first "motor skills" are
    a. fine motor skills.   c. reflexes.
    b. gross motor skills. d. unpredictable.

12. Which of the following is said to have had the greatest impact on human mortality reduction and population growth?

    a. improvements in infant nutrition

    b. oral rehydration therapy

    c. medical advances in newborn care

    d. childhood immunization

13. Which of the following is true of motor-skill development in healthy infants?

    a. It follows the same basic sequence the world over.

    b. It occurs at different rates from individual to individual.

    c. It follows norms that vary from one ethnic group to another.

    d. All of these statements are true.

14. Most of the nerve cells a human brain will ever need are present

    a. at conception.

    b. about 1 month following conception.

    c. at birth.

    d. at age 5 or 6.

15. Chronically malnourished children suffer in which of the following ways?

    a. They have no body reserves to protect them.

    b. Their brains may not develop normally.

    c. They may die from marasmus.

    d. All of these conditions are true of malnourished children.

Matching Items

Match each definition or description with its corresponding term.

Terms

    1. neurons

    2. dendrites

    3. kwashiorkor

    4. marasmus

    5. gross motor skill

    6. fine motor skill

    7. reflex

    8. protein-calorie malnutrition

    9. transient exuberance

    10. prefrontal cortex

    11. self-righting

Definitions or Descriptions

    a. protein deficiency during the first year in which growth stops and body tissues waste away

    b. picking up an object

    c. the most common serious nutrition problem of infancy

    d. protein deficiency during toddlerhood

    e. communication networks among nerve cells

    f. walking or running

    g. an unlearned, involuntary response

    h. the phenomenal increase in neural connections over the first two years

    i. nerve cells

    j. the brain area that specializes in anticipation, planning, and impulse control

    k. the inborn drive to correct a developmental deficit

Progress Test 2

Progress Test 2 should be completed during a final chapter review. Answer the following questions after you thoroughly understand the correct answers for the Chapter Review and Progress Test 1.

Multiple-Choice Questions

1. Dendrite is to axon as neural _____ is to neural _____ .
   a. input; output
   b. output; input
   c. myelin; synapse
   d. synapse; myelin

2. A reflex is best defined as a(n)
   a. fine motor skill.
   b. motor ability mastered at a specific age.
   c. involuntary response to a given stimulus.
   d. gross motor skill.

3. A norm is
   a. a standard, or average, that is derived for a specific group or population.
   b. a point on a ranking scale of 0 to 100.
   c. a milestone of development that all children reach at the same age.
   d. all of the above.

4. (A View from Science) Research studies of the more than 100,000 Romanian children orphaned and severely deprived in infancy reported all of the following EXCEPT
   a. all of the children were overburdened with stress.
   b. after adoption, the children gained weight quickly.
   c. during early childhood, many still showed signs of emotional damage.
   d. most of the children placed in healthy adoptive homes eventually recovered.

5. Regarding the brain's cortex, which of the following is NOT true?
   a. The cortex houses about 70 percent of the brain's neurons.
   b. The cortex is the brain's outer layer.
   c. The cortex is the location of most thinking, feeling, and sensing.
   d. Only primates have a cortex.

6. During the first weeks of life, babies seem to focus reasonably well on
   a. little in their environment.
   b. objects at a distance of 4 to 30 inches.
   c. objects at a distance of 1 to 3 inches.
   d. objects several feet away.

7. Which sleep stage increases markedly at about 3 or 4 months?
   a. REM
   b. transitional
   c. fast-wave
   d. slow-wave

8. An advantage of breast milk over formula is that it
   a. is always sterile and at body temperature.
   b. contains traces of medications ingested by the mother.
   c. can be given without involving the father.
   d. contains more protein and vitamin D than does formula.

9. Synapses are
   a. nerve fibers that receive electrochemical impulses from other neurons.
   b. nerve fibers that transmit electrochemical impulses to other neurons.
   c. intersections between the axon of one neuron and the dendrites of other neurons.
   d. chemical signals that transmit information from one neuron to another.

10. Transient exuberance and pruning demonstrate that
    a. the pace of acquisition of motor skills varies markedly from child to child.
    b. Newborns sleep more than older children because their immature nervous systems cannot handle the higher, waking level of sensory stimulation.
    c. The specifics of brain structure and growth depend partly on the infant's experience.
    d. Good nutrition is essential to healthy biosocial development.

11. Jumping is to using a crayon as _____ is to _____ .
    a. fine motor skill; gross motor skill
    b. gross motor skill; fine motor skill
    c. reflex; fine motor skill
    d. reflex; gross motor skill

12. Some infant reflexes are critical for survival. Hiccups and sneezes help the infant maintain the _____ , and leg tucking maintains _____ .
    a. feeding; oxygen supply
    b. feeding; a constant body temperature
    c. oxygen supply; feeding
    d. oxygen supply; a constant body temperature

13. (A View from Science) Compared with the brains of laboratory rats that were raised in barren cages, those of rats raised in stimulating, toy-filled cages
    a. were better developed and had more dendrites.
    b. had fewer synaptic connections.
    c. showed less transient exuberance.
    d. displayed all of these characteristics.

14. In determining a healthy child's growth, a pediatrician focuses on
    a. the child's past growth.
    b. the growth of others the same age.
    c. growth changes from earlier rankings.
    d. all of these factors.

15. Infant sensory and perceptual abilities appear to be especially organized for
    a. obtaining adequate nutrition and comfort.
    b. comfort and social interaction.
    c. looking.
    d. touching and smelling.

True or False Items

Write T (*true*) or F (*false*) on the line in front of each statement.

_____ 1. Imaging studies have identified a specific area of the brain that specializes in recognizing faces.

_____ 2. Putting babies to sleep on their stomachs increases the risk of SIDS.

_____ 3. Reflexive hiccups, sneezes, and thrashing are signs that the infant's reflexes are not functioning properly.

_____ 4. Infants of all ethnic backgrounds develop the same motor skills at approximately the same age.

_____ 5. The typical 2-year-old is almost one-fifth its adult weight and one-half its adult height.

_____ 6. Vision is better developed than hearing in most newborns.

_____ 7. Today, most infants in industrialized nations are breast-fed up to 6 months.

_____ 8. Certain basic sensory experiences seem necessary to ensure full brain development in the human infant.

_____ 9. Dendrite growth is the major reason that brain weight increases so dramatically in the first two years.

_____ 10. The only motor skills apparent at birth are reflexes.

_____ 11. The prefrontal cortex is one of the first brain areas to mature.

Key Terms

Using your own words, write a brief definition or explanation of each of the following terms on a separate piece of paper.

1. head-sparing
2. norm
3. percentile
4. REM sleep
5. co-sleeping
6. neuron
7. cortex
8. axon
9. dendrite
10. synapse
11. transient exuberance
12. experience-expectant brain functions
13. experience-dependent brain functions
14. prefrontal cortex
15. shaken baby syndrome
16. self-righting
17. sensation
18. perception
19. binocular vision
20. motor skill
21. reflex
22. gross motor skills
23. fine motor skills
24. immunization
25. sudden infant death syndrome (SIDS)
26. protein-calorie malnutrition
27. marasmus
28. kwashiorkor

Answers

CHAPTER REVIEW

1. 20 inches (51 centimeters); 7½ pounds (3,400 grams)
2. 30 pounds (13.5 kilograms); between 32 and 36 inches (81–91 centimeters); 15 to 20; 50
3. head-sparing
4. norm

5. percentile; 0; 100

6. sleep; brain; learning, emotional, psychological

7. stages; dreaming; REM sleep; rapid; decreases; transitional sleep; quiet sleep; 3 or 4

8. do not; Asia; Africa; Latin America; co-sleeping; does not; drugged or drunk

9. 50th. The 50th percentile is the midpoint in a ranking from 0 to 100, which means Rafael is exactly average.

10. d. is the answer. Although slowdowns in growth during infancy are often a cause for concern, their daughter's weight and height are typical of 1-year-old babies.

11. c. is the answer. The dreaming brain is characterized by rapid brain waves.

12. 25; 75; 20

13. neurons; axons; dendrites; brain stem; 70; cortex; 80; thinking; feeling; sensing

14. dendrites; axon

15. synapses; axon; neurotransmitters; synaptic gap; dendrite; myelination; are; far fewer

16. cortex

17. increases; five; transient exuberance; pruning; experience; cortisol

18. experience-expectant; experience-dependent; language; prefrontal cortex; anticipation; planning; impulse control

19. shaken baby syndrome; blood vessels; neural

20. rapid; experience; sequence; growth; connecting; pruning; self-righting

21. genes; prenatal influences; plasticity; a combination of; sensitive periods; dendrites; emotional; improved; were

22. neurotransmitter.

23. a. is the answer. Transient exuberance results in a proliferation of neural connections during infancy, some of which will disappear because they are not used; that is, they are not needed to process information.

24. d. is the answer. Although synapses do form more rapidly in infancy than at any other time, they do not stop forming after infancy.

25. sensation; perception; sensation; perception; cognition; can

26. is; can; meaning; language

27. vision; 4; 30

28. shapes; details; face; binocular vision; 14 weeks

29. function; touch; Brazelton

30. social interaction; comfort

31. motor skills

32. reflex

33. breathing reflex; hiccups; sneezes; thrashing

34. constant body temperature

35. feeding; sucking; rooting; swallowing; crying; spitting up

36. gross motor

37. 8; 10; muscle strength; practice; brain maturation within the motor cortex

On average, a child can walk while holding a hand at 9 months, can stand alone momentarily at 10 months, and can walk well, unassisted, at 12 months.

38. fine motor; 6

39. sequence; age

40. ethnic

41. is; do; cultural pattern

42. a. reflexes that maintain oxygen supply
    b. crying, shivering, tucking in their legs, pushing blankets away
    c. reflexes that facilitate feeding
    d. infants' toes fan upward when their feet are stroked
    e. stepping reflex
    f. infants stretch out their arms and legs when they are held on their stomachs
    g. Palmar grasping reflex
    h. infants fling their arms outward and then clutch them against their chests in response to a loud noise

43. b. is the answer. Answers a. and d. are incorrect because sensation and perception operate in all of these sensory modalities.

44. a. is the answer. Objects more than 30 inches away are out of focus for newborns. The ability to recognize objects by taste or touch does not emerge until about one month of age.

45. b. is the answer. This is true because, at birth, focusing is best for objects between 4 and 30 inches away.

46. twice; oral rehydration therapy

47. do; immunization; immune; smallpox; polio; measles; rotovirus; advances in newborn care, better nutrition, and access to clean water

48. sudden infant death syndrome (SIDS); sleep

49. ethnic; Asian; European; African

Chinese parents tend to their babies periodically as they sleep, which makes them less likely to fall into a deep, nonbreathing sleep. Bangladeshi infants are usually surrounded by many family members in a rich sensory environment, making them less likely to sleep deeply for very long.

50. breast milk; colostrum; the mother is HIV-positive or using toxic or addictive drugs

Breast milk is always sterile and at body temperature; it contains more iron, vitamins, and other nutrients; it contains antibodies that provide the infant some protection against disease; it is more digestible than any formula; and it decreases the risk of many diseases that appear in childhood and adulthood.

51. four to six

52. protein-calorie malnutrition

53. brains; body reserves; marasmus; kwashiorkor

54. marasmus; kwashiorkor

55. four to six months

56. Having had measles, Nell has developed an immunity to the disease. With breast milk, she will pass the resulting antibodies onto her newborn.

PROGRESS TEST 1

Multiple-Choice Questions

1. **b.** is the answer. (p. 131)

2. **a.** is the answer. (p. 131)

3. **b.** is the answer. (p. 146)

   a. The age norm for this skill is 6–7 months.

   c. This is a reflex, not an acquired motor skill.

   d. This skill is acquired between 9 and 14 months.

4. **c.** is the answer. (p. 148)

5. **a.** is the answer. (p. 132)

6. **c.** is the answer. (pp. 132–133)

7. **d.** is the answer. (p. 138)

8. **b.** is the answer. (p. 132)

   a. Experience-dependent functions depend on particular, and variable, experiences in order to develop.

   c. Pruning refers to the process by which some neurons wither because experience does not activate them.

   d. This refers to the great increase in the number of neurons, dendrites, and synapses that occurs in an infant's brain over the first two years of life.

9. **b.** is the answer. This is because breast milk is more digestible than cow's milk or formula. (p. 155)

   a., c., & d. Breast- and bottle-fed babies do not differ in these attributes.

10. **b.** is the answer. (p. 157)

11. **c.** is the answer. (p. 145)

   a. & b. These motor skills do not emerge until somewhat later; reflexes are present at birth.

   d. On the contrary, reflexes are quite predictable.

12. **d.** is the answer. (p. 150)

13. **d.** is the answer. (pp. 148–149)

14. **c.** is the answer. (p. 135)

15. **d.** is the answer. (pp. 156–157)

Matching Items

1. i (p. 135)
2. e (p. 136)
3. d (p. 157)
4. a (p. 157)
5. f (p. 146)
6. b (p. 147)
7. g (p. 145)
8. c (p. 156)
9. h (p. 136)
10. j (p. 134)
11. k (p. 140)

PROGRESS TEST 2

Multiple-Choice Questions

1. **a.** is the answer. (p. 136)

2. **c.** is the answer. (p. 145)

   a., b., & d. Each of these refers to voluntary responses that are acquired only after a certain amount of practice; reflexes are involuntary responses that are present at birth and require no practice.

3. **a.** is the answer. (p. 132)

   b. This defines percentile.

4. **c.** is the answer. (p. 141)

5. **d.** is the answer. All mammals have a cortex. (p. 136)

6. **b.** is the answer. (p. 143)

   a. Although focusing ability seems to be limited to a certain range, babies do focus on many objects in this range.

   c. This is not within the range at which babies *can* focus.

   d. Babies have very poor distance vision.

7. **d.** is the answer. (p. 133)

8. **a.** is the answer. (p. 154)

   b. If anything, this is a potential *disadvantage* of breast milk over formula.

   c. So can formula.

d. Breast milk contains more iron, certain vitamins, and other nutrients than cow's milk; it does not contain more protein and vitamin D, however.

9. **c.** is the answer. (p. 136)

   a. These are dendrites.

   b. These are axons.

   d. These are neurotransmitters.

10. **c.** is the answer. (pp. 136–137)

11. **b.** is the answer. (pp. 146, 147)

   c. & d. Reflexes are involuntary responses; climbing and using a crayon are both voluntary responses.

12. **d.** is the answer. (p. 145)

13. **a.** is the answer. (p. 141)

14. **d.** is the answer. (p. 133)

15. **b.** is the answer. (p. 144)

True or False Items

1. T (p. 136)

2. T (p. 153)

3. F   Hiccups, sneezes, and thrashing are common during the first few days, and they are entirely normal reflexes. (p. 145)

4. F   Although all healthy infants develop the same motor skills in the same sequence, the age at which these skills are acquired can vary greatly from infant to infant. (pp. 148–149)

5. T (p. 132)

6. F   Vision is relatively poorly developed at birth, whereas hearing is well developed. (p. 143)

7. F   Only 36 percent of all babies are breast-fed up to 6 months. (p. 156)

8. T (pp. 138–139)

9. T (p. 136)

10. T (p. 145)

11. F   In fact, the prefrontal cortex is probably the last area of the brain to attain maturity. (p. 139)

KEY TERMS

1. **Head-sparing** is a biological mechanism in which the brain continues to grow even though the body stops growing in a malnourished child. (p. 132)

2. A **norm** is an average, or standard, measurement calculated for a specific population. (p. 132)

3. A **percentile** is any point on a ranking scale of 0 to 100; percentiles are often used to compare a child's development to group norms and to his or her own prior development. (p. 132)

4. **REM sleep,** or rapid eye movement sleep, is a stage of sleep characterized by flickering eyes behind closed eyelids, dreaming, and rapid brain waves. (p. 133)

5. **Co-sleeping** is the custom in which parents and their infants sleep together. (p. 134)

6. A **neuron,** or nerve cell, is the main component of the central nervous system. (p. 135)

7. The **cortex** is the outer layers of the brain that is involved in most thinking, feeling, and sensing. (p. 136)

   Memory aid: Cortex in Latin means "bark." As bark covers a tree, the cortex is the "bark of the brain."

8. An **axon** is the nerve fiber that sends electrochemical impulses from one neuron to the dendrites of other neurons. (p. 136)

9. A **dendrite** is a nerve fiber that receives the electrochemical impulses transmitted from other neurons via their axons. (p. 136)

10. A **synapse** is the point at which the axon of a sending neuron meets the dendrites of a receiving neuron. (p. 136)

11. **Transient exuberance** is the dramatic increase in the number of dendrites that occurs in an infant's brain over the first two years of life. (p. 136)

12. **Experience-expectant brain functions** are those that require basic common experiences (such as having things to see and hear) in order to develop normally. (p. 138)

13. **Experience-dependent brain functions** are those that depend on particular, and variable, experiences (such as experiencing language) in order to develop. (p. 139)

14. The **prefrontal cortex** is the brain area that specializes in anticipation, planning, and impulse control. (p. 139)

15. **Shaken baby syndrome** is a life-threatening condition in which blood vessels in an infant's brain have been ruptured because the infant has been forcefully shaken back and forth. (p. 140)

16. **Self-righting** is the inborn drive to remedy a deficit in development. (p. 140)

17. **Sensation** is the process by which a sensory system detects a particular stimulus. (p. 142)

18. **Perception** is the process by which the brain tries to make sense of a stimulus such that the individual becomes aware of it. (p. 142)

19. **Binocular vision** is the ability to use both eyes in a coordinated fashion in order to see one image. (p. 144)

    Memory aid: Bi- indicates "two"; ocular means something pertaining to the eye. Binocular vision is vision for "two eyes."

20. **Motor skills** are learned abilities to move specific parts of the body. (p. 145)

21. A **reflex** is an unlearned, involuntary action or movement emitted in response to a specific stimulus. (p. 145)

22. **Gross motor skills** are physical abilities that demand large body movements, such as walking, jumping, and running. (p. 146)

23. **Fine motor skills** are physical abilities that require precise, small movements, such as picking up a coin. (p. 147)

24. **Immunization** is the process through which the body's immune system is stimulated (as by a vaccine) to defend against attack by a particular contagious disease. (p. 150)

25. **Sudden infant death syndrome (SIDS)** is a set of circumstances in which a seemingly healthy infant, at least 2 months of age, suddenly stops breathing and dies unexpectedly in his or her sleep. (p. 153)

26. **Protein-calorie malnutrition** results when a person does not consume enough food. (p. 156)

27. **Marasmus** is a disease caused by severe protein-calorie deficiency during the first year of life. Growth stops, body tissues waste away, and the infant dies. (p. 157)

28. **Kwashiorkor** is a disease caused by protein-calorie deficiency during childhood. The child's face, legs, and abdomen swell with fluid; the child becomes more vulnerable to other diseases. Other body parts are degraded, including the hair, which becomes thin, brittle, and colorless. (p. 157)

6

The First Two Years: Cognitive Development

Chapter Overview

Chapter 6 explores the ways in which the infant comes to learn about, think about, and adapt to his or her surroundings. It focuses on the various ways in which infant intelligence is revealed: through sensorimotor intelligence, perception, memory, and language development. The chapter begins with a description of Jean Piaget's theory of sensorimotor intelligence, which maintains that infants think exclusively with their senses and motor skills. Piaget's six stages of sensorimotor intelligence are examined.

The second section discusses the information-processing theory, which compares cognition to the ways in which computers analyze data. Eleanor and James Gibson's influential theory is also described. Central to this theory is the idea that infants gain cognitive understanding of their world through the affordances of objects, that is, the activities they can do with them.

The text also discusses the key cognitive elements needed by the infant to structure the environment discovered through his or her newfound perceptual abilities. Using the habituation procedure, researchers have found that the speed with which infants recognize familiarity and seek something novel is related to later cognitive skill. It points out the importance of memory to cognitive development.

Finally, the chapter turns to the most remarkable cognitive achievement of the first two years: the acquisition of language. Beginning with a description of the infant's first attempts at language, the chapter follows the sequence of events that leads to the child's ability to utter two-word sentences. The chapter concludes with an examination of three classic theories of language acquisition and a fourth, hybrid theory, which combines aspects of each.

NOTE: Answer guidelines for all Chapter 6 questions begin on page 85.

Chapter Review

When you have finished reading the chapter, work through the material that follows to review it. Complete the sentences and answer the questions. In some cases, Study Tips explain how best to learn a difficult concept, while Think About It and Applications help you to know how well you understand the material. As you proceed, evaluate your performance for each section by consulting the answers beginning on page 85. Do not continue with the next section until you understand each answer. If you need to, review or reread the appropriate section in the textbook before continuing.

Sensorimotor Intelligence (pp. 161–168)

1. The first major theorist to realize that infants are active learners was _____ .

2. When infants begin to explore the environment through sensory and motor skills, they are displaying what Piaget called

   _____ intelligence. In number, Piaget described _____ stages of development of this type of intelligence.

3. The first two stages of sensorimotor intelligence are examples of _____

   _____ _____ . Stage one begins with newborns' reflexes, such as

   _____ and _____ , and also the _____ . It lasts from birth to

   _____ of age.

4. Stage two begins when newborns show signs of

   _____ of their _____ and senses to the specifics of the environment. This process involves _____ and

   _____ .

Describe the development of the sucking reflex during stages one and two.

5. In stages three and four, development switches to _____ _____ _____ , involving the baby with an object or with another person. During stage three, which occurs between _____ and _____ months of age, infants repeat a specific action that has just elicited a pleasing response.

Describe a typical stage-three behavior.

6. In stage four, which lasts from _____ to _____ months of age, infants can better _____ events. At this stage, babies also engage in purposeful actions, or _____-directed behavior.

7. (text and A View From Science) A major cognitive accomplishment of infancy is the ability to understand that objects exist even when they are _____ . This awareness is called _____ _____ . To test for this awareness, Piaget devised a procedure to observe whether an infant will _____ for a hidden object. Using this test, Piaget concluded that this awareness does not develop until about _____ of age. More recent research studies have shown that this ability actually begins to emerge at _____ months.

8. During stage five, which lasts from _____ to _____ months, infants begin experimenting in thought and deed. They do so through _____ _____ _____ , which involve taking in experiences and trying to make sense of them.

Explain what Piaget meant when he described the stage-five infant as a "little scientist."

9. Stage six, which lasts from _____ to _____ months, is the stage of anticipating and solving simple problems by using _____ _____ . One sign that children have reached stage six is _____ _____ , which is their emerging ability to imitate behaviors they noticed earlier.

10. Two research tools that have become available since Piaget's time are _____ studies and _____ , which reveals brain activity as cognition occurs.

STUDY TIP: Jean Piaget was the first major theorist to realize that each stage of life has its own characteristic way of thinking. To deepen your understanding of Jean Piaget's stages of sensorimotor development, fill in the missing information in the chart on the next page. See how much you can fill in without reviewing the textbook. To get you started, the first stage has been completed.

11.

Typical Age Range	Stage	Behavior Indicating a Child Is in This Stage
0–1 month	reflexes	reflexive cries
a. 1–4 months		
b. 4–8 months		
c. 8–12 months		
d. 12–18 months		
e. 18–24 months		

12. A 9-month-old repeatedly reaches for his sister's doll, even though he has been told "no" many times. This is an example of _____

_____ .

13. Before putting her dolly to bed, 18-month-old Jessica sings her a song. According to Piaget, Jessica's behavior is an example of the use of
   a. new means through active experimentation.
   b. mental combinations.
   c. new adaptation and anticipation.
   d. first acquired adaptations.

14. Nine-month-old Akshay, who looks out of his crib for a toy that has fallen, is clearly demonstrating an understanding of

_____ .

15. Six-month-old Calysta sucks harder on a nipple, evidences a change in heart rate, or stares longer at one image than at another when presented with a change of stimulus. This indicates that she
   a. is annoyed by the change.
   b. is both hungry and angry.
   c. has become habituated to the new stimulus.
   d. perceives some differences between stimuli.

16. A 20-month-old girl who is able to try out various actions mentally without actually having to perform them is learning to solve simple problems by using _____ .

17. Seven-month-old Francisca is attempting to interact with her smiling mother. She is demonstrating an ability that typically occurs in stage _____ of sensorimotor development.

18. Angelo realizes that sucking a pacifier is different from sucking a nipple. Angelo is in stage _____ of cognitive development.

Information Processing (pp. 168–174)

19. A perspective on human cognition that is modeled on how computers analyze data is the _____-_____ theory. Two aspects of this theory as applied to human development are _____ , which concern perception and so are analogous to computer input, and _____ , which involves storage and retrieval of ideas, or output.

20. Much of the current research in perception and cognition has been inspired by the work of the Gibsons, who stress that perception is a(n) _____ (active/passive/automatic) cognitive phenomenon.

21. According to the Gibsons, any object in the environment offers diverse opportunities for interaction; this property of an object is called an

    _____ .

22. Which of these properties an individual perceives in an object depends on the individual's

    _____ _____ and

    _____ _____ , on his

    or her _____ _____ ,

    and on his or her _____

    _____ of what the object might be

    used for.

23. A firm surface that appears to dropoff is called a

    _____ _____ .

    Although perception of this dropoff was once

    linked to _____ maturity, later

    research found that infants as young as

    _____ are able to perceive the

    dropoff, as evidenced by changes in their

    _____ _____ and their

    wide open eyes.

24. Perception that focuses on movement and change

    is called _____

    _____ . Another universal principle

    of infant perception is _____

    _____ , which may have evolved

    because humans _____ by learning

    to attend to, and rely on, one another.

25. Babies have great difficulty storing new memories in their first _____ (how long?).

26. Research has shown, however, that babies can show that they remember when three conditions are met:

    a. _____

    b. _____

    c. _____

27. When these conditions are met, infants as young

    as _____ months "remembered"

    events from two weeks earlier if they experienced

    a _____ _____ prior to

    retesting.

28. After about _____ months, infants become capable of retaining information for

longer periods of time, with less training, repetition, or reminding.

29. PET scans and fMRI studies reveal that one

    region of the _____ is devoted to

    memory for _____ and other

    regions to memory for _____

    _____ . Memory for routines that

    remains hidden until a stimulus triggers it is

    called _____ _____ .

    Memories that can be recalled on demand are

    referred to as _____

    _____ . The region of the brain that

    this latter type of memory depends on is the

    _____ . This brain region remains

    immature until about age _____ .

According to Eleanor and James Gibson, which of the many affordances people perceive in a given object depends on their developmental level and past experiences, their present needs and motivation, and their sensory awareness of what that object might be used for. To increase your appreciation of the fact that infants are capable of learning about their worlds only by attempting to apply new experiences to a limited repertoire of existing reflexes, conduct a simple observational study with a lollipop. As you employ the sensorimotor reflex of sucking on the treat, consider variations in sucking—for example, licking, chewing—that represent elaborations of the basic action. Consider, too, how the sucking reflex can be adapted to many other objects (just as infants discover)—including a finger, toy, or bottle. Why did Piaget consider such adaptations to be examples of intelligent behavior?

APPLICATIONS:

30. Which of the following is NOT evidence of dynamic perception during infancy?
    a. Natalia prefers looking at her spinning mobile to her stationary teddy bear.
    b. Natalia has formed simple expectations of the path that mobile will follow.
    c. Natalia uses movement cues to discern the boundaries of the moving clown.
    d. Natalia quickly grasps that even though the clown looks different when seen from different viewpoints, it is still the same clown.

31. Eighteen-month-old Emma sees a large, round raised area on her mother's computer modem. She immediately presses the area with her fingers. James Gibson would say that Emma has perceived the modem button's

_____ .

32. Professor Norman frequently uses examples of how computers analyze data to help the class understand how human memory works. Professor Norman evidently is a fan of
   a. Jean Piaget.
   b. James Gibson.
   c. information-processing theory.
   d. dynamic perception theory.

Language: What Develops in the First Two Years?
(pp. 174–184)

33. Children the world over _____ (follow/do not follow) the same sequence of early language development. The timing of this sequence and depth of ability _____ (varies/does not vary).

34. Newborns show a preference for hearing _____ over other sounds, including the high-pitched, simplified adult speech called _____-_____ speech, which is sometimes called

_____ _____ .

35. By 4 months of age, most babies' verbal repertoire consists of _____

_____ .

36. Between _____ and _____ months of age, babies begin to repeat certain syllables, a phenomenon referred to as _____ .

37. Babbling is_____-_____ , so although deaf babies babble at first, they stop because they can't hear responses. Deaf babies may also use

_____ _____ to babble.

38. The average baby speaks a few words at about _____ of age. They understand _____ (more/fewer) words than they speak.

39. Another characteristic of infant language development is the use of the _____ , in which a single word expresses a complete thought. Variations of tone and pitch, called _____ , are extensive in babbling and in this later form of speech.

40. When vocabulary reaches approximately 50 expressed words, it suddenly begins to build rapidly, at a rate of _____ or more words a month. This language spurt is called the _____ _____ because toddlers learn a disproportionate number of _____ .

41. Language acquisition may be shaped by our _____ , as revealed by the fact that English-speaking infants learn more _____ than Chinese or Korean infants, who learn more _____ . Alternatively, the entire _____ _____ may determine language acquisition.

42. Children begin to produce their first two-word sentences at about _____ months, showing a clearly emerging understanding of _____ , which refers to all the methods that languages use to communicate meaning, apart from the words themselves. A child's grammar correlates with the size of his or her

_____ .

43. Reinforcement and other conditioning processes account for language development, according to the learning theory of _____ . One study that followed mother–infant pairs over time found that the frequency of early

_____ _____ predicted the child's rate of language acquisition many months later.

44. The theorist who stressed that language is too complex to be mastered so early and easily through conditioning is _____ .

Because all young children _____ (master/do not master) basic grammar at about the same age, there is, in a sense, a _____ _____ . This theorist also maintained that all children are born with a LAD, or _____ _____ _____ , that enables children to quickly derive the rules of grammar from the speech they hear.

Summarize the research support for theory two.

45. A third, _____-_____ , theory of language proposes that the starting point for language is its social reason for existing: _____ .

46. A new _____ theory combines aspects of several theories. A fundamental aspect of this theory is that _____ _____ .

STUDY TIP: To review the sequences of sensori-motor and language development, and to deepen your understanding of their interrelationship, see if you can fill in the missing information in the chart below. For each listed age (column 1), write down the corresponding sensorimotor stage (column 2) and hallmarks or milestones of language develop-ment (column 3).

47. Age	Sensorimotor Stage	Language Milestones
a. 0–1 month		
b. 1–4 months		
c. 4–8 months		
d. 8–12 months		
e. 12–18 months		
f. 18–24 months		

APPLICATIONS:

48. At about 21 months, Darrell, who is typical of his age group, will
   a. have a vocabulary of between 250 and 350 words.
   b. begin to speak in holophrases.
   c. put words together to form rudimentary sentences.
   d. be characterized by all of these abilities.

49. As an advocate of the social-pragmatic theory, Professor Caruso believes that
   a. infants communicate in every way they can because they are social beings.
   b. biological maturation is a dominant force in language development.
   c. infants' language abilities mirror those of their primary caregivers.
   d. language develops in many ways for many reasons.

50. As soon as her babysitter arrives, 21-month-old Christine holds on to her mother's legs and, in a questioning manner, says "bye-bye." Because Christine clearly is "asking" her mother not to leave, her utterance can be classified as a _____ .

51. Six-month-old Lars continually repeats a variety of sound combinations such as "ba-ba-ba." This form of language is called _____ .

52. Monica firmly believes that her infant daughter "taught" herself language because of the seemingly effortless manner in which she has mastered new words and phrases. Monica is evidently a proponent of the theory proposed by

_____ .

53. Like most Korean toddlers, Noriko has acquired a greater number of _____ (nouns/verbs) in her vocabulary than her North American counterparts, who tend to acquire more _____ (nouns/verbs).

Progress Test 1

Multiple-Choice Questions

Circle your answers to the following questions and check them with the answers on page 87. If your answer is incorrect, read the explanation for why it is incorrect and then consult the appropriate pages of the text (in parentheses following the correct answer).

1. In general terms, the Gibsons' concept of affordances emphasizes the idea that the individual perceives an object in terms of its
   a. economic importance.
   b. physical qualities.
   c. function or use to the individual.
   d. role in the larger culture or environment.

2. According to Piaget, when a baby repeats an action that has just triggered a pleasing response from his or her caregiver, a stage _____ behavior has occurred.
   a. one   c. three
   b. two   d. six

3. Sensorimotor intelligence begins with a baby's first
   a. attempt to crawl.
   b. reflexes.
   c. auditory perception.
   d. adaptation of a reflex.

4. Piaget and the Gibsons would most likely agree that
   a. perception is largely automatic.
   b. language development is biologically predisposed in children.
   c. learning and perception are active cognitive processes.
   d. it is unwise to "push" children too hard academically.

5. Toward the end of the first year, infants usually learn how to
   a. accomplish simple goals.
   b. manipulate various symbols.
   c. solve complex problems.
   d. pretend.

6. When an infant begins to understand that objects exist even when they are out of sight, she or he has begun to understand the concept of object
   a. displacement.   c. permanence.
   b. importance.   d. location.

7. Today, most cognitive psychologists view language acquisition as
   a. primarily the result of imitation of adult speech.
   b. a behavior that is determined primarily by biological maturation.
   c. a behavior determined entirely by learning.
   d. determined by both biological maturation and learning.

8. Despite cultural differences, children all over the world attain very similar language skills
   a. according to ethnically specific timetables.
   b. in the same sequence according to a variable timetable.
   c. according to culturally specific timetables.
   d. according to timetables that vary from child to child.

9. The average baby speaks a few words at about
   a. 6 months.   c. 12 months.
   b. 9 months.   d. 24 months.

10. A single word used by toddlers to express a complete thought is
    a. a holophrase.
    b. child-directed speech.
    c. babbling.
    d. an affordance.

11. A distinctive form of language, with a particular pitch, structure, etc., that adults use in talking to infants is called
    a. a holophrase.
    b. the LAD.
    c. child-directed speech.
    d. conversation.

12. Habituation studies reveal that most infants detect the difference between a pah sound and a bah sound at
    a. birth.   c. 3 months.
    b. 1 month.   d. 6 months.

13. The imaging technique in which the brain's magnetic properties indicate activation in various parts of the brain is called a(n)
    a. PET scan.   c. fMRI.
    b. EEG.   d. MRI.

14. A toddler who taps on the computer's keyboard after observing her mother sending e-mail the day before is demonstrating
    a. assimilation.   c. deferred imitation.
    b. accommodation.   d. dynamic perception.

15. In Piaget's theory of sensorimotor intelligence, reflexes that involve the infant's own body are examples of
    a. primary circular reactions.
    b. secondary circular reactions.
    c. tertiary circular reactions.
    d. none of these reactions.

Matching Items

Match each definition or description with its corresponding term.

Terms

_____ 1. people preference
_____ 2. affordances
_____ 3. object permanence
_____ 4. Noam Chomsky
_____ 5. B. F. Skinner
_____ 6. sensorimotor intelligence
_____ 7. babbling
_____ 8. holophrase
_____ 9. habituation
_____ 10. deferred imitation
_____ 11. dynamic perception

Definitions or Descriptions

a. getting used to an object or event after repeated exposure to it
b. repetitive utterance of certain syllables
c. perception that focuses on movement and change
d. the ability to witness, remember, and later copy a behavior
e. the realization that something that is out of sight continues to exist
f. the innate attraction of human babies to humans
g. opportunities for interaction that an object offers
h. theorist who believed that verbal behavior is conditioned
i. a single word used to express a complete thought
j. theorist who believed that language ability is innate
k. thinking through the senses and motor skills

Progress Test 2

Progress Test 2 should be completed during a final chapter review. Answer the following questions after you thoroughly understand the correct answers for the Chapter Review and Progress Test 1.

Multiple-Choice Questions

1. Stage five (12 to 18 months) of sensorimotor intelligence is best described as
   a. first acquired adaptations.
   b. the period of the "little scientist."
   c. procedures for making interesting sights last.
   d. new means through symbolization.

2. Piaget referred to the shift in an infant's behavior from reflexes to deliberate actions as the shift from
   a. secondary circular reactions to primary circular reactions.
   b. first acquired adaptations to secondary circular reactions.
   c. primary circular reactions to tertiary circular reactions.
   d. stage one primary circular reactions to stage two primary circular reactions.

3. (text and A View from Science) Research suggests that the concept of object permanence
   a. fades after a few months.
   b. is a skill some children never acquire.
   c. may occur earlier and more gradually than Piaget recognized.
   d. involves pretending as well as mental combinations.

4. Which of the following is an example of a secondary circular reaction?
   a. 1-month-old infant stares at a mobile suspended over her crib
   b. a 2-month-old infant sucks a pacifier
   c. realizing that rattles make noise, a 4-month-old infant laughs with delight when his mother puts a rattle in his hand
   d. a 12-month-old toddler licks a bar of soap to learn what it tastes like

5. An 18-month-old toddler puts a collar on a stuffed dog, then pretends to take it for a walk. The infant's behavior is an example of a
   a. primary circular reaction.
   b. secondary circular reaction.
   c. tertiary circular reaction.
   d. first acquired adaptation.

6. According to Piaget, the use of deferred imitation is an example of stage _____ behavior.
   a. three   c. five
   b. four   d. six

7. For Noam Chomsky, the language acquisition device refers to
   a. the human predisposition to acquire language.
   b. the portion of the human brain that processes speech.
   c. the vocabulary of the language to which the child is exposed.
   d. all of these.

8. The first stage of sensorimotor intelligence lasts until
   a. infants can anticipate events that will fulfill their needs.
   b. infants begin to adapt their reflexes to the environment.
   c. infants interact with objects to produce exciting experiences.
   d. infants are capable of thinking about past and future events.

9. Whether or not an infant perceives certain characteristics of objects, such as "suckability" or "graspability," seems to depend on
   a. his or her prior experiences.
   b. his or her needs.
   c. his or her sensory awareness.
   d. all of these factors.

10. (A View from Science) Piaget was INCORRECT in his belief that infants do not have
    a. object permanence.
    b. intelligence.
    c. goal-directed behavior.
    d. any of these abilities.

11. The purposeful actions that begin to develop in sensorimotor stage four are called
    a. reflexes.
    b. affordances.
    c. goal-directed behaviors.
    d. mental combinations.

12. What is the correct sequence of stages of language development?
    a. crying, babbling, cooing, first word
    b. crying, cooing, babbling, first word
    c. crying, babbling, first word, cooing
    d. crying, cooing, first word, babbling

13. Compared with hearing babies, deaf babies
    a. are less likely to babble.
    b. are more likely to babble.
    c. typically never babble.
    d. are more likely to babble using hand signals.

14. According to Skinner, children acquire language
    a. as a result of an inborn ability to use the basic structure of language.
    b. through reinforcement and other aspects of conditioning.
    c. mostly because of biological maturation.
    d. in a fixed sequence of predictable stages.

15. A fundamental idea of the hybrid model of language acquisition is that
    a. all humans are born with an innate language acquisition device.
    b. learning some aspects of language is best explained by one theory at one age, by other theories at another age.
    c. language development occurs too rapidly and easily to be entirely the product of conditioning.
    d. imitation and reinforcement are crucial to the development of language.

Matching Items

Match each definition or description with its corresponding term.

Terms

_____ 1. goal-directed behavior
_____ 2. visual cliff
_____ 3. primary circular reaction
_____ 4. child-directed speech
_____ 5. new adaptation and anticipation
_____ 6. "little scientist"
_____ 7. mental combinations
_____ 8. secondary circular reaction
_____ 9. tertiary circular reaction
_____ 10. LAD
_____ 11. grammar

Definitions or Descriptions

a. a device for studying depth perception
b. understanding how to reach a goal
c. able to put two ideas together
d. a feedback loop involving the infant's own body
e. a feedback loop involving people and objects
f. a hypothetical device that facilitates language development
g. also called baby talk or motherese
h. Piaget's term for the stage-five toddler
i. purposeful actions
j. a feedback loop involving active exploration and experimentation
k. all the methods used by a language to communicate meaning

Key Terms

Writing Definitions

Using your own words, write a brief definition or explanation of each of the following terms on a separate piece of paper.

1. sensorimotor intelligence
2. primary circular reactions
3. secondary circular reactions
4. object permanence
5. tertiary circular reactions
6. "little scientist"
7. deferred imitation
8. habituation
9. fMRI
10. information-processing theory
11. affordance
12. visual cliff
13. dynamic perception
14. people preference
15. reminder session
16. child-directed speech
17. babbling
18. holophrase
19. naming explosion
20. grammar
21. language acquisition device (LAD)

Cross-Check

After you have written the definitions of the key terms in this chapter, you should complete the crossword puzzle to ensure that you can reverse the process—recognize the term, given the definition.

ACROSS

6. a brain-imaging technique
7. a circular reaction involving the infant's own body
8. a circular reaction involving people and objects
9. a type of perception primed to focus on movement
11. the process of getting used to an object
12. child-directed speech
14. a sudden increase in an infant's vocabulary

DOWN

1. the methods used by languages to communicate meaning
2. a type of circular reaction that involves active exploration
3. a single word used to express a complete thought
4. Piaget's term for the stage-five toddler
5. an opportunity for perception
9. imitation of something that occurred earlier
10. extended repetition of syllables
13. Chomsky's term for a brain structure that enables language

ANSWERS

CHAPTER REVIEW

1. Piaget
2. sensorimotor; six
3. primary circular reactions; sucking; grasping; senses; 1 month
4. adaptation; reflexes; assimilation; accommodation

Stage-one infants suck everything that touches their lips. By about 1 month, they start to adapt their reflexive sucking. After several months, they have organized the world into objects to be sucked to soothe hunger, objects to be sucked for comfort, and objects not to be sucked at all.

5. secondary circular reactions; 4; 8

A stage-three infant may squeeze a duck, hear a quack, and squeeze the duck again.

6. 8; 12; anticipate; goal
7. no longer in sight; object permanence; search; 8 months; 4½

8. 12; 18; tertiary circular reactions

The stage-five "little scientist" uses trial and error in creative and active exploration.

9. 18; 24; mental combinations; deferred imitation
10. habituation; fMRI
11. 0–1 month: reflexes (Stage 1); reflexive cries
    a. 1–4 months: first acquired adaptations (Stage 2); sucking a thumb for comfort but not sucking a whole hand
    b. 4–8 months: making interesting sights last (Stage 3); shaking a doll that says "Mama"
    c. 8–12 months: new adaptation and anticipation (Stage 4); pointing at a toy to get Dad to bring it to him or her
    d. 12–18 months: new means through active experimentation (Stage 5); pushing all the buttons on the remote control
    e. 18–24 months: new means through mental combinations (Stage 6); learning that the furry little teddy bear isn't real but can be used for cuddling and security

12. goal-directed behavior

13. **b.** is the answer. Jessica realizes the doll isn't real, but she also knows she can do "real things" with the doll.

14. object permanence. Akshay knows that out of sight doesn't mean the object ceases to exist.

15. **d.** is the answer. In these habituation studies, the infant's increased attention indicates he or she perceives a difference from the previous stimulus.

16. mental combinations. The child is able to think about something before actually doing anything, a major advance in cognitive development.

17. four. This is the stage of new adaptation and anticipation. The infant becomes more deliberate and purposeful in responding to people and objects.

18. two. This is the stage of first acquired adaptations, when the infant accommodates and coordinates reflexes.

19. information-processing; affordances; memory

20. active

21. affordance

22. past experience; current development; immediate motivation; sensory awareness

23. visual cliff; visual; 3 months; heart rate

24. dynamic perception; people preference; survived

25. year

26. (a) experimental conditions are similar to real life; (b) motivation is high; (c) retrieval is strengthened by reminders and repetition

27. 3; reminder session

28. 6

29. brain; faces; sounds, events, sights, phrases, and much more; implicit memory; explicit memory; hippocampus; 5 or 6

30. **d.** is the answer. This is perceptual constancy.

31. affordance

32. **c.** is the answer. Information-processing theory compares human thinking processes, by analogy, to computer analysis of data.

33. follow; varies

34. speech; child-directed; baby talk (or motherese)

35. squeals, growls, gurgles, grunts, croons, and yells

36. 6; 9; babbling

37. experience-expectant; hand gestures

38. 1 year; more

39. holophrase; intonation

40. 50 to 100; naming explosion; nouns

41. culture; nouns; verbs; social context

42. 21; grammar; vocabulary

43. B. F. Skinner; maternal responsiveness

44. Noam Chomsky; master; universal grammar; language acquisition device

Support for this theory comes from the fact that all babies babble ma-ma and da-da sounds at about 6 to 9 months. No reinforcement is needed. Infants merely need dendrites to grow, mouth muscles to strengthen, neurons to connect, and speech to be heard.

45. social-pragmatic; communication

46. hybrid; some learning of language is best explained by one theory at one age and other aspects by another perspective at another age

47. **a.** 0–1 month: reflexes (Stage 1); crying, facial expressions

   b. 1–4 months: first acquired adaptations (Stage 2); cooing, laughing, squealing, growling, crooning, vowel sounds

   c. 4–8 months: making interesting sights last (Stage 3); babbling at 6 months

   d. 8–12 months: new adaptation and anticipation (Stage 4); at 10 months, comprehension of simple words; speechlike intonations

   e. 12–18 months: new means through active experimentation (Stage 5); first spoken words at 12 months; vocabulary growth up to about 50 words

   f. 18–24 months: new means through mental combinations (Stage 6); three or more words learned per day, first two-word sentence at 21 months, multiword sentences at 24 months

48. **c.** is the answer. The first two-word sentence is uttered at about 21 months.

49. **a.** is the answer. b. is more consistent with Noam Chomsky's theory, c. would be based on B. F. Skinner's learning theory, and d. is consistent with the hybrid theory.

50. holophrase. These are one-word utterances that express a complete, meaningful thought.

51. babbling. This form of speech, which begins between 6 and 9 months of age, is characterized by the extended repetition of certain syllables (such as "ma-ma").

52. Noam Chomsky. Chomsky and his followers believe that language is too complex to be learned through reinforcement alone.

53. verbs; nouns. Korean is considered a verb-friendly language, because verbs appear at the beginning of sentences. North Americans use nouns first in their sentences.

PROGRESS TEST 1

Multiple-Choice Questions

1. **c.** is the answer. (p. 169)
2. **c.** is the answer. (p. 163)
3. **b.** is the answer. This was Piaget's most basic contribution to the study of infant cognition—that intelligence is revealed in behavior at every age. (p. 162)
4. **c.** is the answer. (pp. 161, 169)

    b. This is Chomsky's position.

    d. This issue was not discussed in the text.
5. **a.** is the answer. (p. 163)

    b. & c. These abilities are not acquired until children are much older.

    d. Pretending is associated with stage six (18 to 24 months).
6. **c.** is the answer. (p. 163)
7. **d.** is the answer. (pp. 182–183)
8. **b.** is the answer. (p. 175)

    a., c., & d. Children the world over follow the same sequence, but the timing of their accomplishments may vary considerably.
9. **c.** is the answer. (pp. 175, 176)
10. **a.** is the answer. (p. 177)

    b. Child-directed speech is the speech adults use with infants.

    c. Babbling refers to the first syllables a baby utters.

    d. An affordance is an opportunity for perception and interaction.
11. **c.** is the answer. (pp. 175–176)

    a. A holophrase is a single word uttered by a toddler to express a complete thought.

    b. According to Noam Chomsky, the LAD, or language acquisition device, is an innate ability in humans to acquire language.

    d. These characteristic differences in pitch and structure are precisely what distinguish child-directed speech from regular conversation.
12. **b.** is the answer. (p. 167)
13. **c.** is the answer. (p. 167)
14. **c.** is the answer (p. 166)

a. & b. In Piaget's theory, these refer to processes by which mental concepts incorporate new experiences (assimilation) or are modified in response to new experiences (accommodation).

d. Dynamic perception is perception that is primed to focus on movement and change.

15. **a.** is the answer. (p. 162)

    b. Secondary circular reactions involve the baby with an object or with another person.

    c. Tertiary circular reactions involve active exploration and experimentation, rather than mere reflexive action.

Matching Items

1. f (p. 171)	5. h (p. 180)	9. a (p. 166)
2. g (p. 169)	6. k (p. 161)	10. d (p. 166)
3. e (p. 163)	7. b (p. 176)	11. c (p. 171)
4. j (p. 181)	8. i (p. 177)	

PROGRESS TEST 2

Multiple-Choice Questions

1. **b.** is the answer. (p. 162)

    a. & c. These are stages two and three.

    d. This is not one of Piaget's stages of sensorimotor intelligence.
2. **d.** is the answer. Thinking is more innovative in stage four because adaptation is more complex. (p. 163)
3. **c.** is the answer. (p. 164)
4. **c.** is the answer. (p. 163)

    a. & b. These are examples of primary circular reactions.

    d. This is an example of a tertiary circular reaction.
5. **c.** is the answer. (p. 166)
6. **d.** is the answer. (p. 166)
7. **a.** is the answer. Chomsky believed that this device is innate. (p. 181)
8. **b.** is the answer. (p. 162)

    a. & c. Both of these occur later than stage one.

    d. This is a hallmark of stage six.
9. **d.** is the answer. (p. 169)
10. **a.** is the answer. (pp. 164–165)
11. **c.** is the answer. (p. 163)

    a. Reflexes are involuntary (and therefore unintentional) responses.

b. Affordances are perceived opportunities for interaction with objects.

d. Mental combinations are actions that are carried out mentally, rather than behaviorally. Moreover, mental combinations do not develop until a later age, during sensorimotor stage six.

12. **b.** is the answer. (p. 175)

13. **d.** is the answer. (p. 176)

a. & b. Hearing and deaf babies do not differ in the overall likelihood that they will babble.

c. Deaf babies definitely babble.

14. **b.** is the answer. (pp. 180–181)

a., c., & d. These views on language acquisition describe the theory offered by Noam Chomsky.

15. **b.** is the answer. (p. 182)

a. & c. These ideas are consistent with Noam Chomsky's theory.

d. This is the central idea of B. F. Skinner's theory.

Matching Items

1. i (p. 163)
2. a (p. 170)
3. d (p. 162)
4. g (p. 176)
5. b (p. 163)
6. h (p. 165)
7. c (p. 165)
8. e (p. 163)
9. j (p. 165)
10. f (p. 181)
11. k (p. 178)

KEY TERMS

1. Piaget's stages of **sensorimotor intelligence** (from birth to about 2 years old) are based on his theory that infants think exclusively with their senses and motor skills. (p. 161)

2. In Piaget's theory, **primary circular reactions** are a type of feedback loop in sensorimotor intelligence involving the infant's own body, in which infants take in experiences (such as sucking and grasping) and try to make sense of them. (p. 162)

3. **Secondary circular reactions** are a type of feedback loop in sensorimotor intelligence involving the infant's responses to objects and other people. (p. 163)

4. **Object permanence** is the understanding that objects continue to exist even when they cannot be seen, touched, or heard. (p. 163)

5. In Piaget's theory, **tertiary circular reactions** are the most sophisticated type of infant feedback loop in sensorimotor intelligence, involving active exploration and experimentation. (p. 165)

6. **"Little scientist"** is Piaget's term for the stage-five toddler who learns about the properties of objects in his or her world through active experimentation. (p. 165)

7. **Deferred imitation** is the ability of infants to perceive and later copy a behavior they noticed hours or days earlier. (p. 166)

8. **Habituation** is the process of getting used to an object or event through repeated exposure to it. (p. 166)

9. **fMRI** (functional magnetic resonance imaging) is a measuring technique in which the brain's electrical excitement indicates activation anywhere in the brain. (p. 167)

10. **Information-processing theory** is a theory of human cognition that compares thinking to the ways in which a computer analyzes data, through the processes of sensory input, connections, stored memories, and output. (p. 168)

11. **Affordances** are perceived opportunities for interacting with people, objects, or places in the environment. Infants perceive sucking, grasping, noisemaking, and many other affordances of objects at an early age. (p. 169)

12. A **visual cliff** is an experimental apparatus that provides the illusion of a sudden dropoff between one horizontal surface and another. (p. 170)

13. **Dynamic perception,** a universal principle of infant perception, is perception that is primed to focus on movement and change. (p. 171)

14. **People preference,** a universal principle of infant perception, is the innate attraction that human babies have to other humans. (p. 171)

15. A **reminder session** is any perceptual experience that helps people recollect an idea, a thing, or an experience. (p. 173)

16. **Child-directed speech** is a form of speech used by adults when talking to infants. It is simplified, it has a higher pitch, and it is repetitive; it is also called *baby talk* or *motherese*. (p. 176)

17. **Babbling,** which begins between 6 and 9 months of age, is characterized by the extended repetition of certain syllables (such as "ma-ma"). (p. 176)

18. Another characteristic of infant speech is the use of the **holophrase,** in which a single word is used to convey a complete, meaningful thought. (p. 177)

19. The **naming explosion** refers to the dramatic increase in the infant's vocabulary that begins at about 18 months of age. (p. 177)

20. The **grammar** of a language includes rules of word order, verb forms, and all other methods used to communicate meaning apart from words themselves. (p. 178)

21. According to Chomsky, children possess an innate **language acquisition device (LAD),** which is a hypothesized mental structure that enables them to acquire language, including the basic aspects of grammar, vocabulary, and intonation. (p. 181)

Cross-Check

ACROSS

6. fMRI
7. primary
8. secondary
9. dynamic
11. habituation
12. baby talk
14. naming explosion

DOWN

1. grammar
2. tertiary
3. holophrase
4. little scientist
5. affordance
9. deferred
10. babbling
13. LAD

7

The First Two Years: Psychosocial Development

Chapter Overview

Chapter 7 describes the emotional and social life of the developing person during infancy. It begins with a description of the infant's emerging emotions and how they reflect mobility and social awareness. Two emotions, pleasure and pain, are apparent at birth and are soon joined by anger and fear. As self-awareness develops, many new emotions emerge, including embarrassment, shame, guilt, and pride.

The second section explores theories of infant psychosocial development. These include the psycho-analytic theories of Freud and Erikson along with behaviorist, cognitive, epigenetic, and sociocultural theories, which help us understand how the infant's emotional and behavioral responses begin to take on the various patterns that form personality. Temperament, which affects later personality and is primarily inborn, is influenced by the individual's interactions with the environment.

The third section explores the social context in which emotions develop. Emotions and relationships are then examined from the perspective of parent–infant interaction. Videotaped studies of parents and infants, combined with laboratory studies of attachment, have greatly expanded our understanding of psychosocial development. By referencing their caregivers' signals, infants learn when and how to express their emotions. This section concludes by exploring the impact of day care on infants.

NOTE: Answer guidelines for all Chapter 7 questions begin on page 100.

Chapter Review

When you have finished reading the chapter, work through the material that follows to review it. Complete the sentences and answer the questions. In some cases, Study Tips explain how best to learn a difficult concept, while Think About It and Applications help you to know how well you understand the material. As you proceed, evaluate your performance for each section by consulting the answers beginning on page 100 . Do not continue with the next section until you understand each answer. If you need to, review or reread the appropriate section in the textbook before continuing.

Introduction and *Emotional Development* (pp. 187–193)

1. Psychosocial development includes _____ development and _____ development.

2. The first emotions that can be reliably discerned in infants are _____ and _____ . Other early infant emotions include _____ and _____ . Infants' pleasure in seeing faces is first expressed by the _____ _____ , which appears at about _____ weeks.

3. Anger becomes evident at about _____ months. During infancy, anger _____ (is/is not) a healthy response, and usually occurs in response to _____ . In contrast, sadness indicates _____ and is accompanied by an increase in the stress hormone _____ .

4. Fully formed fear emerges at about _____ months. One expression of this new emotion is _____ _____ ; another is _____ _____ , or fear of abandonment, which is normal at age _____ year(s) and intensifies by age _____ year(s). During the second year, anger and fear typically _____ (increase/decrease) and become more _____ toward specific things.

5. Toward the end of the second year, the new emotions of _____ , _____ , _____ , and _____ become apparent. These emotions require an awareness of _____ _____ .

6. An important foundation for emotional growth is _____ ; very young infants have no sense of _____ . This emerging sense of "me" and "mine" leads to a new _____ of others. This sense usually emerges at the same time as advances in _____ and using _____-_____ pronouns.

7. Pride is linked with the infant's maturing _____ . Telling toddlers that they are strong or smart may _____ (help/hinder) their self-awareness, making it seem as if pride comes from _____ _____ .

8. Emotional development depends partly on maturation of the developing _____ , along with having varied _____ and good _____ . The stimulation of one sensory stimulus to the brain by another is called _____ . This type of experience is partly _____ and less common among _____ (infants/older children) than it is among _____ (infants/older children).

9. As emotional development proceeds, specific emotions come to be aroused by particular _____ . This indicates that infant emotional reactions depend partly on _____ .

10. Chronic early stress can impair the brain's _____ , which regulates various bodily functions and hormone production. Children of _____ mothers seem to experience more stress. Helpful behaviors such

as _____ _____ demonstrate the crucial role fathers can play in helping new mothers.

STUDY TIP/APPLICATION: Most students (in fact, most people) find it difficult to understand how young children cannot be self-aware. To enhance your understanding of this limitation in young children, first briefly describe the nature and findings of the classic rouge-and-mirror experiment on self-awareness in infants. Then, try it out with young children of different ages.

APPLICATIONS:

11. Chella and David are planning a night out for the first time since their infant was born nine months ago. As they prepare to leave, baby Lili begins to cry, indicating _____ . Then, when the unfamiliar babysitter approaches her, she cries and clings tightly to her mother, a sign of _____ .

Theories About Infant Psychosocial Development (pp. 193–201)

12. In Freud's theory, development begins with the _____ stage, so named because the _____ is the infant's prime source of gratification and pleasure.

13. According to Freud, in the second year, the prime focus of gratification comes from stimulation and control of the bowels. Freud referred to this period as the _____ stage.

14. Freud believed that the potential conflicts of these stages had _____ (short-term/long-term) consequences. If the conflicts are not resolved, the child may become an adult with, for example, an _____ _____ .

15. (A View from Science) To avoid conflict and the development of an "anal personality," _____ theory advised parents to delay toilet training until the child was ready. This theory has been undermined by _____ research that has found that toilet training occurs in a diversity of ways. Another approach based on principles of

_____ claims that toilet training can occur in as short a period of time as one day. The influential theorist _____ believes that toilet training should begin around age _____ , when children are "ready" based on their _____ , _____ , and _____ maturity.

16. The theorist who believed that development occurs through a series of psychosocial crises is _____ . According to his theory, the crisis of infancy is one of

_____ ,

whereas the crisis of toddlerhood is one of

_____ .

17. According to the perspective of _____ , personality is molded through the processes of _____ and _____ of the child's spontaneous behaviors. A strong proponent of this position was _____ .

18. Later theorists incorporated the role of _____ learning, that is, infants' tendencies to observe and _____ the personality traits of their parents. The theorist most closely associated with this type of learning is _____ .

19. Both psychoanalytic and behaviorist theories emphasize the role of _____ , especially the _____ . Newer theories reflect more recent research and believe this focus is too _____ (narrow/broad).

20. According to cognitive theory, a person's _____ and _____ determine his or her perspective on the world. Early experiences are important because _____ , _____ , and _____ make them so. Infants use their early relationships to build a _____ _____ that becomes a frame of reference for organizing perceptions and experiences.

21. According to _____ theory, each infant is born with a _____ predisposition to develop certain emotional traits. Among these are the traits of _____ .

22. These traits are similar to _____ . Although these traits are not learned, their expression is influenced by the _____ .

23. The classic long-term study of children's temperament is the _____ _____ _____ . The study found that by 3 months, infants can be clustered into one of four types: _____ , _____ , _____ , and _____ .

24. Other researchers studied adult personality traits and came up with the Big Five. These include _____ , _____ , _____ , _____ , and _____ .

25. According to _____ theory, the entire _____ context can have a major impact on infant–caregiver relationships and the infant's development. An _____ is a theory of child rearing that underlies the values and practices of a culture or _____ group. As an example, researchers have found that physically close, _____ parenting predicts toddlers who later are less _____ and more _____ , in comparison to physically far, _____ parenting, which produces children with the opposite traits.

STUDY TIP: Several theories of development have provided different explanations for how infants' emotions and temperaments develop. To help you remember the theories, complete the chart on the next page and use it as a study aid. Some elements are filled in to give you a headstart.

26. Theory	Stages or Continuous	Important Concepts	Effects on Emotional Development
Psychoanalytic Theory Freud	stages	Oral and anal stages sexual impulses and unconscious conflicts	If conflicts not resolved, fixation may occur.
Erikson			
Behaviorism	continuous		
Cognitive Theory			
Epigenetic Theory			
Sociocultural Theory			

APPLICATIONS:

27. Professor Kipketer believes that infants' emotions are molded as their parents reinforce or punish their behaviors. Professor Kipketer evidently is a proponent of _____ .

28. Mashiyat, who advocates epigenetic theory in explaining the origins of personality, points to research evidence that
    a. infants are born with definite and distinct temperaments that can change.
    b. early temperamental traits almost never change.
    c. an infant's temperament does not begin to clearly emerge until 2 years of age.
    d. temperament appears to be almost completely unaffected by the social context.

29. Dr. Hidalgo believes that infants use their early relationships to develop a set of assumptions that become a frame of reference for later experiences. Dr. Hidalgo evidently is a proponent of

    _____ .

30. Felix has an unusually strong need to regulate all aspects of his life. Freud would probably say that Felix is
    a. demonstrating the temperament he developed during infancy.
    b. fixated at the anal stage.
    c. fixated in the oral stage.
    d. experiencing the crisis of trust versus mistrust.

The Development of Social Bonds (pp. 202–215)

31. One study of infant temperament identified three distinct types: _____ , _____ , and _____ .

32. An important factor in healthy psychosocial development is _____ _____ _____ between the developing child and the caregiving context.

33. The coordinated interaction of response between infant and caregiver is called _____ . Partly through this interaction, infants learn to

_____
and to develop some of the basic skills of

_____ _____ .

Synchrony usually begins with _____
(infants/parents) imitating _____
(infants/parents).

34. To study the importance of synchrony in development, researchers use an experimental device, called the _____-_____ technique, in which the caregiver _____ (does/does not) show any facial expression.

35. The emotional bond that develops between slightly older infants and their caregivers is called

_____ .

36. Approaching and following the caregiver are signs of _____- _____ behaviors, while snuggling, touching, and holding are signs of

_____ -_____

behaviors.

37. An infant who derives comfort and confidence from the secure base provided by the caregiver is displaying _____ _____ (type B). In this type of relationship, the caregiver acts as a _____

_____ _____ from which the child is willing to venture forth.

38. By contrast, _____

_____ is characterized by an infant's fear, anger, or indifference. Two extremes of this type of relationship are

_____-_____

_____ (type A) and

_____-_____/

_____ _____ (type C).

(text and Table 7.4) Briefly describe the two types of insecure attachment as well as disorganized attachment.

39. The procedure developed by Mary Ainsworth to measure attachment is called the

_____ _____ .

Approximately _____ (what proportion?) of all normal infants tested with this procedure demonstrate secure attachment. When infant–caregiver interactions are inconsistent, infants are classified as _____ .

40. The most troubled infants may be those who are type _____ . Attachment status _____ (can/cannot) change.

41. The search for information about another person's feelings is called _____

_____ .

42. In _____ (most/some/a few) nations and ethnic groups, fathers spend much less time with infants than mothers do.

43. The social information from fathers tends to be more _____ than that from mothers, who are more _____ and _____ . Fathers are more _____ (proximal/distal) in their parenting than mothers.

44. Infant day care programs include _____ day care, in which children of various ages are cared for in a paid caregiver's home, and _____ day care, in which several paid providers care for children in a designated place.

45. Early day care may be detrimental when the mother is _____ and the infant spends more than _____ (how many?) hours each week in a poor-quality program.

46. (Table 7.6) Researchers have identified five factors that are essential to high-quality day care:

a. _____

b. _____

c. _____

d. _____

e. _____

Most students find it easier to remember the characteristics associated with secure and insecure attachment and their consequences if they are neatly summarized in a table. Complete the table below as a way of organizing the information.

47. Attachment Style	Characteristic Behavior of Infant	Characteristics of Parents
Secure (Type B)	Infant plays happily and comfortably, sometimes glancing at Mom for reassurance.	Parent is sensitive and responsive to infant's needs; synchrony is high; parents are not stressed; parents have a working model from their own parents.
Insecure-avoidant (Type A)		
Insecure-resistant/ ambivalent (Type C)		
Disorganized		

48. One-year-old Kirsten and her Mom are participating in a laboratory test of attachment. When Mom returns to the playroom after a short absence, Kirsten, who is securely attached, is most likely to
   a. cry and protest her Mom's return.
   b. climb into her Mom's arms, then leave to resume play.
   c. climb into her Mom's arms and stay there.
   d. continue playing without acknowledging her Mom.

49. After a scary fall, 18-month-old Miguel looks to his mother to see if he should cry or laugh. Miguel's behavior is an example of

   _____ .

50. Which of the following is a clear sign of Isabel's attachment to her grandmother, her full-time caregiver?
   a. She turns to her grandmother when distressed.
   b. She protests when Grandma leaves a room.
   c. She may cry when strangers appear.
   d. These are all signs of infant attachment.

51. Concluding her report on the impact of day care on young children, Deborah notes that infants are likely to become insecurely attached if:
   a. their own mothers are insensitive caregivers.
   b. the quality of day care is poor.
   c. more than 20 hours per week are spent in day care.
   d. all of these conditions exist.

52. Kalil's mother left him alone in the room for a few minutes. When she returned, Kalil seemed indifferent to her presence. According to Mary Ainsworth's research with children in the Strange Situation, Kalil is probably
   a. a normal, independent infant.
   b. an abused child.
   c. insecurely attached.
   d. securely attached.

53. Two-year-old Anita and her mother spend many hours together in well-coordinated mutual responding: When Anita smiles, her mother smiles. When Anita pouts, her mother shows distress. Their behavior illustrates

   _____ .

Conclusions in Theory and Practice (pp. 213–215)

54. Regarding the major theories of development,
_____ _____ theory
stands out as the best interpretation. Although
the first two years are important, early
_____ and _____
development is influenced by the _____
behavior, the support provided by the
_____ , the quality of
_____ _____ , patterns
within the child's _____ , and traits
that are _____ .

Progress Test 1

Multiple-Choice Questions

Circle your answers to the following questions and
check them with the answers on page 102. If your
answer is incorrect, read the explanation for why it is
incorrect and then consult the appropriate pages of
the text (in parentheses following the correct answer).

1. Newborns have two identifiable emotions
   a. shame and distress.
   b. pleasure and pain.
   c. anger and joy.
   d. pride and guilt.

2. Parenting that results in children who are self-
   aware but less obedient is called
   a. proximal parenting.
   b. distal parenting.
   c. synchrony.
   d. scaffolding.

3. An infant's fear of being left by the mother or
   other caregiver, called _____ , is most obvious
   at about _____ .
   a. separation anxiety; 2 to 4 months
   b. stranger wariness; 2 to 4 months
   c. separation anxiety; 9 to 14 months
   d. stranger wariness; 9 to 14 months

4. Social referencing refers to
   a. parenting skills that change over time.
   b. changes in community values regarding, for
      example, the acceptability of using physical
      punishment with small children.
   c. the support network for new parents provid-
      ed by extended family members.
   d. the infant response of looking to trusted
      adults for emotional cues in uncertain
      situations.

5. A key difference between temperament and personality is that
   a. temperamental traits are learned.
   b. personality includes traits that are primarily
      learned.
   c. personality is more stable than temperament.
   d. personality does not begin to form until much
      later, when self-awareness emerges.

6. The concept of a working model is most consistent with
   a. psychoanalytic theory.
   b. behaviorism.
   c. cognitive theory.
   d. sociocultural theory.

7. Freud's oral stage corresponds to Erikson's crisis
   of
   a. orality versus anality.
   b. trust versus mistrust.
   c. autonomy versus shame and doubt.
   d. secure versus insecure attachment.

8. Erikson believed that the development of a sense
   of trust in early infancy depends on
   a. the quality of the infant's food.
   b. the child's genetic inheritance.
   c. consistency, continuity, and sameness of expe-
      rience.
   d. the introduction of toilet training.

9. Keisha is concerned that her 15-month-old
   daughter, who no longer seems to enjoy face-to-
   face play, is showing signs of insecure attachment. You tell her
   a. not to worry; face-to-face play almost disap-
      pears toward the end of the first year.
   b. she may be right to worry, because face-
      to-face play typically increases throughout
      infancy.
   c. not to worry; attachment behaviors are unreli-
      able until toddlerhood.
   d. that her child is typical of children who spend
      more than 20 hours in day care each week.

10. "Easy," "slow to warm up," and "difficult" are
    descriptions of different
    a. forms of attachment.
    b. types of temperament.
    c. types of parenting.
    d. toddler responses to the Strange Situation.

11. The more physical play of fathers has been described as
    a. proximal parenting.
    b. distal parenting.
    c. disorganized parenting.
    d. insecure parenting.

12. *Synchrony* is a term that describes
    a. the carefully coordinated interaction between caregiver and infant.
    b. a mismatch of the temperaments of caregiver and infant.
    c. a research technique involving videotapes.
    d. the concurrent evolution of different species.

13. The emotional tie that develops between an infant and his or her primary caregiver is called
    a. self-awareness.   c. affiliation.
    b. synchrony.   d. attachment.

14. Research studies using the still-face technique have demonstrated that
    a. a parent's responsiveness to an infant aids development.
    b. babies become more upset when a parent leaves the room than when the parent's facial expression is not synchonized with the infant's.
    c. beginning at about 2 months, babies become very upset by a still-faced caregiver.
    d. beginning at about 10 months, babies become very upset by a still-faced caregiver.

15. Interest in people, as evidenced by the social smile, appears for the first time when an infant is _____ weeks old.
    a. 3   c. 9
    b. 6   d. 12

True or False Items

Write T (*true*) or F (*false*) on the line in front of each statement.

_____ 1. The major developmental theories all agree that maternal care is better for children than nonmaternal care.

_____ 2. Approximately 25 percent of infants display secure attachment.

_____ 3. A baby at 11 months is likely to display both stranger wariness and separation anxiety.

_____ 4. Emotional development is affected by maturation of conscious awareness.

_____ 5. A securely attached toddler is most likely to stay close to his or her mother even in a familiar environment.

_____ 6. Current research shows that the majority of infants in day care are slow to develop cognitive skills.

_____ 7. Infants use their fathers for social referencing when they look for encouragement.

_____ 8. Temperament is genetically determined and is unaffected by environmental factors.

_____ 9. Self-awareness enables toddlers to feel pride as well as guilt.

_____ 10. Synesthesia (one sense triggering another) is a normal brain process.

Progress Test 2

Progress Test 2 should be completed during a final chapter review. Answer the following questions after you thoroughly understand the correct answers for the Chapter Review and Progress Test 1.

Multiple-Choice Questions

1. Infant–caregiver interactions that are marked by inconsistency are usually classified as
   a. disorganized.
   b. insecure-avoidant.
   c. insecure-resistant.
   d. insecure-ambivalent.

2. Freud's anal stage corresponds to Erikson's crisis of
   a. autonomy versus shame and doubt.
   b. trust versus mistrust.
   c. orality versus anality.
   d. identity versus role confusion.

3. Not until the sense of self begins to emerge do babies realize that they are seeing their own faces in the mirror. This realization usually occurs
   a. shortly before 3 months.
   b. at about 6 months.
   c. between 15 and 24 months.
   d. after 24 months.

4. When there is goodness of fit, the parents of a slow-to-warm-up boy will
   a. give him extra time to adjust to new situations.
   b. encourage independence in their son by frequently leaving him for short periods of time.
   c. put their son in regular day care so other children's temperaments will "rub off" on him.
   d. do all of these things.

5. Emotions such as shame, guilt, embarrassment,

and pride emerge at the same time that

a. the social smile appears.
b. aspects of the infant's temperament can first be discerned.
c. self-awareness begins to emerge.
d. parents initiate toilet training.

6. Research by the NYLS on temperamental characteristics indicates that:

a. temperament is probably innate.
b. the interaction of parent and child determines later personality.
c. parents pass their temperaments on to their children through modeling.
d. self-awareness contributes to the development of temperament.

7. In the second six months, stranger wariness is a

a. result of insecure attachment.
b. result of social isolation.
c. normal emotional response.
d. setback in emotional development.

8. The caregiving environment can affect a child's temperament through **change b-d in case these questions go into the testing system**

a. the child's temperamental pattern and the demands of the home environment.
b. parental expectations.
c. both a. and b.
d. neither a. nor b.

9. While observing mothers playing with their infants in a playroom, you notice one mother who often teases her son, ignores him when he falls down, and tells him to "hush" when he cries. Mothers who display these behaviors usually have infants who exhibit which type of attachment?

a. secure
b. insecure-avoidant
c. insecure-resistant
d. disorganized

10. The later consequences of secure attachment and insecure attachment for children are

a. balanced by the child's current rearing circumstances.
b. irreversible, regardless of the child's current rearing circumstances.
c. more significant in girls than in boys.
d. more significant in boys than in girls.

11. The attachment pattern marked by anxiety and uncertainty is

a. insecure-avoidant.
b. insecure-resistant/ambivalent.
c. disorganized.
d. type B.

12. Compared with mothers, fathers are more likely to

a. engage in more imaginative, exciting play.
b. encourage intellectual development in their children.
c. encourage social development in their children.
d. read to their toddlers.

13. Like Freud, Erikson believed that:

a. problems arising in early infancy last a lifetime.
b. inability to resolve a conflict in infancy may result in later fixation.
c. human development can be viewed in terms of psychosexual stages.
d. all of these are true.

14. Which of the following is an example of social learning?

a. Sue discovers that a playmate will share a favorite toy if she asks politely.
b. Jon learns that other children are afraid of him when he raises his voice.
c. Zach develops a hot temper after seeing his father regularly display anger and, in turn, receive respect from others.
d. All of these are examples of social learning.

15. Which of the following is NOT true regarding synchrony?

a. There are wide variations in the frequency of synchrony from baby to baby.
b. Synchrony appears to be uninfluenced by cultural differences.
c. The frequency of mother–infant synchrony has varied over historical time.
d. Parents and infants spend about one hour a day in face-to-face play.

Matching Items
Match each theorist, term, or concept with its corresponding description or definition.

Theorists, Terms, or Concepts

_____ 1. temperament
_____ 2. Erikson
_____ 3. Strange Situation
_____ 4. synchrony
_____ 5. trust versus mistrust
_____ 6. Freud
_____ 7. social referencing
_____ 8. autonomy versus shame and doubt
_____ 9. self-awareness
_____ 10. Ainsworth
_____ 11. proximity-seeking behaviors
_____ 12. contact-maintaining behaviors

Descriptions or Definitions

a. looking to caregivers for emotional cues
b. the crisis of infancy
c. the crisis of toddlerhood
d. approaching and following
e. theorist who described psychosexual stages of development
f. researcher who devised a laboratory procedure for studying attachment
g. laboratory procedure for studying attachment
h. a person's relatively consistent inborn traits
i. touching, snuggling, and holding
j. coordinated interaction between parent and infant
k. theorist who described psychosocial stages of development
l. a person's sense of being distinct from others

Key Terms

Using your own words, write a brief definition or explanation of each of the following terms on a separate piece of paper.

 1. social smile
 2. stranger wariness
 3. separation anxiety
 4. self-awareness
 5. trust versus mistrust
 6. autonomy versus shame and doubt
 7. social learning
 8. working model
 9. temperament
10. Big Five
11. ethnotheory
12. proximal parenting
13. distal parenting
14. goodness of fit
15. synchrony

16. still-face technique
17. attachment
18. secure attachment
19. insecure-avoidant attachment
20. insecure-resistant/ambivalent attachment
21. disorganized attachment
22. Strange Situation
23. social referencing
24. family day care
25. center day care

Answers

CHAPTER REVIEW

1. emotional; social
2. pleasure; pain; curiosity; happiness; social smile; 6
3. 6; is; frustration; withdrawal; cortisol
4. 9; stranger wariness; separation anxiety; 1; 2; decrease; targeted (focused)

5. pride, shame, embarrassment, guilt; other people

6. self-awareness; self; consciousness; pretending; first-person

7. self-concept; hinder; pleasing other people

8. brain; experiences; nutrition; synesthesia; genetic; older children; infants

9. people; memory

10. hypothalamus; teenage; kangaroo care

Study Tip: In the classic self-awareness experiment, babies look in a mirror after a dot of rouge is put on their nose. If the babies react to the mirror image by touching their noses, it is clear they know they are seeing their own faces. Most babies demonstrate this self-awareness between 15 and 24 months of age.

11. separation anxiety; stranger wariness

12. oral; mouth

13. anal

14. long-term; oral fixation

15. psychoanalytic; cross-cultural; behaviorism; Barry Brazelton; 2; cognitive; emotional; biological

16. Erikson; trust versus mistrust; autonomy versus shame and doubt

17. behaviorism; reinforcement; punishment; John Watson

18. social; imitate; Albert Bandura

19. parents; mother; narrow

20. values; thoughts; beliefs; perceptions; memories; working model

21. epigenetic; genetic; temperament

22. personality; environment

23. New York Longitudinal Study (NYLS); easy; difficult; slow to warm up; hard to classify

24. openness; conscientiousness; extroversion; agreeableness; neuroticism

25. sociocultural; social; ethnotheory; ethnic; proximal; self-aware; compliant; distal

26. Only Freud and Erikson proposed stage theories. Other theories see development as continuous throughout the lifespan.

Erikson emphasized psychosocial conflicts at each stage. If the conflicts are not resolved, the effects could last a lifetime, for example, creating a suspicious and pessimistic adult (mistrusting).

Behaviorism emphasizes that emotions and personality are molded as parents reinforce or punish a child's spontaneous behavior. The result can last a lifetime if no other reinforcement or punishment changes the behavior.

Cognitive theory believes that infants develop a working model that serves as a frame of reference later in life. They use this model to organize their perceptions and experiences.

Epigenetic theory holds that each person is born with a unique temperament that affects and is affected by life's experiences.

Sociocultural theory contends that social and cultural factors have a significant influence on development and continue throughout the life span.

27. behaviorism. Behaviorists focus on learning through reinforcement or punishment and by observing others.

28. a. is the answer. Epigenetic theory holds that every human characteristic is strongly influenced by each person's unique genotype.

29. cognitive theory. Cognitive theory holds that thoughts and values determine a person's perspective.

30. c. is the answer. According to Freud, if the conflict at a particular stage is not resolved, the person becomes fixated at that stage. So, being fixated at the anal stage, Felix has a strong need for self-control.

31. positive; negative; inhibited

32. goodness of fit

33. synchrony; read other people's emotions; social interaction; parents; infants

34. still-face; does not

35. attachment

36. proximity-seeking; contact-maintaining

37. secure attachment; base for exploration

38. insecure attachment; insecure-avoidant attachment; insecure-resistant/ambivalent attachment

Some infants are avoidant: They engage in little interaction with their mothers before and after her departure. Others are anxious and resistant: They cling nervously to their mothers, are unwilling to explore, become very upset when she leaves, and refuse to be comforted when she returns. Others are disorganized: They show an inconsistent mixture of behaviors toward their mothers.

39. Strange Situation; two-thirds; disorganized

40. D; can

41. social referencing

42. most

43. encouraging; cautious; protective; proximal

44. family; center

45. insensitive; 20

46. (a) adequate attention to each infant; (b) encouragement of sensorimotor and language development; (c) attention to health and safety; (d) well-trained and professional caregivers; (e) warm and responsive caregivers

47. Insecure-avoidant: They have less confidence and play independently without maintaining contact with the parent. Parents are neglectful, stressed, intrusive, and controlling, and father is an active alcoholic.

    Insecure-resistant/ambivalent: This child is unwilling to leave the parent's lap. Parent is abusive and depressed.

    Disorganized: This type has elements of the other types; the infant shifts between hitting and kissing the parent, from staring to crying. The most troubled children are classified as type D. The parent is abusive, paranoid, and stressed. The mother is an active alcoholic.

48. **b.** is the answer. Securely attached infants use their caregiver as a secure base. Kirsten returns to her mother for reassurance, so we can then resume play.

49. social referencing. Miguel is asking his mother how he should react by looking at her after the fall.

50. **d.** is the answer.

51. **d.** is the answer.

52. **c.** is the answer. Insecure-resistant ambivalent infants usually become upset when the caregiver leaves but may resist or seek contact when she returns.

53. synchrony. Synchrony is a coordinated and smooth exchange of responses between a caregiver and an infant. Usually, it begins with the caregiver imitating the infant's behavior.

54. no single; emotional; social; parents'; day care; culture; inborn

PROGRESS TEST 1

Multiple-Choice Questions

1. **b.** is the answer. (p. 188)

    a., c., & d. These emotions emerge later in infancy, at about the same time as self-awareness emerges.

2. **b.** is the answer. (p. 200)

3. **c.** is the answer. (p. 189)

4. **d.** is the answer. (p. 208)

5. **b.** is the answer. (p. 197)

6. **c.** is the answer. (p. 196)

7. **b.** is the answer. (pp. 194, 195)

    a. Orality and anality refer to personality traits that result from fixation in the oral and anal stages, respectively.

    c. According to Erikson, this is the crisis of toddlerhood, which corresponds to Freud's anal stage.

    d. This is not a developmental crisis in Erikson's theory.

8. **c.** is the answer. (p. 195)

9. **a.** is the answer. (p. 204)

    c. Attachment behaviors are reliably found during infancy.

    d. There is no indication that the child attends day care.

10. **b.** is the answer. Another type is "hard to classify." (p. 198)

    a. "Secure" and "insecure" are different forms of attachment.

    c. The chapter does not describe different types of parenting.

    d. The Strange Situation is a test of attachment rather than of temperament.

11. **a.** is the answer. (p. 210)

    c. & d. These terms were not used to describe parenting styles.

12. **a.** is the answer. (p. 203)

13. **d.** is the answer. (p. 205)

    a. Self-awareness refers to the infant's developing sense of "me and mine."

    b. Synchrony describes the coordinated interaction between infant and caregiver.

    c. Affiliation describes the tendency of people at any age to seek the companionship of others.

14. **a.** is the answer. (p. 204)

    b. In fact, just the opposite is true.

    c. & d. Not usually at 2 months, but clearly at 6 months, babies become very upset by a still-faced caregiver.

15. **b.** is the answer. (p. 188)

True or False Items

1. F Sociocultural theorists contend that the entire social context can have an impact on the infant's development. (p. 199)
2. F About two-thirds of infants display secure attachment. (p. 206)
3. T (p. 189)
4. T (p. 190)
5. F A securely attached toddler is most likely to explore the environment, with the mother's presence being enough to give him or her the courage to do so. (pp. 206–207)
6. F Researchers believe that high-quality day care is not likely to harm the child. In fact, it is thought to be beneficial to the development of cognitive and social skills. (pp. 211–212)
7. T (p. 210)
8. F Temperament is a product of both genes and experience. (p. 197)
9. T (p. 190)
10. T (p. 191)

PROGRESS TEST 2

Multiple-Choice Questions

1. **a.** is the answer. (p. 206)
2. **a.** is the answer. (pp. 194, 195)
3. **c.** is the answer. (p. 190)
4. **a.** is the answer. (p. 202)
5. **c.** is the answer. (pp. 189–190)

   a. & b. The social smile, as well as temperamental characteristics, emerge well before the first signs of self-awareness.

   d. Contemporary developmentalists link these emotions to self-consciousness, rather than any specific environmental event such as toilet training.
6. **a.** is the answer. (p. 198)

   b. & c. Although environment, especially parents, affects temperamental tendencies, the study noted that temperament was established within 3 months of birth.

   d. Self-awareness is not a temperamental characteristic.
7. **c.** is the answer. (p. 189)
8. **c.** is the answer. (pp. 197–198)
9. **d.** is the answer. (p. 206)

10. **a.** is the answer. (p. 208)

    c. & d. The text does not suggest that the consequences of secure and insecure attachment differ in boys and girls.
11. **b.** is the answer. (pp. 206–207)

    a. Insecure-avoidant attachment is marked by behaviors that indicate an infant is uninterested in a caregiver's presence or departure.

    c. Disorganized attachment is marked only by the inconsistency of infant–caregiver behaviors.

    d. Type B, or secure attachment, is marked by behaviors that indicate an infant is using a caregiver as a base from which to explore the environment.
12. **a.** is the answer. (p. 210)
13. **a.** is the answer. (p. 195)

    b. & c. Freud alone would have agreed with these statements.
14. **c.** is the answer. (p. 196)

    a. & b. Social learning involves learning by observing others. In these examples, the children are learning directly from the consequences of their own behavior.
15. **b.** is the answer. (pp. 203–204)

Matching Items

1. h (p. 197)
2. k (p. 195)
3. g (p. 207)
4. j (p. 203)
5. b (p. 195)
6. e (p. 193)
7. a (p. 208)
8. c (p 195)
9. l (p. 190)
10. f (p. 206)
11. d (p. 206)
12. i (p. 206)

KEY TERMS

1. A **social smile** occurs when an infant smiles in response to a human face; evident in infants about 6 weeks after birth. (p. 188)
2. A common early fear in response to some person, thing, or situation, **stranger wariness** (also called *fear of strangers*) is first noticeable at about 9 months. (p. 189)
3. **Separation anxiety**, which is the infant's fear of being left by a familiar caregiver, is usually strongest at 9 to 14 months. (p. 189)
4. **Self-awareness** refers to a person's realization that he or she is a distinct individual, whose body, mind, and actions are separate from other people. Self-awareness makes possible many new self-conscious emotions, including shame, embarrassment, and pride. (p. 190)

5. In Erikson's theory, the psychosocial crisis of infancy is one of **trust versus mistrust,** in which the infant learns whether the world is essentially a secure place in which basic needs will be met. (p. 195)

6. In Erikson's theory, the psychosocial crisis of toddlerhood is one of **autonomy versus shame and doubt,** in which toddlers strive to rule their own actions and bodies. (p. 195)

7. **Social learning** is learning by observing others. (p. 196)

8. According to cognitive theory, infants use early social relationships to develop a set of assumptions called a **working model** that organizes their perceptions and experiences. (p. 196)

9. **Temperament** refers to the "constitutionally based individual differences" in emotions, activity, and self-regulation. (p. 197)

10. The **Big Five** are stable, basic clusters of personality traits that include openness, conscientiousness, extroversion, agreeableness, and neuroticism. (p. 198)

11. An **ethnotheory** is a theory of child rearing that underlies the values and practices of an ethnic group or culture. It is usually not apparent to the people within the culture. (p. 199)

12. **Proximal parenting** practices involve close physical contact between child and parent. (p. 199)

13. **Distal parenting** practices involve remaining distant from a baby. (p. 199)

14. **Goodness of fit** is the pattern of smooth interaction between the individual and the social context. (p. 202)

15. **Synchrony** refers to a coordinated, rapid, and smooth interaction between caregiver and infant that helps infants learn to express and read emotions. (p. 203)

16. The **still-face technique** is an experimental device in which an adult keeps his or her face unmoving and without expression in face-to-face interaction with an infant. (p. 204)

17. According to Mary Ainsworth, **attachment** is the enduring emotional bond that a person forms with another. (p. 205)

18. A **secure attachment** is one in which the infant obtains comfort and confidence from the base of exploration provided by a caregiver. (p. 206)

19. **Insecure-avoidant attachment** is the pattern of attachment in which the infant seems uninterested in the caregiver's presence, departure, or return. (p. 206)

20. **Insecure-resistant/ambivalent attachment** is the pattern of attachment in which an infant resists active exploration, becomes very upset when the caregiver leaves, and both resists and seeks contact when the caregiver returns. (p. 206)

21. **Disorganized attachment** is the pattern of attachment that is neither secure nor insecure and is marked by inconsistent infant–caregiver interactions. (p. 206)

22. The **Strange Situation** is a laboratory procedure developed by Mary Ainsworth for assessing attachment. Infants are observed in a playroom, in several successive episodes, while the caregiver (usually the mother) and a stranger move in and out of the room. (p. 207)

23. When infants engage in **social referencing,** they are looking to trusted adults for emotional cues on how to react to unfamiliar or ambiguous objects or events. (p. 208)

24. **Family day care** is regular care provided for several children in a paid nonrelative's home. (p. 210)

25. **Center day care** is regular care provided for children by several paid adults in a place designed for that purpose. (p. 211)

8

Early Childhood: Biosocial Development

Chapter Overview

Chapter 8 introduces the developing person between the ages of 2 and 6. These years were once called the preschool years or the play years, but those terms are misnomers because school in all its varieties and playfulness are essential to development at every age.

The chapter begins by outlining growth rates and the changes in shape that occur from ages 2 through 6, as well as the toddler's eating habits. This is followed by a look at brain growth and development and its role in physical and cognitive development. The developing limbic system is also described, along with its role in the expression and regulation of emotions during early childhood. A description of the acquisition of gross and fine motor skills follows, noting that mastery of such skills develops steadily during these years along with intellectual growth.

The next section begins with a discussion of the important issues of injury control and accidents, the major cause of childhood death. This section concludes with an in-depth exploration of child maltreatment, including its prevalence, contributing factors, consequences for future development, treatment, and prevention.

NOTE: Answer guidelines for all Chapter 8 questions begin on page 113.

Chapter Review

When you have finished reading the chapter, work through the material that follows to review it. Complete the sentences and answer the questions. In some cases, Study Tips explain how best to learn a difficult concept, while Think About It and Applications help you to know how well you understand the material. As you proceed, evaluate your performance for each section by consulting the answers beginning on page 113. Do not continue with the next section until you understand each answer. If you need to, review or reread the appropriate section in the textbook before continuing.

Body Changes (pp. 221–224)

1. In early childhood, from age _____ to _____ , children add almost _____ in height and gain about _____ in weight per year. By age 6, the average child in a developed nation weighs about _____ and measures _____ in height.

2. In multiethnic countries, children of _____ descent tend to be tallest, followed by _____ , then _____ , and then _____ .

3. Height differences _____ (between/within) groups are greater than the average differences _____ (between/within) groups.

4. Household _____ also affects physical growth. In Brazil, for instance, whereas low income once correlated with _____ , (undernutrition/overnutrition), today it also correlates with more _____ (undernutrition/overnutrition).

5. Overfed children _____ (tend/do not necessarily tend) to become overweight adults. Overweight children often have early symptoms of two chronic illnesses: _____ disease and _____ _____ _____ . During early childhood, children need _____ (fewer/more) calories per pound than they did as infants.

6. The most prevalent nutritional problem in early childhood is an insufficient intake of

_____ , _____ , and

_____ . An additional problem for American children is that they consume too many

_____ . One

result of too much sugar is _____

_____ , the most common disease of young children in developed nations.

7. Young children generally insist that a particular experience occur in an exact sequence and man-

ner, a phenomenon called _____

_____ . By age _____ ,

this rigidity fades.

Learning (and remembering) developmental changes in height, weight, brain maturation, and other aspects of biosocial development requires a lot of rote memorization. A good way to facilitate your learning is to design and complete a simple organizational chart. Your chart might look something like the one below. Continue adding to the chart as you work your way through the chapter.

8. Physical Changes in Early Childhood (2–6 years)

	Changes	Description
Height (in inches)	3 inches per year	The child is taller and thinner and, on average, 46 inches by 6 years of age.
Weight (in pounds)		
Brain functions General		
Limbic system		
Prefrontal cortex		
Motor skills Gross		
Fine		

APPLICATION:

9. Three-year-old Kyle's parents are concerned because Kyle, who generally seems healthy, doesn't seem to have the hefty appetite he had as an infant. Should they be worried?
   a. Yes, because appetite normally increases throughout early childhood.
   b. Yes, because appetite remains as good during early childhood as it was earlier.
   c. No, because caloric need is less during early childhood than during infancy.

d. There is not enough information to determine whether Kyle is developing normally.

Brain Development (pp. 225–231)

10. By age 2, most pruning of the brain's

_____ has occurred, and the brain

weighs _____ percent of its adult

weight. By age 5, the brain has attained about

_____ percent of its adult weight.

11. Some of the brain's increase in size during child-hood is due to the proliferation of _____ pathways, but most of it occurs because of the ongoing process of _____ .

12. The long, thick band of nerve fibers that connects the right and left sides of the brain, called the _____ _____ , grows and _____ rapidly during early childhood. This helps children better coordinate functions that involve _____ _____ .

13. The two sides of the body and brain _____ (are/are not) identical. The specialization of the two sides of the body and brain is called _____ . Throughout the world, societies are organized to favor _____-handedness. Developmentalists _____ (advise against/advise) trying to switch a child's handed-ness.

14. Adults who are _____ (right-/left-) handed tend to have a thicker corpus callosum, probably because as children they had a greater need to _____ both sides of the body in a right-handed world.

15. The left hemisphere of the brain controls the _____ side of the body and contains areas dedicated to _____ , detailed _____ , and the basics of _____ . The right hemisphere con-trols the _____ side of the body and contains brain areas dedicated to generalized _____ and _____ impulses. As a rule, though, every cognitive skill requires _____ (the right/the left/both) side(s) of the brain.

16. In older children, the corpus callosum is more _____ , which partly explains why their behaviors sometimes are less clumsy.

17. The part of the brain that shows the most pro-longed period of postnatal development is the _____ _____ .

Development of this brain area increases throughout _____ . This area is sometimes called the _____ because all other areas of the brain are ruled by its deci-sions.

18. Two signs of an undeveloped prefrontal cortex are _____ and _____ , which is the tendency to stick to a thought or action for a long time.

19. The part of the brain that plays a crucial role in the expression and regulation of emotions is the _____ _____ . Within this system is the _____ , which reg-isters emotions, particularly _____ and _____ . Next to this area is the _____ , which is a central processor of _____ , especially of _____ . Another structure in this brain region is the_____ , which produces _____ that activate other parts of the brain and body.

THINK ABOUT IT: Students, and people in general, often have difficulty understanding the limitations of the young child's thinking and emotional impulsive-ness. To increase your understanding, make a list of behaviors that demonstrate the child's immaturity, then observe and compare 2- or 3-year-olds with 6-year-olds.

APPLICATIONS:

20. Rodesia is a left-handed adult. It is most likely that she
   a. has a thinner corpus callosum.
   b. has a thicker corpus callosum.
   c. experienced delayed maturation of her prefrontal cortex.
   d. experienced accelerated maturation of her prefrontal cortex.

21. Following an automobile accident, Amira devel-oped severe problems with her speech. Her doc-tor believes that the accident injured the _____ of her brain.

22. Yolanda, who is 5 years old, has improved dramatically in her ability to throw and catch a baseball. Which aspect of her brain development contributed most to enable these abilities by enhancing communication among the brain's various specialized areas?
a. increasing brain weight
b. proliferation of dendrite networks
c. myelination
d. increasing specialization of brain areas

Improved Motor Skills (pp. 231–236)

23. Large body movements such as running, climbing, jumping, and throwing are called _____ _____ skills.

24. Most children learn these skills best from _____ (other children/parents).

25. Skills that involve small body movements, such as pouring liquids and cutting food, are called _____ _____ skills. Most 2-year-olds have greater difficulty with these skills primarily because they have not developed the _____ control, patience, or _____ needed—in part because of the immaturity of the _____ _____ and _____ _____ .

26. Fine motor skills are useful in almost all forms of _____ _____ , yet such skills are far from perfect. These skills typically mature _____ (earlier/later), by about _____ months, in _____ (girls/boys). The pictures children draw often reveal the _____ of these skills as well as their unique _____ and _____ .

APPLICATIONS:

27. Two-year-old Ali is quite clumsy, falls down frequently, and often bumps into stationary objects. Ali most likely
a. has a neuromuscular disorder.
b. has an underdeveloped right hemisphere of the brain.
c. is suffering from an iron deficiency.
d. is a normal 2-year-old whose gross motor skills will improve dramatically during early childhood.

28. Climbing a fence is an example of a _____ .

29. Which of the following activities would probably be the most difficult for a 5-year-old child?
a. climbing a ladder
b. catching a ball
c. throwing a ball
d. pouring juice from a pitcher without spilling it

30. A factor that would figure very little into the development of fine motor skills, such as drawing and writing, is
a. strength.   c. judgment.
b. muscular control.   d. short, fat fingers.

Injuries and Abuse (pp. 236–246)

31. The leading cause of childhood death is _____ .

32. Not until age _____ does any disease become a greater cause of mortality.

33. Instead of "accident prevention," many experts speak of _____ _____ (or _____ _____), an approach based on the belief that most accidents _____ (are/are not) preventable.

34. Preventive community actions that reduce everyone's chance of injury are called _____ _____ . Preventive actions that avert harm in a high-risk situation constitute _____ _____ . Actions aimed at minimizing the impact of an adverse event that has already occurred constitute _____ _____ .

35. Until about 1960, the concept of child maltreatment was mostly limited to rare and _____ outbursts of a disturbed stranger. Today, it is known that most perpetrators of maltreatment are the child's _____ .

36. Intentional harm to or avoidable endangerment of someone under age 18 defines child _____ . Actions that are deliberately harmful to a child's well-being are classified as _____ . A failure to act appropriately to meet a child's basic needs is classified as _____ .

37. Since 1993, the ratio of the number of cases of
_____ _____ , in
which authorities have been officially notified, to
cases of _____ _____ ,
which have been reported, investigated, and verified, has been about _____ (what
ratio?).

38. Often the first sign of maltreatment is
_____ _____ , such as
slow growth or lack of curiosity.

39. Signs of maltreatment may be symptoms of
_____-_____
_____ _____ , which
was first described in combat victims.

40. (A View from Science) Abused and neglected
children are more often _____ ,
_____ , and _____ .

41. Maltreated children suffer substantial
_____ and _____
handicaps. However, deficits in their
_____ _____ are even
more apparent.
Describe other deficits of children who have been
maltreated.

42. Public policy measures and other efforts designed
to prevent maltreatment from ever occurring are
called _____ _____ .
An approach that focuses on spotting and treating the first symptoms of maltreatment is called
_____ _____ . Last-
ditch measures, such as removing a child from an
abusive home, jailing the perpetrator, and so
forth, constitute _____
_____ .

43. Once maltreatment has been substantiated, the
first priority is _____
_____ for the child's long-term care.

44. Some children are officially removed from their
biological parents and placed in a _____
_____ arrangement with another
adult or family who is paid to nurture them.

45. In another type of foster care, called
_____ _____ , a rela-
tive of the maltreated child becomes the
approved caregiver. A final option is
_____ .

46. Two-year-old Carrie is hyperactive, often con-
fused between fantasy and reality, and jumps at
any sudden noise. Her pediatrician suspects that
she is suffering from
a. perseveration.
b. child abuse.
c. post-traumatic stress disorder.
d. child neglect.

47. To prevent accidental death in childhood, some
experts urge forethought and planning for safety
and measures to limit the damage of such accidents when they do occur. This approach is
called _____ .

48. After his daughter scraped her knee, Ben gently
cleansed the wound and bandaged it. Ben's
behavior is an example of _____
prevention.

49. Helga comes to school with large black-and-blue
marks on her arm. Her teacher suspects
a. ongoing abuse and neglect by Helga's own
parents.
b. a rare outburst from a unfamiliar perpetrator.
c. abuse by a neighbor or friend of Helga's
family.
d. abuse by a mentally ill perpetrator.

50. A mayoral candidate is calling for sweeping policy changes to help ensure the well-being of children by promoting home ownership, high-quality
community centers, and more stable neighborhoods. If these measures are effective in reducing child maltreatment, they would be classified
as _____ prevention.

Progress Test 1

Multiple-Choice Questions

Circle your answers to the following questions and check them with the answers on page 115. If your answer is incorrect, read the explanation for why it is incorrect and then consult the appropriate pages of the text (in parentheses following the correct answer).

1. During early childhood, the most common disease of young children in developed nations is
    a. undernutrition.
    b. malnutrition.
    c. tooth decay.
    d. diabetes.

2. The brain center for the basics of language is usually located in the
    a. right hemisphere.
    b. left hemisphere.
    c. corpus callosum.
    d. space just below the right ear.

3. Which of the following is an example of tertiary prevention of child maltreatment?
    a. removing a child from an abusive home
    b. home visitation of families with infants by a social worker
    c. new laws establishing stiff penalties for child maltreatment
    d. public policy measures aimed at creating stable neighborhoods

4. The brain area that registers emotions is the
    a. hippocampus.
    b. hypothalamus.
    c. amygdala.
    d. prefrontal cortex.

5. Children's problems with tooth decay result primarily from their having too much _____ in their diet.
    a. iron
    b. sugar
    c. fat
    d. carbohydrates

6. Skills that involve large body movements, such as running and jumping, are called
    a. activity-level skills.
    b. fine motor skills.
    c. gross motor skills.
    d. left-brain skills.

7. The brain's ongoing myelination during childhood helps children
    a. control their actions more precisely.
    b. react more quickly to stimuli.
    c. control their emotions.
    d. do all of these things.

8. The leading cause of death in childhood is
    a. accidents.
    b. untreated diabetes.
    c. malnutrition.
    d. cancer.

9. Regarding lateralization, which of the following is NOT true?
    a. Some cognitive skills require only one side of the brain.
    b. Brain centers for generalized emotional impulses can be found in the right hemisphere.
    c. The left hemisphere contains brain areas dedicated to logical reasoning.
    d. The right side of the brain controls the left side of the body.

10. In young children, perseveration is a sign of
    a. immature brain functions.
    b. maltreatment.
    c. abuse.
    d. amygdala.

11. The area of the brain that directs and controls the other areas is the
    a. corpus callosum.
    b. myelin sheath.
    c. prefrontal cortex.
    d. amygdala.

12. (A View from Science) The relationship between physical abuse and neglect and income can be described as
    a. a positive correlation.
    b. a negative correlation.
    c. curvilinear.
    d. no correlation.

13. Which of the following is true of the corpus callosum?
    a. It enables short-term memory.
    b. It connects the two halves of the brain.
    c. It must be fully myelinated before gross motor skills can be acquired.
    d. All of these statements are correct.

14. The improvements in eye–hand coordination that allow young children to catch and then throw a ball occur, in part, because
    a. the brain areas associated with this ability become more fully myelinated.
    b. the corpus callosum begins to function.
    c. fine motor skills have matured by age 2.
    d. gross motor skills have matured by age 2.

15. During early childhood, inadequate lateralization of the brain and immaturity of the prefrontal cortex may contribute to deficiencies in
    a. cognition.
    b. peer relationships.
    c. emotional control.
    d. all of these abilities.

True or False Items

Write T (*true*) or F (*false*) on the line in front of each statement.

_____ 1. Growth between ages 2 and 6 results in body proportions more similar to those of an adult.

_____ 2. During childhood, the legs develop rapidly.

_____ 3. For most people, the brain center for language is located in the left hemisphere.

_____ 4. At age 5, the body mass index is lower than at any other age.

_____ 5. Overweight children tend to become overweight adults.

_____ 6. Fine motor skills are usually easier for preschoolers to master than are gross motor skills.

_____ 7. Most serious childhood injuries truly are "accidents."

_____ 8. Children often fare as well in kinship care as they do in conventional foster care.

_____ 9. (A Personal Perspective) Laws are generally more effective than educational campaigns in preventing childhood injuries.

_____ 10. Myelination is essential for basic communication between neurons.

Progress Test 2

Progress Test 2 should be completed during a final chapter review. Answer the following questions after you thoroughly understand the correct answers for the Chapter Review and Progress Test 1.

Multiple-Choice Questions

1. Each year from ages 2 to 6, the average child gains and grows, respectively,
   a. 2 pounds and 1 inch.
   b. 3 pounds and 2 inches.
   c. 4½ pounds and 3 inches.
   d. 6 pounds and 6 inches.

2. The center for appreciation of music, art, and poetry is usually located in the brain's
   a. right hemisphere.
   b. left hemisphere.
   c. right or left hemisphere.
   d. corpus callosum.

3. Regarding handedness, which of the following is NOT true?
   a. Infants and toddlers usually show a preference for grabbing with either the right or the left hand.
   b. Some societies favor left-handed people.
   c. Experience can influence hand development.
   d. Language, customs, tools, and taboos all illustrate social biases toward right-handedness.

4. A nutritional problem of young children in developed nations is
   a. too much salt.
   b. too little iron.
   c. too much zinc.
   d. too much calcium.

5. Seeing her toddler reach for a brightly glowing burner on the stove, Sheila grabs his hand and says, "No, that's very hot." Sheila's behavior is an example of
   a. primary prevention.
   b. secondary prevention.
   c. tertiary prevention.
   d. none of these types of prevention.

6. When parents or caregivers do not meet a child's basic physical, educational, or emotional needs, it is referred to as:
   a. abuse.   c. endangering.
   b. neglect.   d. maltreatment.

7. Which of the following is true of a developed nation in which many ethnic groups live together?
   a. Ethnic variations in height and weight disappear.
   b. Ethnic variations in stature persist, but are substantially smaller.
   c. Children of African descent tend to be tallest, followed by Europeans, Asians, and Latinos.
   d. Cultural patterns exert a stronger-than-normal impact on growth patterns.

8. Which of the following is an example of perseveration?
   a. 2-year-old Jason sings the same song over and over
   b. 3-year-old Kwame falls down when attempting to kick a soccer ball
   c. 4-year-old Kara pours water very slowly from a pitcher into a glass
   d. None of these is an example.

9. Which of the following is an example of a fine motor skill?
   a. kicking a ball
   b. running
   c. drawing with a pencil
   d. jumping

10. Children who have been maltreated often
   a. regard other children and adults as hostile and exploitative.
   b. are less friendly and more aggressive.
   c. are more isolated than other children.
   d. have all of these characteristics.

11. The left half of the brain contains areas dedicated to all of the following EXCEPT
   a. language.
   b. logic.
   c. analysis.
   d. creative impulses.

12. Most gross motor skills can be learned by healthy children by about age
   a. 2.   c. 5.
   b. 3.   d. 7.

13. Andrea is concerned because her 3-year-old daughter has been having nightmares. Her pediatrician tells her
   a. not to worry, because nightmares are often caused by increased activity in the amygdala, which is normal during early childhood.
   b. nightmares are a possible sign of an overdeveloped prefrontal cortex.
   c. to monitor her daughter's diet, because nightmares are often caused by too much sugar.
   d. to consult a neurologist, because nightmares are never a sign of healthy development.

14. The brain area that is a central processor for memory is the
   a. hippocampus.   c. hypothalamus.
   b. amygdala.   d. prefrontal cortex.

15. The appetites of young children seem _____ they were in the first two years of life.
   a. larger than
   b. smaller than
   c. about the same as
   d. erratic, sometimes smaller and sometimes larger than

Matching Items

Match each term or concept with its corresponding description or definition.

Terms or Concepts

_____ **1.** corpus callosum
_____ **2.** gross motor skills
_____ **3.** fine motor skills
_____ **4.** kinship care
_____ **5.** foster care
_____ **6.** injury control
_____ **7.** right hemisphere
_____ **8.** left hemisphere
_____ **9.** child abuse
_____ **10.** child neglect
_____ **11.** primary prevention
_____ **12.** secondary prevention
_____ **13.** tertiary prevention

Descriptions or Definitions

a. brain area that is primarily responsible for processing language
b. brain area that is primarily responsible for generalized creative impulses
c. legal placement of a child in the care of someone other than his or her biological parents
d. a form of care in which a relative of a maltreated child takes over from the biological parents
e. procedures to prevent unwanted events or circumstances from ever occurring
f. running and jumping
g. actions that are deliberately harmful to a child's well-being
h. actions for averting harm in the immediate situation
i. painting a picture or tying shoelaces
j. failure to appropriately meet a child's basic needs
k. an approach emphasizing accident prevention
l. actions aimed at reducing the harm that has occurred
m. band of nerve fibers connecting the right and left hemispheres of the brain

Key Terms

Using your own words, write a brief definition or explanation of each of the following terms on a separate piece of paper.

1. myelination
2. corpus callosum
3. lateralization
4. perseveration
5. amygdala
6. hippocampus
7. hypothalamus
8. injury control/harm reduction
9. primary prevention
10. secondary prevention
11. tertiary prevention
12. child maltreatment
13. child abuse
14. child neglect
15. reported maltreatment
16. substantiated maltreatment
17. post-traumatic stress disorder

18. permanency planning
19. foster care
20. kinship care
21. adoption

Answers

CHAPTER REVIEW

1. 2; 6; 3 inches (about 7 centimeters); 4½ pounds (2 kilograms); 46 pounds (21 kilograms); 46 inches (117 centimeters)
2. African; Europeans; Asians; Latinos
3. within; between
4. income; undernutrition; overnutrition
5. tend; heart; type 2 diabetes; fewer
6. iron; zinc; calcium; sweetened cereals and drinks; tooth decay
7. just right (just so); 6
8. Weight: Children gain 4½ pounds each year. Because they are also growing rapidly, they are actually thinner than in earlier years.

General brain functions: Increased myelination allows for greater speed of thought and greater motor abilities, such as catching and throwing a ball.

Limbic system: The amygdala, hippocampus, and hypothalamus in the limbic system advance during these years. The amygdala registers emotions; increased activity in this area makes the child sensitive to other people's emotions and subject to strong personal emotions, including fear.

Prefrontal cortex: Said to be the executive of the brain, the prefrontal cortex is responsible for planning and analyzing. It continues to mature through childhood and adolescence, which enables more regular sleep, more nuanced emotions, and fewer temper tantrums and uncontrollable laughter and tears.

Gross motor skills: These large body movements improve markedly in early childhood. Children can climb a ladder, ride a tricycle, throw, catch, and kick a ball, and sometimes ski, skate, and dive.

Fine motor skills: These small body movements are more difficult for young children because of an immature corpus callosum and prefrontal cortex and because of short, stubby fingers. The lack of fine motor skills is one reason 3-year-olds are not allowed in first grade.

9. **c.** is the answer.

10. dendrites; 75; 90

11. communication; myelination

12. corpus callosum; myelinates; both sides of the brain or body

13. are not; lateralization; right; advise against

14. left-; coordinate

15. right; logic; analysis; language; left; emotional; creative; both

16. myelinated

17. prefrontal cortex; adolescence; executive

18. impulsiveness; perseveration

19. limbic system; amygdala; fear; anxiety; hippocampus; memory; locations; hypothalamus; hormones

20. **b.** is the answer. This is probably because, growing up in a right-handed world, they had a greater need to coordinate both sides of the body.

21. left side. The left side of the brain specializes in the basics of language.

22. **c.** is the answer. The greatest myelination in early childhood occurs in the motor and sensory areas, the areas responsible for the skills that develop dramatically during this time.

23. gross motor

24. other children

25. fine motor; muscular; judgment; corpus callosum; prefrontal cortex

26. artistic expression; earlier; 6; girls; immaturity; perception; cognition

27. **d.** is the answer. Because the child has better balance and coordination of both sides of the brain, motor skills improve greatly during this period.

28. gross motor skill

29. **d.** is the answer. Fine motor skills are more difficult for the young child, in part because of their short, stubby fingers.

30. **a.** is the answer.

31. violence

32. 40

33. injury control; harm reduction; are

34. primary prevention; secondary prevention; tertiary prevention

35. sudden; own parents

36. maltreatment; abuse; neglect

37. reported maltreatment; substantiated maltreatment; 3-to-1

38. delayed development

39. post-traumatic stress disorder

40. injured; sick; hospitalized

41. biological; academic; social skills

Maltreated children tend to regard other people as hostile and exploitative, and thus are less friendly, more aggressive, and more isolated than other children. As adolescents and adults, they often use drugs or alcohol, choose unsupportive relationships, become victims or aggressors, sabotage their own careers, eat too much or too little, and generally engage in self-destructive behavior.

42. primary prevention; secondary prevention; tertiary prevention

43. permanency planning

44. foster care

45. kinship care; adoption

46. **c.** is the answer. First identified in combat veterans, PTSD is now evident in some maltreated children.

47. injury control.

48. tertiary. Ben is applying medical treatment after

the adverse event, his daughter scraping her knee.

49. **a.** is the answer. At one time, people thought child maltreatment was a rare situation, perpetrated by a mentally ill stranger. Today, they know it is more likely to be perpetrated by the child's own parents.

50. primary. Primary prevention refers to actions taken to prevent an adverse event from occurring to a child.

PROGRESS TEST 1

Multiple-Choice Questions

1. **c.** is the answer. (p. 223)

   a.. b., & d. All of these conditions are much more likely to occur in infancy or in adolescence than in early childhood.

2. **b.** is the answer. (p. 227)

   a. & d. The right brain is the location of areas associated with generalized emotional and creative impulses.

   c. The corpus callosum helps integrate the functioning of the two halves of the brain; it does not contain areas specialized for particular skills.

3. **a.** is the answer. (p. 244)

   b. This is an example of secondary prevention.

   c. & d. These are examples of primary prevention.

4. **c.** is the answer. (p. 229)

   a. The hippocampus is a central processor of memory.

   b. The hypothalamus produces hormones that activate other parts of the brain and body.

   c. The prefrontal cortex is responsible for regulating attention, among other things. It makes formal education more possible in children.

5. **b.** is the answer. (p. 223)

6. **c.** is the answer. (p. 232)

7. **d.** is the answer. (pp. 225–226)

8. **a.** is the answer. (p. 236)

9. **a.** is the answer. (p. 227)

10. **a.** is the answer. (p. 228)

    b., c.. & d. Although maltreatment, whether in the form of abuse or neglect, may cause brain injury, perseveration is not necessarily a symptom of brain injury from those sources.

11. **c.** is the answer. (p. 227)

    a. The corpus callosum is the band of fibers that link the two halves of the brain.

    b. The myelin sheath is a fatty substance that surrounds some neurons in the brain.

    d. The amygdala registers emotions.

12. **b.** is the answer. Children who live in poor neighborhoods have *higher* rates of abuse and neglect. (p. 242)

13. **b.** is the answer. (p. 226)

    a. The corpus callosum is not directly involved in memory.

    c. Myelination of the central nervous system is important to the mastery of *fine* motor skills.

14. **a.** is the answer. (pp. 232–233)

    b. The corpus callosum begins to function long before the years between 2 and 6.

    c. & d. Neither fine nor gross motor skills have fully matured by age 2.

15. **d.** is the answer. (p. 227)

True or False Items

1. T (p. 221)

2. F During childhood, the brain develops faster than any other part of the body. (p. 225)

3. T (p. 227)

4. T (p. 221)

5. T (p. 222)

6. F Fine motor skills are more difficult for preschoolers to master than are gross motor skills. (p. 234)

7. F Most serious accidents involve someone's lack of forethought. (p. 237)

8. T (p. 245)

9. T (p. 239)

10. F Although myelination is not essential for basic communication between neurons, it is essential for fast and complex communication (p. 225)

PROGRESS TEST 2

Multiple-Choice Questions

1. **c.** is the answer. (p. 222)

2. **a.** is the answer. (p. 227)

   b. & c. The left hemisphere of the brain contains areas associated with language development.

   d. The corpus callosum does not contain areas for specific behaviors.

3. **b.** is the answer. All societies favor right-handed people. (p. 226)

4. **b.** is the answer. (p. 223)

5. **b.** is the answer. (p. 238)

6. **b.** is the answer. (p. 240)

   a. Abuse is deliberate, harsh injury to the body.

   c. Endangerment was not discussed.

   d. Maltreatment is too broad a term.

7. **c.** is the answer. (p. 222)

8. **a.** is the answer. (p. 228)

   b. Kicking a ball is a gross motor skill.

   c. Pouring is a fine motor skill.

9. **c.** is the answer. (p. 234)

   a., b., & d. These are gross motor skills.

10. **d.** is the answer. (p. 243)

11. **d.** is the answer. Brain areas that control generalized creative and emotional impulses are found in the right hemisphere. (p. 227)

12. **c.** is the answer. (p. 232)

13. **a.** is the answer. (p. 229)

   b. Nightmares generally occur when activity in the amygdala overwhelms the slowly developing prefrontal cortex.

   c. There is no indication that nightmares are caused by diet.

   d. Increased activity in the amygdala is normal during early childhood, as are the nightmares that some children experience.

14. **a.** is the answer. (p. 229)

   b. The amygdala is responsible for registering emotions.

   c. The hypothalamus produces hormones that activate other parts of the brain and body.

   d. The prefrontal cortex is involved in planning and goal-directed behavior.

15. **b.** is the answer. (p. 223)

Matching Items

1. m (p. 226)
2. f (p. 232)
3. i (p. 234)
4. d (p. 245)
5. c (p. 245)
6. k (p. 237)
7. b (p. 227)
8. a (p. 227)
9. g (p. 240)
10. j (p. 240)
11. e (p. 238)
12. h (p. 238)
13. l (p. 238)

KEY TERMS

1. **Myelination** is the process by which axons become coated with myelin, a fatty substance speeds up the transmission of nerve impulses between neurons. (p. 225)

2. The **corpus callosum** is a long, thick band of nerve fibers that connects the right and left hemispheres of the brain. (p. 226)

3. **Lateralization** refers to the specialization in certain functions by each side of the brain. (p. 226)

4. **Perseveration** is the tendency to stick to one thought or action for a long time. In young children, perseveration is a normal product of immature brain functions. (p. 228)

   Memory Aid: To *persevere* is to continue, or persist, at something.

5. A part of the brain's limbic system, the **amygdala** registers emotions, particularly fear and anxiety. (p. 229)

6. The **hippocampus** is the part of the brain's limbic system that is a central processor of memory, especially memory for locations. (p. 229)

7. The **hypothalamus** is the brain structure that produces hormones that activate other parts of the brain and body. (p. 230)

8. **Injury control/harm reduction** is the practice of limiting the extent of injuries by anticipating, controlling, and preventing dangerous activities. (p. 237)

9. **Primary prevention** refers to actions that change overall background conditions to prevent some unwanted event or circumstance. (p. 238)

10. **Secondary prevention** involves actions that avert harm in a high-risk situation. (p. 238)

11. **Tertiary prevention** involves actions taken after an adverse event occurs, aimed at reducing the harm or preventing disability. (p. 238)

12. **Child maltreatment** is intentional harm to or avoidable endangerment of anyone under age 18. (p. 240)

13. **Child abuse** refers to deliberate actions that are harmful to a child's physical, emotional, or sexual well-being. (p. 240)

14. **Child neglect** refers to failure to appropriately meet a child's basic physical, educational, or emotional needs. (p. 240)

15. Child maltreatment that has been officially reported to the police or other authorities is called **reported maltreatment**. (p. 240)

16. Child maltreatment that has been officially reported to authorities, investigated, and verified is called **substantiated maltreatment**. (p. 240)

17. **Post-traumatic stress disorder (PTSD)** is an anxiety disorder triggered by exposure to an extreme traumatic stressor. Symptoms of PTSD include hyperactivity and hypervigilance, sleeplessness, sudden terror or anxiety, and confusion between fantasy and reality. (p. 241)

18. **Permanency planning** is planning for the long-term care of a child who has experienced substantiated maltreatment. (p. 244)

19. **Foster care** is a legally sanctioned, publicly supported arrangement in which children are removed from their biological parents and temporarily given to another adult to nurture. (p. 245)

20. **Kinship care** is a form of foster care in which a relative of a maltreated child becomes the child's approved caregiver. (p. 245)

21. **Adoption** is a legal procedure in which an adult or couple is granted the obligations and joys of being the parent(s) of an unrelated child. (p. 245)

9

Early Childhood: Cognitive Development

Chapter Overview

In countless everyday instances, as well as in the findings of numerous research studies, young children reveal themselves to be remarkably thoughtful, insightful, and perceptive thinkers whose grasp of the causes of everyday events, memory of the past, and mastery of language are sometimes astonishing. Chapter 9 begins with Piaget's and Vygotsky's views of cognitive development at this age. According to Piaget, young children's thought is prelogical: Between the ages of about 2 and 6, they are capable of symbolic thought but unable to perform many logical operations and are limited by irreversible, centered, and static thinking. Lev Vygotsky, a contemporary of Piaget's, saw learning as a social activity more than as a matter of individual discovery. Vygotsky focused on the child's zone of proximal development and the relationship between language and thought.

The next section focuses on what young children can do, including their emerging abilities to theorize about the world. This leads into a section on language development during early childhood. Although young children demonstrate rapid improvement in vocabulary and grammar, they have difficulty with comparisons and certain rules of grammar. A discussion of whether bilingualism in young children is useful concludes the section on language.

The chapter ends with a discussion of preschool education, including a description of "quality" preschool programs and an evaluation of their impact on children.

NOTE: Answer guidelines for all Chapter 9 questions begin on page 127.

Chapter Review

When you have finished reading the chapter, work through the material that follows to review it. Complete the sentences and answer the questions. In some cases, Study Tips explain how best to learn a difficult concept, while Think About It and

Applications help you to know how well you understand the material. As you proceed, evaluate your performance for each section by consulting the answers beginning on page 127. Do not continue with the next section until you understand each answer. If you need to, review or reread the appropriate section in the textbook before continuing.

1. Young children are sometimes _____ , understanding only their own perspective. As a result of their experiences with others, however, they also acquire a _____ _____ _____ that reflects their understanding of how minds work.

Piaget and Vygotsky (pp. 249–256)

2. Piaget referred to cognitive development between the ages of 2 and 6 as _____ intelligence.

3. Young children's tendency to contemplate the world exclusively from their personal perspective is referred to as _____ . Their tendency think about one aspect of a situation at a time is called _____ . This tendency _____ (is/is not) equated with selfishness. Children also tend to focus on _____ to the exclusion of other attributes of objects and people.

4. Young children's understanding of the world tends to focus on _____ (static/dynamic) reasoning, which means that they tend to think of their world as _____ . Another characteristic of preoperational thinking is _____ —the inability to recognize that reversing a process will restore the original conditions from which the process began. The idea that amount is unaffected by changes in appearance is called _____ .

5. Researchers now believe that Piaget _____ (overestimated/underestimated) conceptual ability during early childhood.

6. Yet another characteristic of preoperational thought is _____ , or the belief that natural objects and phenomena are alive. Research demonstrates that many children simultaneously hold ideas that are both _____ and _____ .

7. Much of the research from the sociocultural perspective on the young child's emerging cognition is inspired by the Russian psychologist _____ . According to this perspective, a child is an _____ _____ _____ , whose intellectual growth is stimulated by older and more skilled members of society.

8. Vygotsky believed that adults can most effectively help a child solve a problem by presenting _____ , by offering _____ , by providing _____ , and by encouraging _____ . This emphasizes that children's intellectual growth is stimulated by their _____ _____ in _____ experiences of their environment. The critical element in this process is that the mentor and the child _____ to accomplish a task.

9. Vygotsky suggested that for each developing individual there is a _____ _____ _____ , a range of skills that the person can exercise with assistance but is not yet able to perform independently.

10. How and when new skills are developed depends, in part, on the willingness of tutors to _____ the child's participation in the learning process.

11. Vygotsky believed that language is essential to the advancement of thinking in two crucial ways. The first is through the internal dialogue in which a person talks to himself or herself, called _____ _____ . In young children, this dialogue is likely to be _____ (expressed silently/uttered aloud).

12. According to Vygotsky, another way language advances thinking is as the _____ of the social interaction.

STUDY TIP: When many students first read Piaget's description of the limits of preoperational thought, they have the same reaction many developmentalists did—they don't believe it. To bring to life the fact that the preoperational child sees the world from his or her own perspective (egocentrism) and has not yet mastered the principle of conservation (the idea that properties such as mass, volume, and number remain the same despite changes in appearance), you might try one of Piaget's classic tests with a younger sibling, relative, or friend—for example, cut two hot dogs into different numbers of pieces or pour milk from a tall, thin glass into a short, fat glass and ask the child which hot dog is bigger or which glass has more milk in it.

APPLICATIONS:

13. An experimenter first shows a child two rows of checkers that each have the same number of checkers. Then, with the child watching, the experimenter elongates one row and asks the child if each of the two rows still has an equal number of checkers. This experiment tests the child's understanding of _____ .

14. Five-year-old Dani believes that a "party" is the one and only attribute of a birthday. She says that Daddy doesn't have a birthday because he never has a party. This thinking demonstrates the tendency Piaget called _____ .

15. Darrell understands that 6 + 3 = 9 means that 9 − 6 = 3. He has mastered the concept of _____ .

16. Which of the following terms does NOT belong with the others?
    a. focus on appearances
    b. static reasoning
    c. reversibility
    d. centration

17. In describing the limited logical reasoning of young children, a developmentalist is LEAST likely to emphasize
    a. irreversibility.
    b. centration.
    c. its action-bound nature.
    d. its static nature.

18. A young child fails to put together a difficult puzzle on her own, so her mother encourages her to try again, this time guiding her by asking questions such as, "For this space, do we need a big piece or a little piece?" With Mom's help, the child successfully completes the puzzle. Lev Vygotsky would attribute the child's success to
    a. additional practice with the puzzle pieces.
    b. imitation of her mother's behavior.
    c. the social interaction with her mother that restructured the task to make its solution more attainable.
    d. modeling and reinforcement.

19. Comparing the views of Piaget with those of Vygotsky, active learning is to guided participation as egocentrism is to
    a. apprenticeship.
    b. structure.
    c. scaffold.
    d. fast-mapping.

Children's Theories (pp. 256–260)

20. The term _____-_____ highlights the idea that children attempt to construct theories to explain everything they see and hear.

21. At about _____ years, young children acquire an understanding of others' thinking, or a _____ _____ _____ .

Describe the theory of mind of children between the ages of 3 and 6.

22. Most 3-year-olds _____ (have/do not have) difficulty realizing that a belief can be false.

23. Research studies reveal that theory-of-mind development depends partly on _____ maturation, particularly of the brain's _____ _____ . General _____ ability is also important in strengthening young children's theory of mind. A third helpful factor is having at least one _____ _____ . Finally, _____ may be a factor.

THINK ABOUT IT: One theory of how people acquire a theory of mind is that it is inborn. However, there are many reasons to suppose that as children grow into different cultures, their theories of mind emerge. Cultural variations in theories of mind are often revealed through language. For example, children in Samoa typically do not try to get out of trouble by saying, "I did not do it on purpose," as they often do in European American cultures; instead, they deny having done the deed at all.

APPLICATIONS:

24. A 4-year-old tells the teacher that a clown should not be allowed to visit the class because "Pat is 'fraid of clowns." The 4-year-old thus shows that he can anticipate how another will feel. This is evidence of the beginnings of _____ .

25. When asked "Where do dreams come from?," 5-year-old Rhoda is likely to answer
    a. "from God."
    b. "from the sky."
    c. "from my pillow."
    d. "from inside my head."

Language (pp. 260–267)

26. Two aspects of development that make ages 2 to 6 the prime time for learning language are _____ and _____ in the language areas of the brain. Another is the characteristic _____ interaction of early childhood.

27. Although early childhood does not appear to be a _____ period for language development, it does seem to be a _____ period for the learning of vocabulary, grammar, and pronunciation.

28. During early childhood, a dramatic increase in language occurs, with _____ increasing rapidly.

29. Through the process called _____-_____ , young children often learn words after only one or two hearings. A closely related process is _____ _____ , by which children are able to apply newly learned words to other objects in the same category.

30. Because young children do not understand that word meaning depends on context, they have difficulty with words that express _____ . They also have trouble with words expressing relationships of _____ and _____ .

31. The structures, techniques, and rules that a language uses to communicate meaning define its _____ .

32. How much a child talks is strongly influenced by _____ . The particular words and constructions a child understands is more strongly determined by the child's _____ .

33. Young children's tendency to apply rules of grammar when they should not is called _____ .

Give an example of this tendency.

34. Most developmentalists agree that bilingualism _____ (is/is not necessarily) an asset to children in today's world. Even so, language-minority children are at a(n) _____ (advantage/disadvantage) in most ways. Bilingual children typically process the two languages in _____ (the same/different) areas of their brains. For most

people, pronunciation of a second language is particularly difficult to master after age _____ .

35. Advocates of bilingualism note that children who speak two languages by age 5 often are less _____ in their understanding of language and more advanced in their _____ _____ _____ . Advocates of monolingualism point out that bilingual proficiency comes at the expense of _____ in one or both languages, slowing down the development of _____ and other linguistic skills.

36. Some immigrant parents are saddened when their children make a _____ _____ and become more fluent in the school language than that of their home culture. The best solution is for children to become _____ _____ , who are fluent in both languages.

STUDY TIP: To better understand the cognitive and linguistic processes of young children, you might examine several well-loved children's books. Many characteristics of preoperational thinking and language are reflected in such books. For example, much of the fun in the *Amelia Bedialia* books is based entirely on the main character's literal interpretation of her instructions.

APPLICATIONS:

37. Six-year-old Stefano produces sentences that follow such rules of word order as "the initiator of an action precedes the verb, the receiver of an action follows it." This demonstrates that he has a knowledge of _____ .

38. Two-year-old Amelia says, "We goed to the store." She is making a grammatical _____ .

39. Dr. Jones, who believes that children's language growth greatly contributes to their cognitive growth, evidently is a proponent of the ideas of
    a. Piaget.   c. Flavell.
    b. Chomsky.   d. Vygotsky.

Early-Childhood Education (pp. 267–274)

40. Compared to a hundred years ago, when children didn't start school until _____

_____ , today most

_____ - to _____ -year-

olds are in school.

41. Many new programs use an educational model inspired by _____ that allows children to _____ .
Many programs are also influenced by

_____ , who believed that children learn from other _____ under the watchful guidance of adults.

42. One type of preschool was opened by _____ for poor children in Rome.
This _____ - _____
school was based on the belief that children needed structured, individualized projects in order to give them a sense of _____ .

43. Another new early-childhood curriculum called _____ _____ encourages children to master skills not usually seen in American schools until about age _____ .

44. Other preschool programs are more _____ -directed. These programs explicitly teach basic skills, including

_____ , _____ , and

_____ , typically using

_____ _____ by a

teacher.

45. In 1965, _____ _____

_____ was inaugurated to give low-income children some form of compensatory education during early childhood.

46. (A View from Science) Longitudinal research found that graduates of similar but more intensive, well-evaluated programs scored

_____ (higher/no higher) on achievement tests and were more likely to attend college and less likely to go to jail.

STUDY TIP: To help you understand why an early-education program does not succeed, refer back to Chapter 7. List several characteristics of high-quality early childhood education.

APPLICATION:

47. Noreen, a nursery school teacher, is given the job of selecting holiday entertainment for a group of young children. If Noreen agrees with the ideas of Vygotsky, she is most likely to select
   a. a simple TV show that every child can understand.
   b. a hands-on experience that requires little adult supervision.
   c. brief, action-oriented play activities that the children and teachers will perform together.
   d. holiday puzzles for children to work on individually.

Progress Test 1

Multiple-Choice Questions

Circle your answers to the following questions and check them with the answers beginning on page 128. If your answer is incorrect, read the explanation for why it is incorrect and then consult the appropriate pages of the text (in parentheses following the correct answer).

1. Piaget believed that children are in the preoperational stage from ages
   a. 6 months to 1 year. c. 2 to 6 years.
   b. 1 to 3 years. d. 5 to 11 years.

2. Which of the following is NOT a characteristic of preoperational thinking?
   a. focus on appearance
   b. static reasoning
   c. abstract thinking
   d. centration

3. Which of the following provides evidence that early childhood is a sensitive period, rather than a critical period, for language learning?
   a. People can and do master their native language after early childhood.
   b. Vocabulary, grammar, and pronunciation are acquired especially easily during early childhood.
   c. Neurological characteristics of the young child's developing brain facilitate language acquisition.
   d. All of these abilities provide evidence.

4. According to Vygotsky, children learn because adults do all of the following except
   a. present challenges.
   b. offer assistance.
   c. encourage motivation.
   d. provide reinforcement.

5. Reggio Emilia is
   a. the educator who first opened nursery schools for poor children in Rome.
   b. the early-childhood curriculum that allows children to discover ideas at their own pace.
   c. a new form of early-childhood education that encourages children to master skills not usually seen until age 7 or so.
   d. the Canadian system for promoting bilingualism in young children.

6. The vocabulary of young children consists primarily of
   a. metaphors.
   b. self-created words.
   c. abstract nouns.
   d. verbs and concrete nouns.

7. Young children sometimes apply the rules of grammar even when they shouldn't. This tendency is called
   a. overregularization.   c. practical usage.
   b. literal language.   d. single-mindedness.

8. The Russian psychologist Vygotsky emphasized that
   a. language helps children form ideas.
   b. children form concepts first, then find words to express them.
   c. language and other cognitive developments are unrelated at this stage.
   d. preschoolers learn language only for egocentric purposes.

9. Private speech can be described as
   a. a way of formulating ideas to oneself.
   b. fantasy.
   c. an early learning difficulty.
   d. the beginnings of deception.

10. The child who has not yet grasped the principle of conservation is likely to
   a. insist that a tall, narrow glass contains more liquid than a short, wide glass, even though both glasses actually contain the same amount.
   b. be incapable of egocentric thought.
   c. be unable to reverse an event.
   d. do all of these things.

11. (A View from Science) In later life, High/Scope graduates showed
   a. better report cards, but more behavioral problems.
   b. significantly higher IQ scores.
   c. higher scores on math and reading achievement tests.
   d. alienation from their original neighborhoods and families.

12. A quality preschool program is generally one that
   a. involves behavioral control.
   b. has teachers who know how to respond to the needs of children.
   c. focuses on instruction in conservation and other logical principles.
   d. has professionals demonstrate toys to the children.

13. Many preschool programs that are inspired by Piaget stress _____ , in contrast to alternative programs that stress _____ .
   a. academics; school readiness
   b. readiness; academics
   c. child development; school readiness
   d. academics; child development

14. Young children can succeed at tests of conservation when
   a. they are allowed to work cooperatively with other children.
   b. the test is presented as a competition.
   c. they are informed that they are being observed by their parents.
   d. the test is presented in a simple, nonverbal, and gamelike way.

15. Through the process called fast-mapping, children
   a. immediately assimilate new words by connecting them through their assumed meaning to categories of words they have already mastered.
   b. acquire the concept of conservation at an earlier age than Piaget believed.
   c. are able to move beyond egocentric thinking.
   d. become skilled in the practical use of language.

True or False Items

Write *T (true)* or *F (false)* on the line in front of each statement.

_____ 1. Early childhood is a prime learning period for every child.

_____ 2. In conservation problems, many young children are unable to understand the transformation because they focus exclusively on appearances.

_____ 3. Young children use private speech more selectively than older children.

_____ 4. Children typically develop a theory of mind at about age 7.

_____ 5. Preoperational children tend to focus on one aspect of a situation to the exclusion of all others.

_____ 6. Piaget focused on what children cannot do rather than what they can do.

_____ 7. With the beginning of preoperational thought, most young children can understand words that express comparison.

_____ 8. A young child who says "You comed up and hurted me" is demonstrating a lack of understanding of English grammar.

_____ 9. Successful preschool programs generally have a low adult/child ratio.

_____ 10. Vygotsky believed that cognitive growth is largely a social activity.

_____ 11. *Theory-theory* refers to the tendency of young children to see the world as an unchanging reflection of their current construction of reality.

Progress Test 2

Progress Test 2 should be completed during a final chapter review. Answer the following questions after you thoroughly understand the correct answers for the Chapter Review and Progress Test 1.

Multiple-Choice Questions

1. Children who speak two languages by age 5
   a. are less egocentric in their understanding of language.
   b. are more advanced in their theory of mind.
   c. have somewhat slower vocabulary development in one or both languages.
   d. have all of these characteristics.

2. Piaget believed that preoperational children fail conservation of liquid tests because of their tendency to
   a. focus on appearance.
   b. fast-map.
   c. overregularize.
   d. exhibit all of these behaviors.

3. A young child who focuses his or her attention on only one feature of a situation is demonstrating a characteristic of preoperational thought called
   a. centration.   c. reversibility.
   b. overregularization. d. egocentrism.

4. One characteristic of preoperational thought is
   a. the ability to categorize objects.
   b. the ability to count in multiples of 5.
   c. the inability to perform logical operations.
   d. difficulty adjusting to changes in routine.

5. The zone of proximal development represents the
   a. skills or knowledge that are within the potential of the learner but are not yet mastered.
   b. influence of a child's peers on cognitive development.
   c. explosive period of language development during the play years.
   d. normal variations in children's language proficiency.

6. According to Vygotsky, language advances thinking through private speech and by
   a. helping children to privately review what they know.
   b. helping children explain events to themselves.
   c. serving as a mediator of the social interaction that is a vital part of learning.
   d. facilitating the process of fast-mapping.

7. Irreversibility refers to the
   a. inability to understand that other people view the world from a different perspective than one's own.
   b. inability to think about more than one idea at a time.
   c. failure to understand that changing the arrangement of a group of objects doesn't change their number.
   d. failure to understand that undoing a process will restore the original conditions.

8. According to Piaget
   a. it is impossible for preoperational children to grasp the concept of conservation, no matter how carefully it is explained.
   b. young children fail to solve conservation problems because they center their attention on the transformation that has occurred and ignore the changed appearances of the objects.
   c. with special training, even preoperational children are able to grasp some aspects of conservation.
   d. young children fail to solve conservation problems because they have no theory of mind.

9. Scaffolding of a child's cognitive skills can be provided by
   a. a mentor.
   b. the objects or experiences of a culture.
   c. the child's past learning.
   d. all of these answers.

10. Which theorist would be most likely to agree with the statement, "Adults should focus on helping children learn rather than on what they cannot do"?
    a. Piaget
    b. Vygotsky
    c. Montessori
    d. Emilia

11. Children first demonstrate some understanding of grammar
    a. as soon as the first words are produced.
    b. once they begin to use language for practical purposes.
    c. through the process called fast-mapping.
    d. in their earliest sentences.

12. Seeing his cousin Jack for the first time in several months, 3-year-old Zach notices how long Jack's hair has become. "You're turning into a girl," he exclaims. Zach's comment reflects the preoperational child's
    a. egocentrism.
    b. tendency to focus on appearance.
    c. static reasoning.
    d. irreversibility.

13. Most 5-year-olds have difficulty understanding comparisons because:
    a. they have not yet begun to develop grammar.
    b. they don't understand that meaning depends on context.
    c. of their limited vocabulary.
    d. of their tendency to overregularize.

14. Overregularization indicates that a child
    a. is clearly applying rules of grammar.
    b. persists in egocentric thinking.
    c. has not yet mastered the principle of conservation.
    d. does not yet have a theory of mind.

15. Regarding the value of preschool education, most developmentalists believe that
    a. most disadvantaged children will not benefit from an early preschool education.
    b. most disadvantaged children will benefit from an early preschool education.
    c. the early benefits of preschool education are likely to disappear by grade 3.
    d. the relatively small benefits of antipoverty measures such as Head Start do not justify their huge costs.

Matching Items

Match each term or concept with its corresponding description or definition.

Terms or Concepts

_____ 1. static reasoning
_____ 2. scaffold
_____ 3. theory of mind
_____ 4. zone of proximal development
_____ 5. overregularization
_____ 6. fast-mapping
_____ 7. irreversibility
_____ 8. centration
_____ 9. conservation
_____ 10. private speech
_____ 11. guided participation

Descriptions or Definitions

a. the idea that amount is unaffected by changes in shape or placement
b. the tendency to see the world as an unchanging place
c. the cognitive distance between a child's actual and potential levels of development
d. the tendency to think about one aspect of a situation at a time
e. the process whereby the child learns through social interaction with a mentor
f. our understanding of mental processes in ourselves and others
g. the process by which words are learned after only one hearing
h. an inappropriate application of rules of grammar
i. the internal use of language to form ideas
j. the inability to understand that original conditions are restored by the undoing of some process
k. to structure a child's participation in learning encounters

Key Terms

Using your own words, write a brief definition or explanation of each of the following terms on a separate piece of paper.

1. preoperational intelligence
2. centration
3. egocentrism
4. focus on appearance; conservation
5. underestimated
6. animism; rational; irrational
7. conservation
8. animism
9. apprentice in thinking
10. guided participation
11. zone of proximal development
12. scaffolding
13. private speech
14. social mediation
15. theory-theory
16. theory of mind
17. fast-mapping

18. overregularization
19. balanced bilingual
20. Montessori schools
21. Reggio Emilia approach

Answers

CHAPTER REVIEW

1. egocentric; theory of mind
2. preoperational
3. egocentrism; centration; is not; appearance
4. static; unchanging; irreversibility; conservation
5. underestimated
6. animism; rational; irrational
7. Lev Vygotsky; apprentice in thinking
8. challenges; assistance; instruction; motivation; guided participation; social; interact
9. zone of proximal development
10. scaffold
11. private speech; uttered aloud
12. mediator
13. conservation. This is the principle that properties such as mass, volume, and number remain the

same even though they appear different. In this case, the number of checkers remains the same.

14. centration. This is the tendency to focus on one aspect of a situation while ignoring everything else. Dani equates birthday with party: No party, no birthday.

15. reversibility. Young children are unable to reverse operations, so Darrell must be older than 6 years old.

16. c. is the answer. All of the other choices are aspects of preoperational thinking.

17. c. is the answer. This is typical of cognition during the first two years, when infants think exclusively with their senses and motor skills.

18. c. is the answer. Key to Vygotsky's theory is that children are apprentices in thinking and that they learn best by working with an older and more experienced mentor.

19. c. is the answer. Piaget emphasized the young child's egocentric tendency to perceive everything from his or her own perspective; Vygotsky emphasized the young child's tendency to look to others for insight and guidance.

20. theory-theory

21. 4; theory of mind

Between the ages of 3 and 6, young children come to realize that thoughts may not reflect reality and that individuals can believe various things and, therefore, can be deliberately deceived or fooled.

22. have

23. neurological; prefrontal cortex; language; brother or sister; culture

24. theory of mind

25. a. is the answer. In developing a theory of mind, children also understand that thoughts may not reflect reality and that individuals can believe various things.

26. maturation; myelination; social

27. critical; sensitive

28. vocabulary

29. fast-mapping; logical extension

30. comparisons; time; place

31. grammar

32. genes; experience

33. overregularization

Many English-speaking children overapply the rule of adding "s" to form the plural. Thus, they are likely to say "foots" and "snows."

34. is; disadvantage; the same; 6

35. egocentric; theory of mind; fluency; reading

36. language shift; balanced bilinguals

37. grammar

38. overregularization. This shows that although Amelia is applying the rules of grammar when she should not, she has a basic understanding of those rules.

39. d. is the answer. Vygotsky believed that children used language (private speech, in the beginning) to enhance their cognitive understanding.

40. first grade; 3; 5

41. Piaget; discover ideas at their own pace; Vygotsky; children

42. Maria Montessori; child-centered; accomplishment

43. Reggio Emilia; 7

44. teacher; reading; writing; arithmetic; direct instruction

45. Project Head Start

46. higher

Study Tip: In Chapter 7, high-quality preschools were described as being characterized by (a) a low adult/child ratio, (b) a trained staff (or educated parents) who are unlikely to leave the program, (c) positive social interactions among children and adults, (d) adequate space and equipment, and (e) safety. Continuity also helps, and curriculum is important.

47. c. is the answer. In Vygotsky's view, learning is a social activity. Thus, social interaction that provides motivation and focuses attention facilitates learning.

PROGRESS TEST 1

Multiple-Choice Questions

1. c. is the answer. (p. 249)

2. c. is the answer. Preoperational children have great difficulty understanding abstract concepts. (p. 250)

3. d. is the answer. (p. 260)

4. d. is the answer. (p. 253)

5. c. is the answer. (p. 269)
   a. This describes Maria Montessori.
   b. This refers to Piaget's approach.
   d. The program originated in Italy.

6. d. is the answer. (p. 261)

a. & c. Young children generally have great difficulty understanding, and therefore using, metaphors and abstract nouns.

b. Other than the grammatical errors of overregularization, the text does not indicate that young children use a significant number of self-created words.

7. **a.** is the answer. (p. 264)

b. & d. These terms are not identified in the text and do not apply to the use of grammar.

c. Practical usage, which also is not discussed in the text, refers to communication between one person and another in terms of the overall context in which language is used.

8. **a.** is the answer. (p. 255)

b. This expresses the views of Piaget.

c. Because he believed that language facilitates thinking, Vygotsky obviously felt that language and other cognitive developments are intimately related.

d. Vygotsky did not hold this view.

9. **a.** is the answer. (p. 255)

10. **a.** is the answer. (pp. 250, 251)

b., c., & d. Failure to conserve is the result of thinking that is centered on appearances. Egocentrism and irreversibility are also examples of centered thinking.

11. **c.** is the answer. (p. 273)

b. This is not discussed in the text.

a. & d. There was no indication of greater behavioral problems or alienation in graduates of this program.

12. **b.** is the answer. (p. 273)

13. **c.** is the answer. (pp. 268, 270)

14. **d.** is the answer. (p. 252)

15. **a.** is the answer. (p. 261)

True or False Items

1. T (p. 249)
2. T (p. 250)
3. F In fact, just the opposite is true. (p. 255)
4. F Children develop a theory of mind at about age 4. (p. 258)
5. T (p. 250)
6. T (p. 252)
7. F Young children have difficulty understanding words of comparison such as high and low. (p. 263)

8. F In adding "ed" to form a past tense, the child has indicated an understanding of the grammatical rule for making past tenses in English, even though the construction in these two cases is incorrect. (p. 264)
9. T (p. 274)
10. T (p. 253)
11. F This describes static reasoning; theory-theory is the idea that children attempt to construct a theory to explain all their experiences. (p. 256)

PROGRESS TEST 2

Multiple-Choice Questions

1. **d.** is the answer. (p. 265)
2. **a.** is the answer. (p. 250)

b. & c. Fast-mapping and overregularization are characteristics of language development during the play years; they have nothing to do with reasoning about volume.

3. **a.** is the answer. (p. 250)

b. Overregularization is the child's tendency to apply grammatical rules even when he or she shouldn't.

c. Reversibility is the concept that reversing an operation, such as addition, will restore the original conditions.

d. This term is used to refer to the young child's belief that people think as he or she does.

4. **c.** is the answer. This is why the stage is called *pre*operational. (p. 250)
5. **a.** is the answer. (p. 254)
6. **c.** is the answer. (pp. 255–256)

a. & b. These are both advantages of private speech.

d. Fast-mapping is the process by which new words are acquired, often after only one hearing.

7. **d.** is the answer. (p. 250)

a. This describes egocentrism.

b. This is the opposite of centration.

c. This defines conservation of number.

8. **a.** is the answer. (p. 250)

b. According to Piaget, young children fail to solve conservation problems because they focus on the *appearance* of objects and ignore the transformation that has occurred.

d. Piaget did not relate conservation to a theory of mind.

9. **d.** is the answer. (p. 254)

10. **b.** is the answer. (pp. 253–254)

    a. Piaget focused on what children cannot do.

11. **d.** is the answer. English-speaking children almost always put subject before verb in their two-word sentences. (p. 263)

12. **b.** is the answer. (p. 250)

    a., c., & d. Egocentrism, static reasoning, and irreversibility are all characteristics of preoperational thinking, but noticing the long hair is a matter of attending to appearances.

13. **b.** is the answer. (p. 263)

    a. By the time children are 3 years old, their grammar is quite impressive.

    c. On the contrary, vocabulary develops so rapidly that, by age 5, children seem to be able to understand and use almost any term they hear.

    d. This tendency to make language more logical by overapplying certain grammatical rules has nothing to do with understanding comparisons.

14. **a.** is the answer. (p. 264)

    b., c., & d. Overregularization is a *linguistic* phenomenon rather than a characteristic type of thinking (b. and d.), or a logical principle (c.).

15. **b.** is the answer. (p. 274)

Matching Items

1. b (p. 250)	**5.** h (p. 264)	**9.** a (p. 250)
2. k (p. 254)	**6.** g (p. 261)	**10.** i (p. 255)
3. f (p. 258)	**7.** j (p. 250)	**11.** e (p. 253)
4. c (p. 254)	**8.** d (p. 250)	

KEY TERMS

1. According to Piaget, thinking between the ages of about 2 and 6 is characterized by **preoperational intelligence,** meaning that children cannot yet perform logical operations; that is, they cannot use logical principles. This stage involves language and imagination. (p. 249)

2. **Centration** is the tendency of preoperational children to focus only on a single aspect of a situation or object. (p. 250)

3. **Egocentrism** is Piaget's term for a type of centration in which preoperational children view the world exclusively from their own perspective. (p. 250)

4. **Focus on appearance** refers to the preoperational child's tendency to focus only on apparent attributes and ignore all others. (p. 250)

5. Preoperational thinking is characterized by **static reasoning,** in which the young child sees the world as unchanging. (p. 250)

6. **Irreversibility** is the characteristic of preoperational thought in which the young child fails to recognize that a process can be reversed to restore the original conditions of a situation. (p. 250)

7. **Conservation** is the understanding that the amount or quantity of a substance or object is unaffected by changes in its appearance. (p. 250)

8. **Animism** is the belief that natural objects and phenomena are alive. (p. 252)

9. According to Vygotsky, a young child is an **apprentice in thinking,** whose intellectual growth is stimulated and directed by older and more skilled members of society. (p. 253)

10. According to Vygotsky, **guided participation** is the process by which young children learn to think by having social experiences and by exploring their universe. As mentors, parents, siblings, and peers present challenging tasks, offer assistance (not taking over), maintain enthusiasm, provide instructions, and support the child's interest and motivation. (p. 253)

11. According to Vygotsky, each individual has a **zone of proximal development (ZPD),** which represents the skills that are within the potential of the learner but cannot be performed independently. (p. 254)

12. Tutors who utilize **scaffolding** structure children's learning experiences in order to foster their emerging capabilities. (p. 254)

13. **Private speech** is Vygotsky's term for the internal dialogue in which a person talks to himself or herself. Private speech, which often is uttered aloud, helps young children to think, review, decide, and explain events to themselves. (p. 255)

14. In Vygotsky's theory, **social mediation** is a human interaction that expands and advances understanding, often through words that one person uses to explain something to another. (p. 255)

15. **Theory-theory** is Gopnik's term for the tendency of young children to attempt to construct theories to explain everything they experience. (p. 256)

16. A **theory of mind** is an understanding of human mental processes, that is, of one's own or another's emotions, beliefs, intentions, motives, and thoughts. (p. 258)

17. **Fast-mapping** is the speedy and sometimes imprecise process by which children learn new words by tentatively connecting them to words and categories that they already understand. (p. 261)

18. **Overregularization** occurs when children apply rules of grammar when they should not. It is seen in English, for example, when children add "s" to form the plural even in irregular cases that form the plural in a different way. (p. 264)

19. A **balanced bilingual** is a person who is equally fluent in two languages. (p. 245)

20. **Montessori schools,** which offer early-childhood education based on the philosophy of Maria Montessori, emphasize careful work and tasks that each young child can do. (p. 261)

21. **Reggio Emilia approach** refers to a famous program of early-childhood education that originated in the town of Reggio Emilia, Italy, and that encourages each child's creativity in a carefully designed setting.

10

Early Childhood: Psychosocial Development

Chapter Overview

Chapter 10 explores the ways in which young children begin to relate to others in an ever-widening social environment. The chapter begins where social understanding begins, with emotional development and the emergence of the sense of self. With their increasing social awareness, children become more concerned with how others evaluate them and better able to regulate their emotions.

The next section explores how children use play to help with their emerging ability to regulate their emotions. Although play is universal, its form varies by culture and gender.

The third section discusses Baumrind's parenting patterns and their effects on the developing child. The effects of the media on parenting and family life in general are also explored.

The chapter continues with a discussion of moral development during early childhood, focusing on the origins of helpful, prosocial behaviors in young children, as well as antisocial behaviors such as the different forms of aggressive behavior. The usefulness of the different forms of discipline, including punishmen, in the child's developing morality is also considered in this section.

The chapter concludes with a description of children's emerging awareness of male–female differences and gender identity. Five major theories of gender-role development are considered.

NOTE: Answer guidelines for all Chapter 10 questions begin on page 143.

Chapter Review

When you have finished reading the chapter, work through the material that follows to review it. Complete the sentences and answer the questions. In some cases, Study Tips explain how best to learn a difficult concept, while Think About It and Applications help you to know how well you under-

stand the material. As you proceed, evaluate your performance for each section by consulting the answers beginning on page 143. Do not continue with the next section until you understand each answer. If you need to, review or reread the appropriate section in the textbook before continuing.

Emotional Development (pp. 277–283)

1. The major psychosocial accomplishment of early childhood is learning _____

   _____ .

   This ability is called _____

   _____ .

2. Between 3 and 6 years of age, according to Erikson, children are in the stage of

   _____ _____

   _____ . As they acquire skills and competencies, children develop

   _____ , a belief in their own abilities. In the process, they develop a positive

   _____ and feelings of

   _____ in their accomplishments.

3. Children also develop a longer

   _____ span that enables concentration, which is made possible by _____ maturity. And they develop naïve predictions, called _____ _____ , which helps them try new things.

4. Erikson also believed that during this stage, children begin to feel _____ when their efforts result in failure or criticism. Many people believe that _____ is a more mature emotion than _____ , because the former emotion is _____ .

5. For the most part, children enjoy learning, playing, and practicing for their own joy; that is, they are _____ _____ .

The importance of this type of motivation is seen when children invent and converse with

_____ _____ .

6. Motivation that comes from the outside is called

_____ _____ .

Providing reinforcement for something a person already enjoys doing _____ (strengthens/may diminish) intrinsic motivation.

7. Emotional regulation _____ (is/is not) valued in all cultures. Cultures _____ (differ/generally do not differ) in the emotions considered most in need of control.

8. An illness or disorder that involves the mind is called _____ . Children who have _____ problems and lash out at other people or things are said to be "_____" (overcontrolled/undercontrolled). Children who have _____ problems tend to be inhibited, fearful, and withdrawn.

9. Neurological advances in the brain's

_____ _____ are partly responsible for the greater capacity for self-control that occurs at about age _____ .

10. Girls generally are better than boys at regulating their _____ (internalizing/externalizing) emotions, but they are less successful with _____ (internalizing/externalizing) ones. For both sexes, though, extreme reactions predict future _____ .

11. Repeated exposure to extreme stress can kill _____ and stop others from developing properly, making some children physiologically unable to regulate their emotions.

12. Another set of influences on emotional regulation is the child's early and current

_____ _____ . Neglect or abuse in the first two years of life is likely to cause later _____ or _____ problems.

To help you understand the difference between internalizing problems and externalizing problems in emotional regulation, you might list several examples of each type. Which have you engaged in? _____

APPLICATIONS:

13. According to Erikson, 5-year-old Samantha is incapable of feeling guilt because
    a. guilt depends on a sense of self, which is not sufficiently established in young children.
    b. she does not yet understand that she is female for life.
    c. this emotion is unlikely to have been reinforced at such an early age.
    d. guilt is associated with the resolution of the Electra complex, which occurs later in life.

14. Three-year-old Ali, who is fearful and withdrawn, is displaying signs of _____ problems, which suggests that he is emotionally

_____ .

15. Summarizing her report on neurological aspects of emotional regulation, Alycia notes that young children who have externalizing problems tend to lack neurological maturity in the brain's

_____ .

Play (pp. 283–288)

16. Between ages 2 and 6, children learn how to make, and keep, _____ as a consequence of many hours of

_____ _____ .

17. An aspect of culture that shapes play is the nature of the _____ setting. In cities, the scarcity of undeveloped space means that play usually occurs in _____-_____ settings.

18. Another cultural shift that has changed the nature of children's play is the increasing prevalence of _____ , which has resulted in their displaying advanced _____

_____ .

19. The developmentalist who distinguished five kinds of play is _____ . These include _____ play, in which a child plays alone; _____ play, in which a

child watches other children play; _____ play, in which children play together without interacting; _____ play, in which children interact, but their play is not yet mutual and reciprocal; and _____ play, in which children play together and take turns.

20. The type of active play that looks rough is called _____-_____-_____ play. A distinctive feature of this form of play, which _____ (occurs only in some cultures/is universal), is the positive facial expression that characterizes the "_____ _____ ." This type of play, which requires planned _____ and _____ , also fosters _____ , especially if a child is accidentally hurt.

21. In _____ play, children act out various roles and themes in stories of their own creation. This type of play helps them to develop a _____ in a nonthreatening context, for example.

STUDY TIP/APPLICATION: To help you distinguish the different types of play, complete the following table, including the basic characteristics of each type of play. Then, give an example of each type.

22. Type of Play	Characteristics	Examples
a. Solitary play		
b. Onlooker plan		
c. Parallel play		
d. Associative play		
e. Cooperative play		
f. Rough-and-tumble play		
g. Sociodramatic play		

APPLICATION:

23. Although Juvaria and Brittany are sharing drawing materials and watching each other, their play is not yet mutual or reciprocal. Mildred Parten would probably classify this type of play as _____ play.

Challenges for Parents (pp. 288–293)

24. A significant influence on early psychosocial growth is the style of _____ that characterizes a child's family life.

25. The early research on parenting styles, which was conducted by _____ , found that parents varied in four dimensions: their expressions of _____ , their strategies for _____ , their _____ , and their expectations for _____ .

26. Parents who adopt the _____ style demand unquestioning obedience from their children. In this style of parenting, nurturance tends to be _____ (low/high), maturity demands are _____ (low/high), and parent–child communication tends to be _____ (low/high).

27. Parents who adopt the _____ style make few demands on their children and are lax in discipline. Such parents _____ (are/are not very) nurturant, communicate _____ (well/poorly), and make _____ (few/extensive) maturity demands.

28. Parents who adopt the _____ style set limits and enforce rules but also listen to their children. Such parents make _____ (high/low) maturity demands, communicate _____ (well/poorly), and _____ (are/are not) nurturant.

29. Parents who are indifferent toward their children have adopted the _____ / _____ style.

30. Although this classification is generally regarded as _____ (very useful, too simplistic), follow-up studies indicate that children raised by _____ parents are likely to be obedient but unhappy and those raised by _____ parents are likely to lack self-control. Those raised by _____ parents are more likely to be articulate, successful, happy with themselves, and generous with others.

31. An important factor in the effectiveness of parenting style is the child's _____ .

32. Culture _____ (exerts/does not exert) a strong influence on disciplinary techniques. Japanese mothers tend to use _____ as disciplinary techniques more often than do North American mothers. However, discipline methods and family rules are less important than parental _____ .

33. Other effects on child rearing are values, climate, _____ , and _____ .

34. Six major American organizations concerned with the well-being of children urge parents to reduce _____ _____ .

35. Children who watch violence on television _____ (become/do not necessarily become) more violent themselves.

36. Most young children in the United States spend more than _____ (how many?) hours each day using some sort of media.

37. Longitudinal research demonstrates that young children who watched violent television programs tended to become more _____ , less _____ , and _____ - _____ teenagers.

38. Parents and children _____ (rarely/ sometimes/often) watch TV together.

STUDY TIP: Students often confuse *authoritarian* and *authoritative* when studying parenting styles. Although both words have the same root noun, *authority* ("the power or right to give commands and enforce obedience"), their suffixes have very different meanings. The suffix *-arian* denotes an occupation, and the suffix *-ative* denotes a tendency toward something. Thus, authoritative parents don't make an occupation of enforcing obedience; rather, they tend to give commands with some margin for freedom of action.

APPLICATIONS:

39. Yolanda and Tom are strict and aloof parents. Their children are most likely to be
    a. cooperative and trusting.
    b. obedient but unhappy.
    c. violent.
    d. withdrawn and anxious.

40. Which is NOT a feature of parenting used by Baumrind to differentiate authoritarian, permissive, and authoritative parents?
  a. maturity demands for the child's conduct
  b. efforts to control the child's actions
  c. nurturance
  d. adherence to stereotypical gender roles

Moral Development (pp. 294–299)

41. The ability to truly understand the emotions of another, called _____ , often leads to sharing, helping, and other examples of _____ _____ . In contrast, dislike for others, or _____ , may lead to actions that are destructive or deliberately hurtful. Such actions are called _____ _____ .

42. By age _____ , most children can be deliberately prosocial or antisocial. This occurs as a result of _____ maturation, _____ regulation, _____ _____ , and interactions with _____ .

43. Developmentalists distinguish four types of aggression: _____ , used to obtain or retain an object or privilege; _____ , used in angry retaliation against an intentional or accidental act committed by a peer; _____ , which takes the form of insults or social rejection; and _____ , used in an unprovoked attack on a peer.

44. (text and Table 10.3) The form of aggression that often increases from age 2 to 6 is _____ _____ . Of greater concern are _____ _____ , because it can indicate a lack of _____ _____ ; and _____ , which is most worrisome overall.

45. (A View from Science) State four specific recommendations for the use of punishment that are derived from developmental research findings.
  a. _____
  b. _____

  c. _____
  d. _____

46. Physical punishment _____ (seems to increase/does not seem to increase) the possibility of long-term aggression and _____ (temporarily increases/has no effect on) obedience.

47. Another method of discipline, in which children's guilt and gratitude are used to control their behavior, is _____ _____ . This method of discipline has been linked to children's decreased _____ , _____ , and _____ acceptance.

48. The disciplinary technique most often used in North America is the _____-_____ , in which a misbehaving child is asked to sit quietly without toys or playmates. Experts suggest a period of _____ (how many?) minute(s) for each year of the child's age.

49. Another common practice involves the parents explaining to the child why the behavior was wrong, called _____ .

APPLICATIONS:

50. Seeking to discipline her 3-year-old son for snatching a playmate's toy, Cassandra gently says, "How would you feel if Juwan grabbed your car?" Developmentalists would probably say that Cassandra's approach
  a. is too permissive and would therefore be ineffective in the long run.
  b. would probably be more effective with a girl.
  c. will be effective in increasing prosocial behavior because it promotes empathy.
  d. will backfire and threaten her son's self-confidence.

51. When 4-year-old Seema grabs for Vincenzo's Beanie Baby, Vincenzo slaps her hand away, displaying an example of _____ aggression.

52. Five-year-old Curtis, who is above average in height and weight, often picks on children who are smaller than he is. Curtis' behavior is an example of _____ aggression.

53. Four-year-old Eboni shows signs of distrust toward strangers. Eboni's behavior is an example of _____ .

Becoming Boys and Girls (pp. 299–305)

54. Social scientists distinguish between biological, or _____ , differences between males and females, and cultural, or _____ , differences in the _____ and behavior of males and females.

55. By age _____ , children can consistently apply gender labels. By age _____ , children are convinced that certain toys are appropriate for one gender but not the other. Awareness that sex is a fixed biological characteristic does not become solid until about age

    _____ .

56. Freud called the period from age 3 to 6 the _____ _____ . According to his view, boys in this stage develop sexual feelings about their _____ and become jealous of their _____ . Freud called this phenomenon the _____ _____ . Boys also develop, in self-defense, a powerful conscience called the

    _____ .

57. During the phallic stage, little girls may experience the _____ _____ , in which they want to get rid of their mother and become intimate with their father.

58. In Freud's theory, children of both sexes resolve their guilt and fear through _____ with their same-sex parent.

59. According to behaviorism, young children develop a sense of gender by being _____ for behaviors deemed appropriate for their sex and _____ for behaviors deemed inappropriate.

60. Behaviorists also maintain that children learn gender-appropriate behavior not only through direct reinforcement but also through

    _____ _____ .

61. Cognitive theorists focus on children's _____ of male–female differences. This understanding is called a _____

    _____ .

62. The behaviors appropriate for each gender are determined by society, not by biology, according to the _____ theory. Gender distinctions are emphasized in many _____ cultures. This theory points out that children can maintain a balance of male and female characteristics, or _____ , only if their culture promotes that idea.

63. According to _____ theory, gender attitudes and roles are the result of interaction between _____ and _____

    _____ .

64. The idea that is supported by recent research is that some gender differences are _____ based because of differences between male and female _____ .

65. These differences probably result from the differing _____ _____ that influence brain development. However, the theory maintains that the manifestations of biological origins are shaped, enhanced, or halted by _____ _____ . One example of such a factor is that prehistorically, female brains apparently favored _____ , which may have created a genetically inclined tendency for girls to _____ earlier than boys.

APPLICATIONS:

66. Bonita eventually copes with the fear and anger she feels over her hatred of her mother and love of her father by
    a. identifying with her mother.
    b. copying her brother's behavior.
    c. adopting her father's moral code.
    d. competing with her brother for her father's attention.

67. A little girl who says she wants her mother to go on vacation so that she can marry her father is voicing a fantasy consistent with the _____ described by Freud.

68. Leonardo believes that almost all sexual patterns are learned rather than inborn. He is clearly a strong adherent of _____ .

69. In explaining the origins of gender distinctions, Dr. Christie notes that every society teaches its children its values and attitudes regarding pre-ferred behavior for men and women. Dr. Christie is evidently a proponent of _____ .

Progress Test 1

Multiple-Choice Questions

Circle your answers to the following questions and check them with the answers on page 145. If your answer is incorrect, read the explanation for why it is incorrect and then consult the appropriate pages of the text (in parentheses following the correct answer).

1. Young children have a clear (but not necessarily accurate) concept of self. Typically, they believe that they
   a. own all objects in sight.
   b. are great at almost everything.
   c. are much less competent than peers and older children.
   d. are more powerful than their parents.

2. According to Freud, the third stage of psychosexual development, during which the penis is the focus of psychological concern and pleasure, is the
   a. oral stage.   c. phallic stage.
   b. anal stage.   d. latency period.

3. Girls generally are better than boys at regulating their
   a. internalizing emotions.
   b. externalizing emotions.
   c. internalizing and externalizing emotions.
   d. prosocial behaviors.

4. The three *basic* patterns of parenting described by Diana Baumrind are
   a. hostile, loving, and harsh.
   b. authoritarian, permissive, and authoritative.

   c. positive, negative, and punishing.
   d. indulgent, neglecting, and traditional.

5. Authoritative parents are receptive and loving, but they also normally
   a. set limits and enforce rules.
   b. have difficulty communicating.
   c. withhold praise and affection.
   d. encourage aggressive behavior.

6. Children who watch a lot of violent television or play violent video games
   a. are more likely to be violent.
   b. are less creative.
   c. become lower-achieving teens.
   d. have all of these characteristics.

7. (Table 10.3) Between 2 and 6 years of age, the form of aggression that is most likely to increase is
   a. reactive.   c. relational.
   b. instrumental.   d. bullying.

8. During early childhood, a child's self-concept is defined largely by his or her
   a. expanding range of skills and competencies.
   b. physical appearance.
   c. gender.
   d. relationship with family members.

9. Behaviorists emphasize the importance of _____ in the development of the preschool child.
   a. identification   c. initiative
   b. praise and blame   d. a theory of mind

10. Children apply gender labels and have definite ideas about how boys and girls behave as early as age
    a. 2.   c. 5.
    b. 4.   d. 7.

11. Developmentalists agree that punishment should be
    a. avoided at all costs.
    b. immediate and harsh.
    c. delayed until emotions subside.
    d. rare and limited to behaviors the child understands and can control.

12. Six-year-old Marco has superior verbal ability rivaling that of most girls his age. Although Marco's sex is predisposed to slower language development, Dr. Laurent believes that Marco's upbringing in a linguistically rich home enhanced his biological capabilities. Dr. Laurent is evidently a proponent of
    a. cognitive theory.
    b. psychoanalytic theory.
    c. sociocultural theory.
    d. epigenetic theory.

13. Three-year-old Jake, who lashes out at the family pet in anger, is displaying signs of _____ problems, which suggests that he is emotionally

    _____ .

    a. internalizing; overcontrolled
    b. internalizing; undercontrolled
    c. externalizing; overcontrolled
    d. externalizing; undercontrolled

14. Compared to North American mothers, Japanese mothers are more likely to:
    a. use reasoning to control their children's social behavior.
    b. use expressions of disappointment to control their children's social behavior.
    c. express empathy for their children.
    d. use all of these techniques.

15. (Table 10.3) When her friend hurts her feelings, Maya shouts that she is a "mean old stinker!" Maya's behavior is an example of
    a. instrumental aggression.
    b. reactive aggression.
    c. bullying aggression.
    d. relational aggression.

True or False Items

Write *T* (*true*) *or* *F* (*false*) on the line in front of each statement.

_____ 1. According to Diana Baumrind, only authoritarian parents make maturity demands on their children.

_____ 2. Children of authoritative parents tend to be successful, happy with themselves, and generous with others.

_____ 3. Not until age 4 can children apply gender labels.

_____ 4. Empathy is the same as sympathy.

_____ 5. Many gender differences are genetically based.

_____ 6. Children can be truly androgynous only if their culture promotes such ideas and practices.

_____ 7. Developmentalists do not agree about how children acquire gender roles.

_____ 8. By age 4, most children have definite ideas about what toys are appropriate for each gender.

_____ 9. Identification was defined by Freud as a means of defending one's self-concept by taking on the attitudes and behaviors of another person.

_____ 10. By adolescence, undercontrolled boys may be delinquents.

Progress Test 2

Progress Test 2 should be completed during a final chapter review. Answer the following questions after you thoroughly understand the correct answers for the Chapter Review and Progress Test 1.

Multiple-Choice Questions

1. Children of permissive parents are *most* likely to lack
   a. social skills.   c. initiative and guilt.
   b. self-control.   d. care and concern.

2. The major psychosocial accomplishment of early childhood is
   a. learning when and how to express emotions.
   b. developing an internalized sense of initiative.
   c. developing an identity.
   d. forging positive self-esteem.

3. Which area of the brain plays an important role in the child's greater capacity for self-control that appears at age 4 or 5?
   a. temporal lobe   c. prefrontal cortex
   b. occipital lobe   d. hippocampus

4. Generally speaking, the motivation of young children
   a. is intrinsic.
   b. is extrinsic.
   c. is the desire to gain praise or some other reward from someone else.
   d. varies too much from country to country to be characterized.

5. Which of the following best summarizes the current view of developmentalists regarding gender differences?
   a. Developmentalists disagree on the proportion of gender differences that are biological in origin.
   b. Most gender differences are biological in origin.
   c. Nearly all gender differences are cultural in origin.
   d. There is no consensus among developmentalists regarding the origin of gender differences.

6. According to Freud, a young boy's jealousy of his father's relationship with his mother, and the guilt feelings that result, are part of the
   a. Electra complex.
   b. Oedipus complex.
   c. phallic complex.
   d. penis envy complex.

7. The style of parenting in which the parents make few demands on children, the discipline is lax, and the parents are nurturant and accepting is
   a. authoritarian.
   b. authoritative.
   c. permissive.
   d. traditional.

8. Cooperating with a playmate is to _____ as insulting a playmate is to _____ .
   a. antisocial behavior; prosocial behavior
   b. prosocial behavior; antisocial behavior
   c. emotional regulation; antisocial behavior
   d. prosocial behavior; emotional regulation

9. Antipathy refers to a person's
   a. understanding of the emotions of another person.
   b. self-understanding.
   c. feelings of anger or dislike toward another person.
   d. tendency to internalize emotions or inhibit their expression.

10. Which of the following theories advocates the development of gender identification as a means of avoiding guilt over feelings for the opposite-sex parent?
    a. behaviorism
    b. sociocultural
    c. psychoanalytic
    d. social learning

11. A parent who wishes to use a time-out to discipline her son for behaving aggressively on the playground would be advised to:
    a. have the child sit quietly indoors for a few minutes.
    b. tell her son that he will be punished later at home.
    c. tell the child that he will not be allowed to play outdoors for the rest of the week.
    d. choose a different disciplinary technique because time-outs are ineffective.

12. The young child's readiness to learn new tasks and play activities reflects his or her
    a. emerging competency and self-awareness.
    b. theory of mind.
    c. relationship with parents.
    d. growing identification with others.

13. Emotional regulation is in part related to maturation of a specific part of the brain in the
    a. prefrontal cortex.
    b. parietal cortex.
    c. temporal lobe.
    d. occipital lobe.

14. In which style of parenting is the parents' word law and misbehavior strictly punished?
    a. permissive
    b. authoritative
    c. authoritarian
    d. traditional

15. Erikson noted that young children eagerly begin many new activities but are vulnerable to criticism and feelings of failure; they experience the crisis of
    a. identity versus role confusion.
    b. initiative versus guilt.
    c. basic trust versus mistrust.
    d. efficacy versus helplessness.

Matching Items

Match each term or concept with its corresponding description or definition.

Terms or Concepts

_____ **1.** empathy
_____ **2.** androgyny
_____ **3.** antipathy
_____ **4.** prosocial behavior
_____ **5.** antisocial behavior
_____ **6.** Electra complex
_____ **7.** Oedipus complex
_____ **8.** authoritative
_____ **9.** authoritarian
_____ **10.** identification
_____ **11.** instrumental aggression

Descriptions or Definitions

a. forceful behavior that is intended to get or keep something that another person has
b. Freudian theory that every daughter secretly wishes to replace her mother
c. parenting style associated with high maturity demands and low parent–child communication
d. an action performed for the benefit of another person without the expectation of reward
e. Freudian theory that every son secretly wishes to replace his father
f. parenting style associated with high maturity demands and high parent–child communication
g. understanding the feelings of others
h. an action that is intended to harm someone else
i. dislike of others
j. the way children cope with their feelings of guilt during the phallic stage
k. a balance of traditional male and female characteristics in an individual

Key Terms

Writing Definitions

Using your own words, write a brief definition or explanation of each of the following terms on a separate piece of paper.

1. emotional regulation
2. initiative versus guilt
3. self-esteem
4. self-concept
5. intrinsic motivation
6. extrinsic motivation
7. psychopathology
8. externalizing problems
9. internalizing problems
10. rough-and-tumble play
11. sociodramatic play
12. authoritarian parenting
13. permissive parenting
14. authoritative parenting
15. neglectful/uninvolved parenting
16. empathy
17. antipathy
18. prosocial behavior
19. antisocial behavior
20. instrumental aggression
21. reactive aggression
22. relational aggression
23. bullying aggression
24. psychological control
25. time-out
26. sex differences
27. gender differences
28. phallic stage
29. Oedipus complex
30. superego
31. Electra complex
32. identification
33. gender schema
34. androgyny

Cross-Check

After you have written the definitions of the key terms in this chapter, you should complete the crossword puzzle to ensure that you can reverse the process—recognize the term, given the definition.

ACROSS

1. A balance of traditionally male and female characteristics.
3. A behavior, such as cooperating or sharing, performed to benefit another person without the expectation of a reward.
8. In psychoanalytic theory, the judgmental part of personality that internalizes the moral standards set by parents and society.
12. Behavior that takes the form of insults or social rejection is called _____ aggression.
14. Act intended to obtain or retain an object desired by another is called _____ aggression.
15. Style of parenting in which parents make few demands on their children, yet are nurturant and accepting and communicate well with their children.

DOWN

2. Cultural differences in the roles and behaviors of males and females.
4. Means of defending one's self-concept by taking on the behaviors and attitudes of someone else.
5. Ability to manage and modify one's feelings, particularly feelings of fear, frustration, and anger.
6. In Freud's phallic stage of psychosexual development, a boy's sexual attraction toward the mother and resentment of the father.
7. Style of child rearing in which the parents show little affection or nurturance for their children, parents have high behavioral standards, and parent–child communication is low.
9. In Freud's phallic stage of psychosexual development, a girl's sexual attraction toward the father and resentment of the mother.
10. Style of parenting in which the parents set limits and enforce rules but do so more democratically than do authoritarian parents.
11. Form of aggression involving an unprovoked attack on another child.
13. Aggressive behavior that is an angry retaliation for some intentional or incidental act by another person.

Answers

CHAPTER REVIEW

1. when and how to express emotions; emotional regulation
2. initiative versus guilt; self-esteem; self-concept; pride
3. attention; neurological; protective optimism
4. guilt; guilt; shame; internalized
5. intrinsically motivated; imaginary friends
6. extrinsic motivation; may diminish
7. is; differ
8. psychopathology; externalizing; undercontrolled; internalizing
9. prefrontal cortex; 4 or 5
10. externalizing; internalizing; psychopathology
11. neurons
12. care experiences; internalizing; externalizing

13. **a.** is the answer. Erikson did not equate gender constancy with the emergence of guilt (b); (c) and (d) reflect the viewpoints of learning theory and Freud, respectively.

14. internalizing; overcontrolled. Usually, with maturity, extreme fears and shyness diminish.

15. prefrontal cortex. Emotional regulation requires thinking before acting, which is the province of the prefrontal cortex. Lack of maturity there results in externalizing problems.

16. friends; social play

17. physical; child-care

18. television; sexual awareness

19. Mildred Parten; solitary; onlooker; parallel; associative; cooperative

20. rough-and-tumble; is universal; play face; provocation; self-control; caregiving

21. sociodramatic; self-concept

22. No answer is right or wrong. Some examples follow.

    a. Solitary play: playing alone. A girl playing with her doll in her room or a boy with his truck

    b. Onlooker play: watching other children play. Sitting on a bench in the playground watching children on the see-saw.

    c. Parallel play: playing with similar toys in similar ways, but not together. Two girls playing with their own dolls in different areas of a dollhouse or two boys building blocks.

    d. Associative play: interactive play, but not yet mutual and reciprocal. A group of children drawing with crayons.

    e. Cooperative play: playing together. Playing tag.?

    f. Rough-and-tumble play: mimicking aggression but without intent to harm. Imitating a boxing match.

    g. Sociodramatic play: acting out various roles and themes in stories they create. Pretend-racing cars or playing house.

23. parallel

24. parenting

25. Diana Baumrind; warmth; discipline; communication; maturity

26. authoritarian; low; high; low

27. permissive; are; well; few

28. authoritative; high; well; are

29. neglectful/uninvolved

30. too simplistic; authoritarian; permissive; authoritative

31. temperament

32. exerts; reasoning, empathy, and expressions of disappointment; warmth, support, and concern

33. economy; history

34. television watching

35. become

36. three

37. violent; creative; lower-achieving

38. rarely

39. **b.** is the answer. Authoritarian parents have behavior standards and require obedience without question. So, their children to be obedient but unhappy.

40. **d.** is the answer. Baumrind's categories have nothing to do with gender roles.

41. empathy; prosocial behaviors; antipathy; antisocial behavior

42. 4 or 5; brain; emotional; theory of mind; caregivers

43. instrumental; reactive; relational; bullying

44. instrumental aggression; reactive aggression; emotional regulation; bullying aggression

45. **a.** Remember theory of mind.

    b. Remember emerging self-concept.

    c. Remember fast-mapping.

    d. Remember that young children are not logical.

46. seems to increase; temporarily increases

47. psychological control; achievement; creativity; social

48. time-out; one

49. induction

50. **c.** is the answer.

51. instrumental. This kind of aggression involves trying to get or keep something someone else has, as Seema is doing here.

52. bullying. This kind of aggression involves repeated, unprovoked physical or verbal attacks on other people.

53. antipathy.

54. sex; gender; roles

55. 2; 4; 8

56. phallic stage; mothers; fathers; Oedipus complex; superego

57. Electra complex

58. identification

59. reinforced; punished

60. social learning

61. understanding; gender schema

62. sociocultural; traditional; androgyny

63. epigenetic; genes; early experience

64. biologically; brains

65. sex hormones; environmental factors; language; speak

66. **a.** is the answer. According to Freud, children identify with the same-sex parents because of their guilt in hating that parent.

67. Electra complex. Resolution of this complex results in the identification noted in 66.

68. behaviorists. Behaviorists believe that children learn through rewards and punishments.

69. sociocultural theory. Sociocultural theorists contend that children learn from society, not biology.

PROGRESS TEST 1

Multiple-Choice Questions

1. **b.** is the answer. (pp. 278–279)

2. **c.** is the answer. (p. 300)

   a. & b. In Freud's theory, the oral and anal stages are associated with infant development.

   d. In Freud's theory, the latency period is associated with development during the school years.

3. **b.** is the answer. (p. 281)

4. **b.** is the answer. (p. 289)

   d. Traditional is a variation of the basic styles. Indulgent and neglecting are abusive styles and clearly harmful, unlike the styles initially identified by Baumrind.

5. **a.** is the answer. (p. 289)

   b. & c. Authoritative parents communicate very well and are quite affectionate.

   d. This is not typical of authoritative parents.

6. **d.** is the answer. (p. 292)

7. **b.** is the answer. (p. 295)

8. **a.** is the answer. (p. 278)

9. **b.** is the answer. (p. 301)

   a. This is the focus of Freud's phallic stage.

   c. This is the focus of Erikson's psychosocial theory.

   d. This is the focus of cognitive theorists.

10. **a.** is the answer. (p. 299)

11. **d.** is the answer. (p. 297)

12. **d.** is the answer. In accounting for Marco's verbal ability, Dr. Laurent alludes to both genetic and environmental factors, a giveaway for epigenetic theory. (pp. 303–304)

    a., b., & c. These theories do not address biological or genetic influences on development.

13. **d.** is the answer. (p. 281)

    a. & b. Children who display internalizing problems are withdrawn and bottle up their emotions.

    c. Jake is displaying an inability to control his negative emotions.

14. **d.** is the answer. (p. 291)

15. **d.** is the answer. (p. 295)

True or False Items

1. F   All parents make some maturity demands on their children; maturity demands are high in both the authoritarian and authoritative parenting styles. (p. 289)

2. T (p. 290)

3. F   Children can apply gender labels by age 2. (p. 299)

4. F   Sympathy is feeling sorry *for* someone; empathy is feeling sorry *with* someone. (p. 294)

5. T (p. 303)

6. T (p. 303)

7. T (pp. 300–304)

8. T (p. 299)

9. T (p. 300)

10. T (p. 282)

PROGRESS TEST 2

Multiple-Choice Questions

1. **b.** is the answer. (p. 290)

2. **a.** is the answer. (p. 277)

   b. & d. Developing a sense of initiative and positive self-esteem are aspects of emotional regulation.

   c. Developing a sense of identity is the task of adolescence.

3. **c.** is the answer. (p. 281)

4. **a.** is the answer. (p. 280)

5. **a.** is the answer. (pp. 299–300)

6. **b.** is the answer. (p. 300)

   a. & d. These are Freud's versions of phallic-stage development in little girls.

   c. There is no such thing as the "phallic complex."

7. **c.** is the answer. (p. 289)

   a. & b. Both authoritarian and authoritative parents make high demands on their children.

   d. This is not one of the three parenting styles. Traditional parents could be any one of these types.

8. **b.** is the answer. (p. 294)

9. **c.** is the answer. (p. 294)

   a. This describes empathy.

   b. This describes self-concept.

   d. This describes an internalizing problem.

10. **c.** is the answer. (p. 300)

    a. & d. Behaviorism, which includes social learning, emphasizes that children learn about gender by rewards and punishments and by observing others.

    b. Sociocultural theory focuses on the impact of the environment on gender identification.

11. **a.** is the answer. (p. 298)

    b. & c. Time-outs involve removing a child from a situation in which misbehavior has occurred. Moreover, these threats of future punishment would likely be less effective because of the delay between the behavior and the consequence.

    d. Although developmentalists stress the need to prevent misdeeds instead of punishing them and warn that time-outs may have unintended consequences, they nevertheless can be an effective form of discipline.

12. **a.** is the answer. (pp. 278–279)

    b. This viewpoint is associated only with cognitive theory.

    c. Although parent–child relationships are important to social development, they do not determine readiness.

    d. Identification is a Freudian defensive behavior.

13. **a.** is the answer. (p. 281)

14. **c.** is the answer. (p. 289)

15. **b.** is the answer. (p. 278)

    a. & c. According to Erikson, these are the crises of adolescence and infancy, respectively.

    d. This is not a crisis described by Erikson.

Matching Items

1. g (p. 294)	**5.** h (p. 294)	**9.** c (p. 289)
2. k (p. 303)	**6.** b (p. 300)	**10.** j (p. 300)
3. i (p. 294)	**7.** e (p. 300)	**11.** a (p. 295)
4. d (p. 294)	**8.** f (p. 289)	

KEY TERMS

Writing Definitions

1. **Emotional regulation** is the ability to control when and how emotions are expressed. (p. 277)

2. According to Erikson, the crisis of early childhood is **initiative versus guilt**. In this crisis, young children eagerly take on new skills and activities and feel guilty when their efforts result in failure or criticism. (p. 278)

3. **Self-esteem** is the belief in one's own ability. (p. 278)

4. **Self-concept** refers to people's understanding of who they are. (p. 278)

5. **Intrinsic motivation** is the internal goals or drives to accomplish something for the joy of doing it. (p. 279)

6. **Extrinsic motivation** is the need for rewards from outside, such as material possessions. (p. 279)

7. **Psychopathology** is an illness or disorder of the mind. (p. 281)

8. Young children who have **externalizing problems** have trouble regulating emotions and uncontrollably lash out at other people or things. (p. 281)

9. Children who have **internalizing problems** tend to be fearful and withdrawn as a consequence of their tendencies to keep their emotions bottled up inside themselves. (p. 281)

10. **Rough-and-tumble play** is physical play that often mimics aggression but involves no intent to harm. (p. 286)

11. In **sociodramatic play,** children act out roles and themes in stories of their own creation, allowing them to rehearse social roles, practice regulating their emotions, tet their ability to convince others of their ideas, and develop a self-concept in a nonthreatening context. (p. 287)

12. **Authoritarian parenting** is Baumrind's term for a style of child rearing in which the parents show little affection or nurturance for their children, maturity demands are high, and parent–child communication is low. (p. 289)

Memory aid: Someone who is an authoritarian demands unquestioning obedience and acts in a dictatorial way.

13. **Permissive parenting** is Baumrind's term for a style of child rearing in which the parents make few demands on their children, yet are nurturant and accepting and communicate well with their children. (p. 289)

14. **Authoritative parenting** is Baumrind's term for a style of child rearing in which the parents set limits and enforce rules but are willing to listen to the child's ideas and are flexible. (p. 289)

Memory aid: Authoritative parents act as authorities do on a subject—by discussing and explaining why certain family rules are in place.

15. **Neglectful/uninvolved parenting** is Baumrind's term for an approach to child rearing in which the parents are indifferent toward their children. (p. 289)

16. **Empathy** is a person's understanding of other people's feelings and concerns. (p. 294)

17. **Antipathy** is a person's feelings of dislike or even hatred of another person. (p. 294)

18. **Prosocial behavior** is feelings and actions that are helpful and kind but without any obvious benefit. (p. 294)

19. **Antisocial behavior** is feelings and actions that are deliberately hurtful or destructive. (p. 294)

20. **Instrumental aggression** is hurtful behavior that is intended to get or keep something that another person has. (p. 295)

21. **Reactive aggression** is impulsive retaliation for some intentional or accidental act, verbal or physical, by another person. (p. 295)

Memory aid: Instrumental aggression is behavior that is *instrumental* in allowing a child to retain a favorite toy. **Reactive aggression** is a *reaction* to another child's behavior.

22. **Relational aggression** involves insults, and other nonphysical acts, aimed at harming the social connection between the victim and other people. (p. 295)

23. An unprovoked, repeated physical or verbal attack on another person is an example of **bullying aggression**. (p. 295)

24. **Psychological control** is a form of discipline that involves threatening to withdraw love and support from a child. (p. 298)

25. A **time-out** is a form of discipline in which a child is required to stop all activity and sit quietly apart from other people for a few minutes. (p. 298)

26. **Sex differences** are biological differences between females and males. (p. 299)

27. **Gender differences** are cultural differences in the roles and behavior of males and females. (p. 299)

28. In psychoanalytic theory, the **phallic stage** is the third stage of psychosexual development, in which the penis becomes the focus of concern and pleasure. (p. 300)

29. According to Freud, boys in the phallic stage of psychosexual development develop a collection of feelings, known as the **Oedipus complex**, that center on sexual attraction to the mother and resentment of the father. (p. 300)

30. In psychoanalytic theory, the **superego** is the judgmental part of personality that internalizes the moral standards of the parents. (p. 300)

31. Girls in Freud's phallic stage may develop a collection of feelings, known as the **Electra complex**, that center on sexual attraction to the father and resentment of the mother. (p. 300)

32. In Freud's theory, **identification** is a means of defending one's self-concept by taking on the behaviors and attitudes of another person. (p. 300)

33. In cognitive theory, **gender schema** is the child's understanding of sex differences. (p. 302)

34. **Androgyny** is a balance of traditionally female and male psychological characteristics in one person. (p. 303)

Cross-Check

ACROSS

1. androgyny
3. prosocial
8. superego
12. relational
14. instrumental
15. permissive

DOWN

2. gender difference
4. identification
5. emotional regulation
6. Oedipus complex
7. authoritarian
9. Electra complex
10. authoritative
11. bullying
13. reactive

11

Middle Childhood: Biosocial Development

Chapter Overview

This chapter introduces middle childhood, the years from 7 to 11. Changes in physical size and shape are described, and the problems of obesity and asthma are addressed.

The discussion then turns to the continuing development of intellectual skills during the school years, culminating in an evaluation of intelligence testing.

A final section examines the experiences of children with special needs, such as children with attention-deficit/hyperactivity disorder, those with learning disabilities, and children with autism. The causes of and treatments for these problems are discussed, with emphasis placed on insights arising from the developmental psychopathology perspective. This perspective makes it clear that the manifestations of any special childhood problem will change as the child grows older and that treatment must also consider the social context.

NOTE: Answer guidelines for all Chapter 11 questions begin on page 158.

Chapter Review

When you have finished reading the chapter, work through the material that follows to review it. Complete the sentences and answer the questions. In some cases, Study Tips explain how best to learn a difficult concept, while Think About It and Applications help you to know how well you understand the material. As you proceed, evaluate your performance for each section by consulting the answers beginning on page 158. Do not continue with the next section until you understand each answer. If you need to, review or reread the appropriate section in the textbook before continuing.

A Healthy Time (pp. 311–316)

1. Compared with biosocial development during other periods of the life span, biosocial development during this time, known as

_____ _____ , is

_____ (relatively smooth/often fraught with problems). For example, disease and death during these years are _____ (common/rare).

2. Children grow at a _____ (faster/ slower) rate during middle childhood than they did earlier.

Describe several other features of physical development during middle childhood.

3. Compared to the past, middle childhood is now a healthier time _____ (in every nation of the world/only in developed nations). Two areas of improvement are the reduced danger of exposure to _____ and better _____ care.

State two important strategies for preventing many adult health problems in children.

State some of the benefits and hazards of childhood sports.

4. Especially for low-income children, participating in structured sports activities correlates with improved _____ achievement, less _____ , and better _____ _____ .

5. Jethro plays on a Little League baseball team and enjoys casual sports with his schoolfriends. Jethro will
    a. enjoy better overall health.
    b. learn to appreciate fair play.
    c. exhibit improved problem-solving abilities.
    d. accomplish all of these things.

6. Summarizing physical development during middle childhood, Professor Wilson notes each of the following except that
    a. it is the healthiest period of the life span.
    b. mortal injuries are unusual during this time.
    c. most fatal childhood diseases occur during middle childhood.
    d. growth is slower than during early childhood.

Two Common Health Problems (pp. 316–321)

7. Every physical and psychological characteristic affects and is affected by the _____ context.

8. The number that expresses the relationship of height to weight is the _____ _____ _____ .

    Children are said to be overweight when their body mass index is above the _____ (what number?) percentile of the growth chart for their age. Obesity is defined as having a BMI above the _____ (what number?) percentile. Because body shape and depression are partly _____ , obesity may be considered a _____ disease.

9. The rate of increase in childhood obesity is slowest in nations located in _____ _____ . This is due to a decline in _____ availability. In the United States, the highest rates of childhood obesity occur among _____ - _____ children and _____ _____ children.

10. Overweight children are more likely to have _____ , high _____ _____ , and elevated levels of bad _____ . As weight increases, school achievement and self-esteem _____ (increase/decrease), and _____ increases.

11. People who inherit a gene allele called _____ are more likely to be obese and suffer from diabetes.

State several parenting practices that protect against childhood obesity.

12. A chronic inflammatory disorder of the airways is called _____ . This disorder is _____ (more common/less common) today than in the past.

13. The causes or triggers of asthma include _____ , not getting the infections and childhood diseases that would strengthen their _____ systems, and exposure to _____ such as pet hair.

14. The use of injections and inhalers to treat asthma is an example of _____ prevention. Less than _____ (how many?) of all asthmatic children in the United States benefit from this type of treatment. The best approach to treating childhood diseases is _____ _____ , which in the case of asthma includes proper _____ of homes and schools, decreased _____ , eradication of cockroaches, and safe outdoor _____ _____ .

To help you differentiate and remember the various middle childhood experiences that protect against or promote adult health problems, make a list that describes your own experiences during middle childhood. For example, did your parents promote regular exercise? Excessive television watching?

APPLICATIONS:

15. Because 11-year-old Wayne is obese, he runs a greater risk of developing
    a. heart problems.
    b. diabetes.
    c. psychological problems.
    d. all of these problems.

16. Harold weighs about 20 pounds more than his friend Jay. During school recess, Jay can usually be found playing soccer with his classmates, while Harold sits on the sidelines by himself. Harold's rejection is likely due to his
    a. being physically different.
    b. being dyslexic.
    c. intimidation of his schoolmates.
    d. being hyperactive.

17. Concluding her presentation on "Asthma During Middle Childhood," Amanda mentions each of the following except that
    a. asthma is much more common today than 20 years ago.
    b. genetic vulnerability is rarely a factor in a child's susceptibility to developing asthma.
    c. the incidence of asthma continues to increase.
    d. carpeted floors, airtight windows, and less outdoor play increase the risk of asthma attacks.

Brain Development (pp. 316–326)

18. Advances in brain development during early childhood enables emerging _____ regulation and _____ _____. Left–right coordination also emerges as the _____ _____ strengthens connections between the brain's two _____. The executive functions of the brain also begins developing, along with maturation of the _____ _____.

19. The length of time it takes a person to respond to a particular stimulus is called _____ _____.

20. Two other advances in brain function at this time include the ability to pay special heed to one source of information among many, called _____ _____, and the _____ of thoughts and actions that are repeated in sequence.

21. The potential to master a specific skill or to learn a certain body of knowledge is a person's _____. The most commonly used tests to measure this potential are _____ _____. In the original version of the most commonly used test of this type, a person's score was calculated as a _____ (the child's _____ divided by the child's _____ _____ and multiplied by 100 to determine his or her _____).

22. Tests that are designed to measure what a child has learned are called _____ tests.

23. Two highly regarded IQ tests are the _____ _____ _____ _____ _____ and the _____-_____.

24. The average IQ scores of nations have _____ (increased/decreased), a phenomenon called the _____ _____.

25. To be classified as _____ _____, children must have IQs below _____ and be unusually low in _____.

26. IQ testing is controversial in part because no test can measure _____ without also measuring _____ or without reflecting the _____. Another reason is that a child's intellectual potential _____ (changes/does not change) over time.

27. Many critics of IQ testing contend that we have _____ _____. Robert Sternberg believes that there are three distinct types of intelligence: _____, _____, and _____.

Similarly, Howard Gardner describes

_____ (how many?) distinct

intelligences.

THINK ABOUT IT: The board of directors for a new private school is considering the pros and cons of using IQ testing to admit and place students. Help them out by listing the major advantages and disadvantages of IQ testing as identified by developmental psychologists.

_____

APPLICATIONS:

28. Angela was born in 1984. In 1992, she scored 125 on an intelligence test. Using the original formula, what was Angela's mental age when she took the test? _____

29. Of the following individuals, who is likely to have the fastest reaction time?
    a. a 7-year-old
    b. a 9-year-old
    c. an 11-year-old
    d. a 60-year-old

30. Concluding his presentation on the Flynn Effect, Kwame notes that the reasons for this trend include all of the following except
    a. better health.
    b. genetic vulnerability.
    c. more schooling.
    d. smaller families.

31. Professor Allenby teaches in a public school in a large city. Following the views of Howard Gardner and Robert Sternberg , the professor is most critical of traditional aptitude and achievement tests because they
    a. inadvertently reflect certain nonacademic competencies.
    b. do not reflect knowledge of cultural ideas.
    c. measure only a limited set of abilities.
    d. underestimate the intellectual potential of disadvantaged children.

Children with Special Needs (pp. 326–334)

32. Among the conditions that give rise to "special needs" are _____

    _____

    _____

    _____ .

33. Down syndrome and other conditions that give rise to "special needs" begin with a

    _____ anomaly.

34. The field of study that is concerned with childhood psychological disorders is

    _____ _____ . This

    perspective has provided several lessons that apply to all children. Three of these are that _____ is normal, disability _____ (changes/does not change) over time, and adolescence and adulthood may be _____ .

35. This perspective also has made diagnosticians much more aware of the _____ _____ of childhood problems. This awareness is reflected in the official diagnostic guide of the American Psychiatric Association, which is the _____

    _____ .

36. A condition that manifests itself in a difficulty in concentrating for more than a few moments is called _____-_____

    _____ .

37. The most common type of this disorder, which includes a need to be active, often accompanied by excitability and impulsivity, is called

    _____-_____/

    _____ _____ .

    Children suffering from this disorder can be

    _____ , _____ , and

    _____ .

38. Other disorders often occur together with (that is, are _____ with) ADHD. Examples of these conditions include _____

    _____ .

39. In childhood, the most effective forms of treatment for ADHD are _____ ,

    _____ , and special _____

    for parents and teachers.

40. Certain drugs that stimulate adults, such as

    _____ and _____ ,

    have a reverse effect on many hyperactive children.

41. Children who have difficulty acquiring a particular skill that others acquire easily are said to have a _____ _____ . These deficits usually _____ (do/do not) result in lifelong impediments.

42. A disability in reading is called_____ .

43. The most severe disturbance of early childhood is _____ , which is used to describe children who have extremely inadequate _____ skills. Children who are less withdrawn are usually diagnosed with

_____ _____

_____ .

44. In autistic spectrum disorder, deficiencies appear in three areas: delayed _____ , impaired _____ _____ , and unusual _____ .

45. Children who have autistic symptoms but are unusually intelligent in some area and have close-to-normal speech are sometimes diagnosed with _____ _____ , also called _____-_____

_____ .

State three possible reasons for the increased incidence of autistic spectrum disorder.

46. Another possibility is that some new _____ harms their developing brains. One suspected toxin was the antiseptic _____ , which is used in childhood _____ . Other possible toxins are

_____

_____ .

47. The process of formally identifying a child with special needs usually begins with a teacher _____ , which may ultimately lead to agreement on an _____ _____ _____ for the child.

48. In response to a 1975 act requiring that children with special needs be taught in the

_____ _____

_____ , the strategy of not separating special-needs children into special classes, called _____ , emerged. More recently, some schools have developed a _____ _____ , in which such children spend part of each day with a teaching specialist. In the most recent approach, called _____ , learning-disabled children receive targeted help within the setting of a regular classroom.

STUDY TIP: Complete the following chart as a way of organizing your understanding of the differences among children with special needs.

Category	Characteristics	Suggested Treatment
Attention-deficit disorder		
Attention-deficit/ hyperactivity disorder		
Learning disability		
Autism		
Autistic spectrum disorder		
Asperger syndrome		

49. Dr. Rutter, who believes that knowledge about normal development can be applied to the study and treatment of psychological disorders, evidently is working from the _____ perspective.

50. Ten-year-old Clarence is quick-tempered, easily frustrated, and is often disruptive in the classroom. Clarence may be suffering from

    _____ .

51. In determining whether her 8-year-old student has a learning disability, the teacher looks primarily for
    a. poor performance in all subject areas.
    b. the exclusion of other explanations.
    c. a family history of the learning disability.
    d. an inability to communicate.

52. Although 9-year-old Carl has severely impaired social skills, his intelligence and speech are normal. Carl is evidently displaying symptoms of

    _____ .

53. Jennifer displays inadequate social skills and is extremely self-absorbed. It is likely that she suffers from _____ .

54. Danny has been diagnosed as having attention-deficit/hyperactivity disorder. Every day, his parents make sure that he takes the proper dose of Ritalin. His parents should
    a. continue this behavior until Danny is an adult.
    b. try different medications when Danny seems to be reverting to his normal overactive behavior.
    c. also make sure that Danny has psychotherapy and that they and Danny's teachers receive training.
    d. not worry about Danny's condition; he will outgrow it.

Progress Test 1

Multiple-Choice Questions

Circle your answers to the following questions and check them with the answers on page 159. If your answer is incorrect, read the explanation for why it is incorrect and then consult the appropriate pages of the text (in parentheses following the correct answer).

1. As children move into middle childhood
   a. the rate of accidental death increases.
   b. sexual urges intensify.
   c. the rate of weight gain increases.
   d. biological growth slows and steadies.

2. Ongoing maturation of which brain area contributes most to left–right coordination?
   a. corpus callosum
   b. prefrontal cortex
   c. brainstem
   d. temporal lobe

3. The ability to filter out distractions and concentrate on relevant details is called
   a. automatization.
   b. reaction time.
   c. selective attention.
   d. inclusion.

4. Dyslexia is a learning disability that affects the ability to
   a. do math.   c. write.
   b. read.   d. speak.

5. The developmental psychopathology perspective is characterized by its
   a. contextual approach.
   b. emphasis on the unchanging nature of developmental disorders.
   c. emphasis on cognitive development.
   d. concern with all of these considerations.

6. The time—usually measured in fractions of a second—it takes for a person to respond to a particular stimulus is called
   a. the interstimulus interval.
   b. reaction time.
   c. the stimulus–response interval.
   d. response latency.

7. The underlying problem in attention-deficit/hyperactivity disorder appears to be
   a. low overall intelligence.
   b. a neurological difficulty in paying attention.
   c. a learning disability in a specific academic skill.
   d. the existence of a conduct disorder.

8. Healthy 6-year-olds tend to have
   a. the lowest body mass index of any age group.
   b. the highest body mass index of any age group.
   c. more short-term illnesses than any other age group.
   d. fewer short-term illnesses than any other age group.

9. Children who have an autistic spectrum disorder have severe deficiencies in
   a. social responses.
   b. language development.
   c. play.
   d. all of these abilities.

10. Although asthma has genetic origins, several environmental factors contribute to its onset, including
    a. urbanization.
    b. airtight windows.
    c. dogs and cats living inside the house.
    d. all of these factors.

11. Psychoactive drugs are most effective in treating attention-deficit/hyperactivity disorder when they are administered
    a. before the diagnosis becomes certain.
    b. for several years after the basic problem has abated.
    c. as part of the labeling process.
    d. with psychotherapy and training of parents and teachers.

12. Tests that measure a child's potential to learn a new subject are called _____ tests.
    a. aptitude
    b. achievement
    c. vocational
    d. intelligence

13. In the earliest aptitude tests, a child's score was calculated by dividing the child's _____ age by his or her _____ age to find the _____ quotient.
    a. mental; chronological; intelligence
    b. chronological; mental; intelligence
    c. intelligence; chronological; mental
    d. intelligence; mental; chronological

14. Selective attention refers to the ability to
    a. choose which of many stimuli to concentrate on.
    b. control emotional outbursts.
    c. persist at a task.
    d. perform a familiar action without much conscious thought.

15. Ongoing maturation of which brain area enables schoolchildren to more effectively analyze the potential consequences of their actions?
    a. corpus callosum
    b. prefrontal cortex
    c. brainstem
    d. temporal lobe

True or False Items

Write *T (true)* or *F (false)* on the line in front of each statement.

_____ 1. The rate of growth in school-age children continues at a rapid pace.

_____ 2. Genes and hereditary differences in taste preferences are the most important factors in promoting childhood obesity.

_____ 3. Childhood obesity increases the risk for serious health problems in adulthood.

_____ 4. The quick reaction time that is crucial in some sports can be readily achieved with practice.

_____ 5. The intellectual performance of children with Asperger syndrome is poor in all areas.

_____ 6. The incidence of children with autistic characteristics is decreasing.

_____ 7. Despite the efforts of teachers and parents, most children with learning disabilities can expect their disabilities to persist and even worsen as they enter adulthood.

_____ 8. Stressful living conditions are an important consideration in diagnosing a learning disability.

_____ 9. The drugs sometimes given to children to reduce hyperactive behaviors have a reverse effect on adults.

_____ 10. Mainstreaming along with use of a resource room is the most effective educational method for children with special needs.

Progress Test 2

Progress Test 2 should be completed during a final chapter review. Answer the following questions after you thoroughly understand the correct answers for the Chapter Review and Progress Test 1.

Multiple-Choice Questions

1. During the years from 7 to 11, the average child
   a. develops stronger muscles.
   b. grows at a rapid rate.
   c. has decreased lung capacity.
   d. is more likely to become obese than at any other period in the life span.

2. Comorbidity refers to the presence of
   a. two or more unrelated disease conditions in the same person.
   b. abnormal neurons in the prefrontal cortex.
   c. developmental delays in physical development.
   d. any of several disorders characterized by inadequate social skills.

3. A specific learning disability that becomes apparent when a child experiences unusual difficulty in learning to read is:
   a. dyslexia.   c. ADHD.
   b. Asperger syndrome. d. ADD.

4. Marked delays in particular areas of learning are collectively referred to as:
   a. learning disabilities.
   b. attention-deficit/hyperactivity disorder.
   c. hyperactivity.
   d. dyslexia.

5. Aptitude and achievement testing are controversial in part because
   a. most tests are unreliable with respect to the individual scores they yield.
   b. a child's intellectual potential often changes over time.
   c. they often fail to identify serious learning problems.
   d. of all of these reasons.

6. The most effective form of help for children with ADHD is
   a. medication.
   b. psychotherapy.
   c. training parents and teachers.
   d. a combination of some or all of these practices.

7. A key factor in reaction time is
   a. whether the child is male or female.
   b. brain maturation.
   c. whether the stimulus to be reacted to is an auditory or visual one.
   d. all of these conditions.

8. One of the first noticeable symptoms of autism is usually
   a. a difficulty with reading.
   b. abnormal social responsiveness.
   c. hyperactivity.
   d. unpredictable.

9. Which of the following is true of children with a diagnosed learning disability?
   a. They may have an average or above-average IQ.
   b. They often have a specific physical handicap, such as hearing loss.
   c. They often lack basic educational experiences.
   d. All of these conditions are true.

10. Most important in the automatization of children's thoughts and actions is
    a. the continuing myelination of neurons.
    b. diet.
    c. activity level.
    d. all of these factors.

11. Which approach to education may best meet the needs of learning-disabled children in terms of both skill remediation and social interaction with other children?
    a. mainstreaming   c. inclusion
    b. special education   d. resource rooms

12. Asperger syndrome is a disorder in which
    a. body weight fluctuates dramatically over short periods of time.
    b. verbal skills seem normal, but social perceptions and skills are abnormal.
    c. an autistic child is extremely aggressive.
    d. a child of normal intelligence has difficulty mastering a specific cognitive skill.

13. Which of the following is NOT evidence of ADHD?
    a. inattentiveness   c. impulsivity
    b. poor language skills d. overreactivity

14. Tests that measure what a child has already learned are called _____ tests.
    a. aptitude   c. achievement
    b. vocational   d. intelligence

15. Which of the following is NOT a type of intelligence identified in Robert Sternberg's theory?
    a. academic   c. achievement
    b. practical   d. creative

Matching Items

Match each term or concept with its corresponding description or definition.

Terms or Concepts

_____ 1. dyslexia
_____ 2. automatization
_____ 3. Asperger syndrome
_____ 4. attention-deficit/hyperactivity disorder
_____ 5. asthma
_____ 6. Flynn Effect
_____ 7. autism
_____ 8. developmental psychopathology
_____ 9. DSM-IV-TR
_____ 10. learning disability
_____ 11. mainstreaming

Descriptions or Definitions

a. set of symptoms in which a child has impaired social skills despite having normal speech and intelligence
b. the rise in IQ score averages that has occurred in many nations
c. the diagnostic guide of the American Psychiatric Association
d. process by which thoughts and actions become routine and no longer require much thought
e. system in which learning-disabled children are taught in general education classrooms
f. disorder characterized by self-absorption
g. chronic inflammation of the airways
h. behavior problem involving difficulty in concentrating, as well as excitability and impulsivity
i. applies insights from studies of normal development to the study of childhood disorders
j. an unexpected difficulty with one or more academic skills
k. difficulty in reading

Key Terms

Using your own words, write a brief definition or explanation of each of the following terms on a separate piece of paper.

1. middle childhood
2. BMI (body mass index)
3. overweight
4. obesity
5. asthma
6. reaction time
7. selective attention
8. automatization
9. aptitude
10. IQ test
11. achievement test
12. Wechsler Intelligence Scale for Children (WISC)
13. Flynn Effect
14. mental retardation
15. child with special needs
16. developmental psychopathology
17. *Diagnostic and Statistical Manual of Mental Disorders* (DSM-IV-R)
18. attention-deficit/hyperactivity disorder (ADHD)
19. comorbidity
20. learning disability
21. dyslexia
22. autism
23. autistic spectrum disorder
24. Asperger syndrome
25. individual education plan (IEP)
26. least restrictive environment (LRE)
27. resource room
28. inclusion

Answers

CHAPTER REVIEW

1. middle childhood; relatively smooth; rare

2. slower

During middle childhood, children grow taller, muscles become stronger, and lung strength and capacity expand.

3. in every nation of the world; lead; oral

Parents must be diligent in providing regular preventive care, and children must develop the habit of taking care of their health.

The benefits of sports include better overall health, less obesity, an appreciation of cooperation and fair play, improved problem-solving ability, and respect for teammates and opponents of many ethnicities and nationalities. The hazards may include loss of self-esteem as a result of criticism, injuries, reinforcement of existing prejudices, increased stress, and time taken away from learning academic skills.

4. academic; delinquency; social relationships

5. d. is the answer. Participation in sports during middle childhood helps children develop not only biologically but also cognitively and socially.

6. c. is the answer. Just the opposite is true.

7. social

8. body mass index; 85th; 95th; genetic; family

9. eastern Europe; food; low-income; African American

10. asthma; blood pressure; cholesterol; decrease; loneliness

11. FTO

Obesity is rare if infants are breast-fed for a year, if preschoolers rarely watch TV or drink soda, and if school-age children exercise for at least an hour every day.

12. asthma; more common

13. genes; immune; allergens

14. tertiary; half; primary prevention; ventilation; pollution; play areas

15. d. is the answer.

16. a. is the answer.

17. b. is the answer. Obese children are no more likely to be dyslexic, physically intimidating, or hyperactive than other children.

18. emotional; theory of mind; corpus callosum; hemispheres; prefrontal cortex

19. reaction time

20. selective attention; automatization

21. aptitude; IQ tests; quotient; mental age; chronological age; IQ

22. achievement

23. Wechsler Intelligence Scale for Children (WISC); Stanford-Binet

24. increased; Flynn Effect

25. mentally retarded; 70; adaptation to daily life

26. potential; achievement; culture; changes

27. multiple intelligences; academic; creative; practical; eight

Think About It: See text pages 324–326 for a discussion of the pros and cons of IQ testing.

28. 10 years old. At the time she took the test, Angela's chronological age was 8. Knowing that her IQ was 125, we can solve the equation to yield a mental age of 10 ($125 = x/8$).

29. d. is the answer. Although reaction time decreases for a time as we age, it slowly lengthens in adulthood.

30. b. is the answer. Genetic variability has not changed in recent decades.

31. c. is the answer. Both Sternberg and Gardner believe that there are multiple intelligences rather than the narrowly defined abilities measured by traditional aptitude and achievement tests.

32. anxiety disorder, autism, conduct disorder, clinical depression, developmental delay, learning or language disability, Down syndrome, attachment disorder, attention-deficit disorder, bipolar disorder, and Asperger syndrome

33. biological

34. developmental psychopathology; abnormality; changes; better or worse

35. social context; *Diagnostic and Statistical Manual of Mental Disorders* (DSM-IV-TR)

36. attention-deficit disorder

37. attention-deficit/hyperactivity disorder; inattentive; impulsive; overactive

38. comorbid; conduct disorder, depression, anxiety, Tourette syndrome, dyslexia, bipolar disorder, autism, and schizophrenia

39. medication; psychotherapy; training

40. amphetamines (e.g., Adderall); methylphenidate (Ritalin)

41. learning disability; do not

42. dyslexia

43. autism; social; autistic spectrum disorder

44. language; social responses; play

45. Asperger syndrome; high-functioning autism

The increase may reflect an expanded definition of the condition, earlier diagnosis, and the greater availability of special education.

46. teratogen; thimerosal; immunizations; pesticides, cleaning chemicals, and some ingredients in nail polish

47. referral; individual education plan (IEP)

48. least restrictive environment (LRE); mainstreaming; resource room; inclusion

Study Tip: Attention-deficit disorder: difficulty paying attention; medication plus psychotherapy

Attention-deficit/hyperactivity disorder: difficulty concentrating plus being inattentive, impulsive, and overactive; medication, psychotherapy, and special training for parents and teachers.

Learning disability, such as dyslexia: marked delay in learning a particular skill that comes easily to others; learning disabilities do not result in lifelong impediments because most people learn how to work around them.

Autism: woefully inadequate social skills, extreme self-absorption, and an inability to acquire normal speech; early training that focuses on each of the specific deficiencies. Some programs emphasize language, others focus on play, and others stress attachment. All autistic spectrum disorders involve these treatments, varying only in the degree of help needed.

Autistic spectrum disorder: inadequate social skills, impaired communication, and unusual play.

Asperger syndrome, or "high-functioning" autism: extreme attention to details and deficient social understanding, but unusually intelligent in some specialized area.

49. developmental psychopathology

50. ADHD. Children with ADHD are inattentive, impulsive, and overactive.

51. b. is the answer.

52. Asperger syndrome. Asperger syndrome is referred to as "high-functioning" autism because the person tends to have normal or above-average intelligence, especially in a particular skill.

53. autism

54. c. is the answer. Medication alone cannot ameliorate all the problems of ADHD.

PROGRESS TEST 1

Multiple-Choice Questions

1. d. is the answer. (p. 311)

2. a. is the answer. (p. 321)

3. c. (p. 322)

a. Automatization is the process in which repetition of a sequence of thoughts and actions makes the sequence routine.

b. Reaction time is the length of time it takes to respond to a stimulus.

d. Inclusion is an approach in which children with special needs are educated in regular classrooms along with all the other children.

4. b. is the answer. (p. 330)

a. Though not defined in the text, this is called dyscalcula.

c. & d. The text does not give labels for learning disabilities in writing or speaking.

5. a. is the answer. (p. 327)

b. & c. Because of its contextual approach, developmental psychopathology emphasizes *all* domains of development. Also, it points out that behaviors change over time.

6. b. is the answer. (p. 321)

7. b. is the answer. (p. 328)

8. a. is the answer. (p. 317)

9. d. is the answer. (p. 330)

10. d. is the answer. (p. 320)

11. d. is the answer. (p. 328)

12. a. is the answer. (p. 323)

b. Achievement tests measure what has already been learned.

c. Vocational tests, which, as their name implies, measure what a person has learned about a particular trade, are achievement tests.

d. Intelligence tests measure general aptitude, rather than aptitude for a specific subject.

13. a. is the answer. (p. 323)

14. a. is the answer. (p. 322)

b. This is emotional regulation.

d. This is automatization.

15. b. is the answer. (p. 321)

a. Maturation of the corpus callosum contributes to left–right coordination.

c. & d. These brain areas, which were not discussed in this chapter, play important roles in regulating sleep–waking cycles (brain stem) and hearing and language abilities (temporal lobe).

True or False Items

1. F The rate of growth slows down during middle childhood. (p. 311)

2. F Environmental factors are more important in promoting obesity during middle childhood. (pp. 318–319)

3. T (p. 318)

4. F Reaction time depends on brain maturation and is not readily affected by practice. (p. 321)

5. F Children with Asperger syndrome show isolated areas of remarkable skill. (p. 331)

6. F Just the opposite is true, possibly because of better diagnoses. (p. 331)

7. F Some children find ways to compensate for their deficiencies, and others are taught effective strategies for learning. (p. 330)

8. F Stressful living conditions must be excluded before diagnosing a learning disability. (p. 330)

9. T (pp. 328–329)

10. F Mainstreaming did not meet all children's educational needs. (p. 333)

PROGRESS TEST 2
Multiple-Choice Questions

1. **a.** is the answer. (p. 312)
   b. & c. During this period, children's growth slows down, and they experience increased lung capacity.
   d. Although childhood obesity is a common problem, the text does not indicate that a person is more likely to become obese at this age than at any other.

2. **a.** is the answer. (p. 328)

3. **a.** is the answer. (p. 330)
   b., c. & d. These disorders do not manifest themselves in a particular academic skill but instead appear in psychological processes that affect learning in general.

4. **a.** is the answer. (p. 330)
   b. & c. ADHD is a disorder that usually does not manifest itself in specific subject areas. Hyperactivity is a facet of this disorder.
   d. Dyslexia is a learning disability in reading only.

5. **b.** is the answer. (p. 325)

6. **d.** is the answer. (pp. 328–329)

7. **b.** is the answer. (p. 321)

8. **c.** is the answer. (p. 331)

9. **a.** is the answer. (p. 330)

10. **a.** is the answer. (p. 322)

11. **c.** is the answer. (p. 333)
    a. Many general education teachers are unable to cope with the special needs of some children.
    b. & d. These approaches undermined the social integration of children with special needs.

12. **b.** is the answer. (p. 331)

13. **b.** is the answer. (p. 328)

14. **c.** is the answer. (p. 323)

15. **c.** is the answer. (p. 325)

Matching Items

1. k (p. 330)
2. d (p. 322)
3. a (p. 331)
4. h (p. 328)
5. g (p. 320)
6. b (p. 324)
7. f (p. 330)
8. i (p. 327)
9. c (p. 328)
10. j (p. 330)
11. e (p. 333)

KEY TERMS

1. **Middle childhood** is the period from early childhood to adolescence, roughly ages 7 to 11. (p. 311)

2. **BMI (body mass index)** is a person's weight in kilograms divided by the square of height in meters. (p. 317)

3. A child whose body mass index (BMI) falls above the 85th percentile for children of a given age is designated as **overweight.** (p. 317)

4. **Obesity** is a body mass index (BMI) above the 95th percentile for children of a given age. (p. 317)

5. **Asthma** is a disorder in which the airways are chronically inflamed. (p. 320)

6. **Reaction time** is the length of time it takes a person to respond to a particular stimulus. (p. 321)

7. **Selective attention** is the ability to concentrate on one stimulus while ignoring others. (p. 322)

8. **Automatization** is the process by which thoughts and actions that are repeated often enough to become routine no longer require much conscious thought. (p. 322)

9. **Aptitude** is the potential to master a specific skill or learn a certain body of knowledge. (p. 323)

10. **IQ tests** are aptitude tests, which were originally designed to yield a measure of intelligence and originally calculated as mental age divided by chronological age, multiplied by 100. (p. 323)

11. **Achievement tests** measure what a child has already learned in a particular academic subject or subjects. (p. 323)

12. The **Wechsler Intelligence Scale for Children (WISC)** is a widely used IQ test for school-age children that assesses vocabulary, general knowledge, memory, and spatial comprehension. (p. 324)

13. The **Flynn Effect** refers to the rise in average IQ scores that has occurred recently in many nations. (p. 324)

14. People are considered **mentally retarded** if their IQs fall below 70 and they are unusually low in adaptation to daily life. (p. 324)

15. A **child with special needs** is one who, because of physical or mental disability, requires extra help in order to learn. (p. 325)

16. **Developmental psychopathology** is a field that applies the insights into typical development to understand and remediate developmental disorders, and vice versa. (p. 327)

17. The fourth edition of the *Diagnostic and Statistical Manual of Mental Disorders* **(DSM-IV-TR),** developed by the American Psychiatric Association, is the leading means of diagnosing mental disorders. (p. 328)

18. **Attention-deficit/hyperactivity disorder (ADHD)** is a behavior problem in which the individual has great difficulty concentrating and is often inattentive, impulsive, and overactive. (p. 328)

19. **Comorbidity** is the presence of two or more unrelated diseases at the same time in the same person. (p. 328)

20. A **learning disability** is a difficulty in a particular area of learning that is not attributable to overall intellectual slowness, a physical disability, or an unusually stressful home environment. (p. 330)

21. **Dyslexia** is a learning disability in reading. (p. 330)

22. **Autism** is a severe disturbance of early childhood characterized by an inability to communicate with others in an ordinary way, by extreme self-absorption, and by an inability to learn normal speech. (p. 330)

23. **Autistic spectrum disorder** is any of several disorders characterized by deficient social skills, unusual communication, and unusual play. (p. 330)

24. **Asperger syndrome** is a type of autistic spectrum disorder characterized by extreme attention to details and poor social skills. (p. 331)

25. An **individual education plan (IEP)** is a legal document that specifies a set of educational goals for a child with special needs. (p. 333)

26. A **least restrictive environment (LRE)** is a legally required school setting that offers special-needs children as much freedom as possible to benefit from the instruction available to other children. (p. 333)

27. A **resource room** is a classroom equipped with special material, in which children with special needs spend part of their day working with a trained specialist in order to learn basic skills. (p. 333)

28. **Inclusion** is an educational approach in which children with special needs receive individualized instruction within a regular classroom setting. (p. 333)

12

Middle Childhood: Cognitive Development

Chapter Overview

Chapter 12 examines the development of cognitive abilities in children from ages 7 to 11. The first section discusses the views of Piaget and Vygotsky regarding cognitive development, which involves the child's growing ability to use logic and reasoning (as emphasized by Piaget) and to benefit from social interactions with skilled mentors (as emphasized by Vygotsky). It also explores information-processing theory, which focuses on changes in the child's processing speed and capacity, control processes, knowledge base, and metacognition.

The second section looks at language development during middle childhood. During this time, children develop a more analytic understanding of words and show a marked improvement in their language skills. This section also discusses the problems of children who speak a minority language.

The third section covers educational and environmental conditions that are conducive to learning by schoolchildren, including how reading, math, and science are best taught.

The chapter concludes with a discussion of the hidden but strong influences of culture on education.

NOTE: Answer guidelines for all Chapter 12 questions begin on page 172.

Chapter Review

When you have finished reading the chapter, work through the material that follows to review it. Complete the sentences and answer the questions. In some cases, Study Tips explain how best to learn a difficult concept, while Think About It and Applications help you to know how well you understand the material. As you proceed, evaluate your performance for each section by consulting the answers beginning on page 172. Do not continue with the next section until you understand each answer. If you need to, review or reread the appropriate section in the textbook before continuing.

Building on Theory (pp. 337–348)

1. According to Piaget, between ages 7 and 11, children are in the stage of _____ _____ _____ .

2. The concept that objects can be organized into categories according to some common property is _____ .
   The ability to figure out an unspoken link between two facts is called _____ _____ . The logical principle that certain characteristics of an object remain the same even when other characteristics change is _____ . The idea that a transformation process can be reversed to restore the original condition is _____ .

3. Although other research has found that classification and other logical abilities may appear _____ (before/after) middle childhood, it nevertheless has supported Piaget's finding that what develops at this time is the ability to use _____ _____ .
   This is in line with a movement away from _____ toward a logic that is more _____ .

4. Unlike Piaget, Vygotsky believed that in the child's _____ _____ _____ _____ instruction by _____ is crucial to cognitive development. In his view, formal education _____ (is/is not) the only context for learning.

5. Vygotsky's emphasis on the _____ context contrasts with Piaget's more _____ approach.

6. Educators', and psychologists', understanding of how children learn is based on the framework that was laid down by _____ and embellished by _____ .

7. The idea that the advances in thinking that accompany middle childhood occur because of basic changes in how children take in, store, and process data is central to the _____-_____ theory.

8. Incoming stimulus information is held for a split second in _____ _____ , after which most of it is lost.

9. Meaningful material is transferred into _____ _____ , which is also called _____-_____ _____ . This part of memory handles mental activity that is _____ . Improvement in this type of memory occurs in two areas: the _____ _____ , which stores sounds, and the _____-_____ _____ , which stores sights.

10. The part of memory that stores information for days, months, or years is _____-_____ _____ . Crucial in this component of the system is not only storage of the material but also its _____ .

11. One reason for the cognitive advances of middle childhood is _____ maturation, especially the _____ of neural axons.

12. Processing capacity also becomes more efficient through _____ , as familiar mental activities become routine.

13. Memory ability improves during middle childhood in part because of the child's expanded _____ _____ .

14. The knowledge base also depends on _____ , current _____ , and personal _____ .

15. The mechanisms of the information-processing system that regulate the analysis and flow of information are the _____ _____ . These include _____ _____ , _____ , and _____ _____ .

16. The ability to evaluate a cognitive task to determine what to do—and to monitor and adjust one's performance—is called _____ .

17. Control processes develop spontaneously with _____ , but they are also taught, either _____ through instruction or through _____ learning.

APPLICATIONS:

18. Of the following statements made by children, which best illustrates the logical principle of identity?
   a. "You can't leave first base until the ball is hit!"
   b. "See how the Jell-O springs back into shape after I poke my finger into it?"
   c. "I know it's still a banana, even though it's mashed down in my sandwich."
   d. "You're my friend, so I don't have to use polite speech like I do with adults."

19. Which of the following statements is the clearest indication that the child has grasped the principle of reversibility?
    a. "See, the lemonade is the same in both our glasses; even though your glass is taller than mine, it's narrower."
    b. "Even though your dog looks funny, I know it's still a dog."
    c. "I have one sister and no brothers. My parents have two children."
    d. "I don't cheat because I don't want to be punished."

20. Dr. Larsen believes that the cognitive advances of middle childhood occur because of basic changes in children's thinking speed, knowledge base, and memory retrieval skills. Dr. Larsen evidently is working from the _____ perspective.

21. Mei-Chin is able to sort her Legos into groups according to size. Clearly, she has an understanding of the principle of _____ .

22. Lana is 4 years old and her brother Roger is 7. The fact that Roger remembers what their mother just told them about playing in the street while Lana is more interested in the children playing across the street is due to improvements in Roger's _____ .

23. For the first time, 7-year-old Nathan can remember his telephone number. This is probably the result of
    a. maturation of the sensory register.
    b. increased capacity of working memory.
    c. increased capacity of long-term memory.
    d. improved speed of processing.

24. Nine-year-old Rachel has made great strides in her ability to evaluate and monitor her learning and mastery of specific tasks. In other words, Rachel has shown great improvement in her _____ .

25. Andy, who is 7 years old, spends many hours playing with Ronny, a friend who lives down the street. Vygotsky would say that this _____ is important to Andy's cognitive development.

Language (pp. 348–352)

26. During middle childhood, some children learn as many as _____ new words a day. Unlike the vocabulary explosion of the play years, this language growth is distinguished by _____ , _____ , _____ , _____ of thinking, _____ , and the ability to make connections between one bit of knowledge and another and later vocabulary performance in school. At this time, children also become much better able to understand _____ , _____ , and _____ .

27. The practical use of language is called _____ .

28. Children are able to change from proper speech, or a _____ _____ , to a colloquial form, or _____ _____ , with their peers.

29. Children who speak a minority language and are learning to speak English are called _____-_____ _____ .

30. Many American children make a _____ _____ as they replace their original language with English. This is especially true of American children from _____ families.

31. The approach to bilingual education in which the child's instruction occurs entirely in the second language is called _____ . In _____ _____ programs, teachers instruct children in both their native language and English.

32. In ESL, or _____ _____ programs, children must master the basics of English before joining regular classes with other children.

33. Any method tends to fail if children feel

_____ , _____ ,

or _____ because of their language.

34. The success of any method seems to depend on home and school environments that are

_____ -rich and on the

_____ status of the family.

THINK ABOUT IT: Imagine that you've been given total control over the educational experiences of a group of 7-year-old children, including microsystem factors and macrosystem factors. What factors will you focus on to promote bilingualism in your group? For example, you might suggest putting English-speaking students in a class with non-English-peaking students so they could help each other out.

APPLICATION:

35. Seven-year-old Kyra has just moved to the United States from Colombia and knows very little English. Her school believes that she will best learn English if classes are in both Spanish, her native language, and English. This strategy is referred to as _____ .

Teaching and Learning (pp. 352–267)

36. Throughout history, children have been given new responsibility and instruction at about age _____ . Today, about _____ percent of children this age attend school.

37. The connection between _____ achievement and _____ status is revealed by the fact that children from _____ - _____ families are least likely to succeed in school. Their difficulty is generally in the area of _____ and includes having smaller _____ and using simpler _____ and _____ sentences.

38. Three factors that contribute to greater school achievement are: early exposure to _____ ; the _____ of teachers and parents; and expectations from the child's larger _____ .

39. Two international approaches to objective assessment of children's achievement are the

_____

_____

and the _____

_____ .

40. Internationally, girls are slightly ahead of boys in _____ skills, while boys are ahead in _____ skills. In the United States, girls tend to catch up to boys in math by age _____ . According to the _____ - _____ hypothesis, males and females are similar on most measures. One exception is in the early grades, when girls typically get higher _____ than boys do. This difference decreases in

_____ .

41. Beyond the basics of reading, writing, and math, national differences in curriculum content _____ (are/are not) notable.

42. In the United States, the _____

_____

Act is a federal law that mandates annual standardized achievement tests for public-school children beginning in the third grade.

43. The _____ is a federal project that measures achievement in reading, mathematics, and other subjects over time.

44. Every culture creates its own _____ _____ , the unofficial rules and priorities that influence every aspect of school learning.

45. Two distinct approaches to teaching reading are the _____ approach, in which children learn the sounds of letters first, and the _____-_____ approach, in which children are encouraged to develop all their language skills at the same time. Most developmentalists believe that _____ (both approaches/neither approach/only the phonics approach/only the whole-language approach) make(s) sense.

46. In the United States, math was traditionally taught by _____ . A more recent approach replaces this type of learning by making instruction more _____ and _____ .

47. Cross-cultural research reveals that U.S. teachers present math at a lower level with more _____ but less _____ to other learning. In contrast, teachers in Japan work more _____ to build children's knowledge.

48. Most people assume that children learn best when class size is _____ . Research studies demonstrate that the relationship between class size and student performance is _____ (clear-cut/complex).

Compare and contrast the educational systems in Japan and the United States as experienced during middle childhood.

49. Japanese children _____ (score about the same as/outscore) U.S. children in math and science. This led to the recent shift toward greater federal involvement in education in the United States, as seen in the almost unanimous passage of the _____ _____ Act.

50. After moving to a new country, Arlene's parents are struck by the greater tendency of math teachers in their new homeland to work collaboratively and to emphasize social interaction in the learning process. To which country have these parents probably moved?
  a. the United States   **c.** Japan
  b. Germany   **d.** Australia

51. During the school board meeting, a knowledgeable parent proclaimed that the board's position on achievement testing and class size was an example of the district's "hidden curriculum." The parent was referring to
  a. the unofficial and unstated educational priorities of the school district.
  b. the political agendas of individual members of the school board.
  c. the legal mandates for testing and class size established by the state board of education.
  d. the federally sponsored measure of children's achievement in reading, math, and other subjects.

52. Four-year-old Tasha, who is learning to read by sounding out the letters of words, evidently is being taught using the _____ approach. Tabatha, on the other hand, is learning by talking and listening, reading and writing. She is being taught using the _____ approach.

Progress Test 1

Multiple-Choice Questions

Circle your answers to the following questions and check them with the answers on page 173. If your answer is incorrect, read the explanation for why it is incorrect and then consult the appropriate pages of the text (in parentheses following the correct answer).

1. According to Piaget, the stage of cognitive development in which a person understands specific logical ideas and can apply them to concrete problems is called
  a. preoperational thought.
  b. operational thought.
  c. concrete operational thought.
  d. formal operational thought.

2. Japanese children outscore children in the United States in math. This difference has been attributed to which of the following?
   a. U.S. teachers present math at a lower level.
   b. Japanese teachers encourage more social interaction among groups of children.
   c. Japanese teachers are more collaborative in their teaching.
   d. Each of these practices has been offered as an explanation of national differences in math scores.

3. The idea that an object that has been transformed in some way can be restored to its original form by undoing the process is
   a. identity.
   b. reversibility.
   c. classification.
   d. automatization.

4. Information-processing theorists contend that major advances in cognitive development occur during the school years because
   a. the child's mind becomes more like a computer as he or she matures.
   b. children become better able to process and analyze information.
   c. most mental activities become automatic by the time a child is about 13 years old.
   d. the major improvements in reasoning that occur during the school years involve increased long-term memory capacity.

5. Cross-cultural research on children's cognition reveals
   a. the same patterns of development worldwide.
   b. significant variations from country to country.
   c. that children's understanding of classification is unrelated to social interaction.
   d. that children's understanding of reversibility is unrelated to social interaction.

6. Some researchers believe that cognitive processing speed and capacity increase during middle childhood because of
   a. the myelination of neural axons.
   b. repetition and practice.
   c. better use of cognitive resources.
   d. all of these reasons.

7. The term for the ability to monitor and adjust one's cognitive performance—to think about thinking—is
   a. pragmatics.
   b. information processing.
   c. selective attention.
   d. metacognition.

8. Long-term memory is _____ permanent and _____ limited than working memory.
   a. more; less
   b. less; more
   c. more; more
   d. less; less

9. Passed in 2001, the federal law that mandates annual standardized achievement tests for public school children is the
   a. Reading First Act.
   b. National Assessment of Educational Progress.
   c. No Child Left Behind Act.
   d. Trends in Math and Science Study.

10. Which theorist believed that cultures (tools, customs, and people) teach children best?
    a. Piaget
    b. Vygotsky
    c. Skinner
    d. Chomsky

11. Which aspect of memory is most likely to change during the school years?
    a. sensory memory
    b. long-term memory
    c. the speed and efficiency of working memory
    d. All of these aspects change.

12. Eight-year-old Cho, who recently emigrated from Mayanmar, attends a school in Canada in which all subjects are taught in English. Cho's school is using which strategy to teach English-language learners?
    a. bilingual education
    b. hidden curriculum
    c. total immersion
    d. ESL

13. Many American children make a language shift. This means that they
    a. do not yet speak English well.
    b. are fluent in their first language and in English.
    c. replace their original language with English rather than becoming fluent in both languages.
    d. experience a language explosion in which they learn as many as 20 new words a day.

14. Which theorist emphasized the critical role of maturation in cognitive development?
    a. Piaget
    b. Vygotsky
    c. Skinner
    d. Chomsky

15. Of the following, which was NOT identified as an important factor in the difference between success and failure in second-language learning?

   a. the age of the child
   b. the attitudes of the parents
   c. community values regarding second-language learning
   d. the difficulty of the language

True or False Items

Write T (*true*) or F (*false*) on the line in front of each statement.

_____ 1. A major objection to Piaget's theory is that he underestimated the influence of context, instruction, and culture.

_____ 2. Immersion is the best strategy for teaching English-language learners.

_____ 3. Vygotsky emphasized the child's own logical thinking.

_____ 4. Japanese children outscore children in the United States in math and science.

_____ 5. Fearing their children were feeling too much academic pressure, the people of Japan recently implemented a more relaxed educational program.

_____ 6. Research evidence consistently demonstrates that children learn best with fewer students in each classroom.

_____ 7. Socioeconomic status does not affect bilingualism.

_____ 8. Most information that comes into the sensory memory is lost or discarded.

_____ 9. Information-processing theorists believe that advances in the thinking of school-age children occur primarily because of changes in long-term memory.

_____ 10. One idea for improving math education involves making each grade of elementary school math build on the previous year's instruction.

Progress Test 2

Progress Test 2 should be completed during a final chapter review. Answer the following questions after you thoroughly understand the correct answers for the Chapter Review and Progress Test 1.

Multiple-Choice Questions

1. The first component of the information-processing system is

   a. sensory memory.   c. long-term memory.
   b. working memory..   d. control process.

2. Research regarding Piaget's theory has found that

   a. cognitive development seems to be considerably less affected by sociocultural factors than Piaget's descriptions imply.
   b. the movement to a new level of thinking is much more erratic than Piaget predicted.
   c. there is no dramatic shift in the thinking of children when they reach the age of 5.
   d. all of these statements are true.

3. The increase in processing speed that occurs during middle childhood is partly the result of

   a. ongoing myelination of axons.
   b. neurological development in the limbic system.
   c. the streamlining of the knowledge base.
   d. all of these events.

4. When psychologists look at the ability of children to receive, store, and organize information, they are examining cognitive development from a view based on

   a. the observations of Piaget.
   b. information processing.
   c. behaviorism.
   d. the idea that the key to thinking is the sensory register.

5. The National Assessment of Educational Progress (NAEP)

   a. measures achievement in reading, mathematics, and other subjects over time.
   b. federally mandates annual achievement testing for public school children.
   c. established a five-year cycle of international trend studies in reading ability.
   d. provides states with funding for early reading instruction.

6. The logical operations of concrete operational thought are particularly important to an understanding of the elementary-school subject of

   a. spelling.   c. math.
   b. reading.   d. social studies.

7. Which of the following is especially helpful in making it easier to master new information in a specific subject?

   a. a large sensory register
   b. a large knowledge base
   c. unlimited long-term memory
   d. working memory

8. Language "codes" include variations in

   a. pronunciation.   c. vocabulary.
   b. gestures.   d. all of these aspects.

9. When we refer to a child's improved memory capacity, we are referring to
   a. the child's ability to selectively attend to more than one thought.
   b. the amount of information the child is able to hold in working memory.
   c. the size of the child's knowledge base.
   d. all of these things.

10. Retaining information in memory is called
    a. retrieval.   c. automatization.
    b. storage.   d. metacognition.

11. Which of the following terms does NOT belong with the others?
    a. selective attention
    b. metacognition
    c. emotional regulation
    d. knowledge base

12. Which aspect of the information-processing system assumes an executive role in regulating the analysis and transfer of information?
    a. sensory register   c. long-term memory
    b. working memory   d. control processes

13. An example of schoolchildren's growth in meta-cognition is their understanding that
    a. transformed objects can be returned to their original state.
    b. rehearsal is a good strategy for memorizing, but outlining is better for understanding.
    c. objects may belong to more than one class.
    d. they can use different language styles in different situations.

14. Which of the following most accurately states the relative merits of the phonics approach and the whole-language approach to teaching reading?
    a. The phonics approach is more effective.
    b. The whole-language approach is the more effective approach.
    c. Both approaches have merit.
    d. Both approaches have been discarded in favor of newer, more interactive methods of instruction.

15. Juan attends a school that offers instruction in both English and Spanish. This strategy for teaching English-language learners is called
    a. bilingual education.
    b. immersion.
    c. heritage language instruction.
    d. ESL.

Matching Items

Match each term or concept with its corresponding description or definition.

Terms or Concepts

_____ 1. working memory
_____ 2. reversibility
_____ 3. classification
_____ 4. identity
_____ 5. information processing
_____ 6. control processes
_____ 7. retrieval
_____ 8. storage
_____ 9. metacognition
_____ 10. total immersion
_____ 11. concrete operational thought

Descriptions or Definitions

a. mechanism for regulating the analysis and flow of information within the information-processing system
b. the idea that a transformation process can be undone to restore the original conditions
c. the idea that certain characteristics of an object remain the same even when other characteristics change
d. developmental perspective that conceives of cognitive development as the result of changes in the processing and analysis of information
e. Piaget's term for the ability to reason logically about direct experiences.
f. an educational technique in which instruction occurs entirely in the second language
g. accessing previously learned information
h. holding information in memory
i. the logical principle that things can be organized into groups
j. area where current, conscious mental activity occurs
k. the ability to evaluate a cognitive task and to monitor one's performance on it

Key Terms

Writing Definitions

Using your own words, write a brief definition or explanation of each of the following terms on a separate piece of paper.

1. concrete operational thought
2. classification
3. identity
4. reversibility
5. information-processing theory
6. sensory memory
7. working memory
8. long-term memory
9. knowledge base
10. control processes
11. metacognition
12. English-language learner (ELL)
13. language shift
14. immersion
15. bilingual education
16. ESL (English as a second language)
17. Progress in International Reading Literacy Study (PIRLS)
18. Trends in Math and Science Study (TIMSS)
19. No Child Left Behind Act
20. National Assessment of Educational Progress (NAEP)
21. hidden curriculum
22. phonics approach
23. whole-language approach

Cross-Check

After you have written the definitions of the key terms in this chapter, you should complete the crossword puzzle to ensure that you can reverse the process—recognize the term, given the definition.

ACROSS

3. The part of memory that stores unlimited amounts of information for days, months, or years.
5. The aspect of memory that holds information for only a split second.
7. Processes that regulate the analysis and flow of information in memory.
8. According to the theorist in 13 across, cognitive development occurs in _____ .
9. The main characteristic of concrete operational thinking is the ability to use _____ .
12. An approach to teaching a second language in which the teacher instructs the children in school subjects using their native language as well as the second language.
13. Psychologist who developed an influential theory of cognitive development.
14. The principle that objects remain the same even if some characteristics change.
15. The principle that things can return to their original state.

DOWN

1. The part of memory that handles current, conscious mental activity.
2. Ongoing neural process that speeds up neural processing.
4. The ability to evaluate a cognitive task in order to determine what to do.
6. English as a second language.
10. According to Piaget, the type of cognitive operations that occur during middle childhood.
11. The body of knowledge that has been learned about a particular area.

Answers

CHAPTER REVIEW

1. concrete operational thought
2. classification; transitive inference; identity; reversibility
3. before; mental categories; egocentrism; flexible
4. zone of proximal development; others; is not
5. sociocultural; maturational
6. Piaget; Vygotsky
7. information-processing
8. sensory memory (the sensory register)
9. working memory; short-term memory; conscious; phonological loop; visual-spatial sketchpad
10. long-term memory; retrieval
11. neurological; myelination
12. automatization
13. knowledge base
14. experience; opportunity; motivation
15. control processes; selective attention; metacognition; emotional regulation
16. metacognition
17. age; explicitly; discovey
18. c. is the answer. Identity is the logical principle that certain characteristics of an object remain the same even when other characteristics change.
19. c. is the answer. Reversibility is the logical principle that something that has been changed (such as the height of lemonade poured from one glass into another) can be returned to its original shape by reversing the process of change (pouring the liquid back into the other glass).
20. information-processing
21. classification. This is the process of organizing things into groups according to some common property.

22. control processes. The control processes, which include selective attention, metacognition, and emotional regulation, are the executives of the information-processing system. They regulate the analysis and flow of information.
23. b. is the answer. The capacity of working memory increases during middle childhood.
24. metacognition. Metacognition has been referred to as "thinking about thinking."
25. social interaction. Vygotsky believed that peers and teachers provide the bridge between the child's developmental potential and the needed skills and knowledge, via guided participation.
26. 20; logic; flexibility; memory; speed; metacognition; metaphors; jokes; puns
27. pragmatics
28. formal code; informal code
29. English-language learners (ELLs)
30. language shift; Asian
31. immersion; bilingual education
32. English as a second language
33. shy; stupid; lonely
34. language; socioeconomic
35. bilingual education
36. 7; 90
37. school; socioeconomic; low-income; language; vocabularies; grammar; shorter
38. language; expectations; macrosystem
39. Progress in International Reading Literacy Study (PIRLS); Trends in Math and Science Study (TIMSS)
40. verbal; math; 9; gender-similarities; grades; adolescence
41. are
42. No Child Left Behind
43. National Assessment of Educational Progress
44. hidden curriculum
45. phonics; whole-language; both approaches
46. rote; active; engaging
47. definitions; connection; collaboratively
48. small; complex

Children in Japan study more than U.S. children and spend more time in school. Teachers are given more respect by students and parents, and they learn from one another. The Japanese government funds and guides education, and the curriculum is universal. Most Japanese children also attend private classes (*juko*).

49. outscore; No Child Left Behind
50. **c.** is the answer.
51. **a.** is the answer.
52. phonics; whole-word

PROGRESS TEST 1

Multiple-Choice Questions

1. **c.** is the answer. (p. 338)

    a. Preoperational thought is "pre-logical" thinking.

    b. There is no such stage in Piaget's theory.

    d. Formal operational thought extends logical reasoning to abstract problems.

2. **d.** is the answer. (p. 365)

3. **b.** is the answer. (p. 339)

    a. This is the concept that certain characteristics of an object remain the same even when other characteristics change.

    c. This is the organization of things into groups.

    d. This is the process by which familiar mental activities become routine and automatic.

4. **b.** is the answer. (p. 342)

    a. Information-processing theorists use the mind–computer metaphor at every age.

    c. Although increasing automatization is an important aspect of development, the information-processing perspective does not suggest that most mental activities become automatic by age 13.

    d. Most of the important changes in reasoning that occur during the school years are due to the improved processing capacity of the person's *working memory*.

5. **a.** is the answer. (p. 341)

6. **d.** is the answer. (pp. 343–344)

7. **d.** is the answer. (p. 345)

    a. Pragmatics refers to the practical use of language to communicate with others.

    b. The information-processing perspective views the mind as being like a computer.

    c. This is the ability to screen out distractions in order to focus on important information.

8. **a.** is the answer. (pp. 343–344)

9. **c.** is the answer. (p. 358)

10. **b.** is the answer. (pp. 340–341)

    a. Piaget emphasized the importance of maturation in cognitive development.

    c. & d. Skinner and Chomsky each developed a theory of language development.

11. **c.** is the answer. During middle childhood, speed of processing increases and automatization improves, thus improving the efficiency of working memory. (p. 343)

12. **c.** is the answer. (p. 351)

    a. In bilingual education, instruction occurs in both languages.

    b. Hidden curriculum is not a method of instruction.

    d. ESL children are taught intensively in English for a few months to prepare them for regular classes. It is not clear that Cho received this type of preparatory instruction.

13. **c.** is the answer. (p. 350)

14. **a.** is the answer. (p. 341)

15. **d.** is the answer. (pp. 350–352)

True or False Items

1. T (p. 340)

2. F No single approach to teaching a second language is best for all children in all contexts. (pp. 351–352)

3. F This is true of Piaget. (p. 338)

4. T (p. 365)

5. T (p. 365)

6. F Research support for this popular assumption is weak. (p. 364)

7. F The likelihood of parents, school, or culture encouraging bilingualism in children depends on the family's socioeconomic status. (p. 352)

8. T (pp. 342–343)

9. F They believe that the changes are due to basic changes in control processes. (pp. 344–346)

10. T (p. 363)

PROGRESS TEST 2

Multiple-Choice Questions

1. **a.** is the answer. (p. 342)

2. **b.** is the answer. (p. 340)

3. **a.** is the answer. (p. 344)

    b. Neurological development in the prefrontal cortex facilitates processing speed during middle childhood. The limbic system, which was not discussed in this chapter, is concerned with emotions.

    c. Processing speed is facilitated by *growth*, rather than streamlining, of the knowledge base.

4. **b.** is the answer. (p. 342)

5. **a.** is the answer. (p. 358)

6. **c.** is the answer. (p. 340)

7. **b.** is the answer. (p. 344)

   a. The sensory register briefly stores incoming sensations. Its capacity does not change with maturation.

   c. & d. Working memory and long-term memory are important in all forms of learning. Unlike a broad knowledge base in a specific area, however, these memory processes do not selectively make it easier to learn more in a specific area.

8. **d.** is the answer. (p. 349)

9. **b.** is the answer. (p. 343)

10. **b.** is the answer. (p. 344)

    a. This is the *accessing* of already learned information.

    c. Automatization is the process by which well-learned activities become routine and automatic.

    d. This is the ability to evaluate a task and to monitor and adjust one's performance on it.

11. **d.** is the answer. (p. 344)

    a., b., & c. Each of these is a control process.

12. **d.** is the answer. (p. 345)

    a. The sensory register stores incoming information for a split second.

    b. Working memory is the part of memory that handles current, conscious mental activity.

    c. Long-term memory stores information for days, months, or years.

13. **b.** is the answer. (p. 346)

14. **c.** is the answer. (pp. 361–362)

15. **a.** is the answer. (p. 351)

Matching Items

1. j (p. 343)	5. d (p. 342)	9. k (p. 345)
2. b (p. 339)	6. a (p. 344)	10. f (p. 351)
3. i (p. 338)	7. g (p. 344)	11. e (p. 338)
4. c (p. 339)	8. h (p. 344)	

KEY TERMS

Writing Definitions

1. During Piaget's stage of **concrete operational thought,** lasting from ages 7 to 11, children can think logically about direct experiences and perceptions but are not able to reason abstractly. (p. 338)

2. **Classification** is the principle that things can be organized into groups according to some common property. (p. 338)

3. In Piaget's theory, **identity** is the logical principle that certain characteristics of an object remain the same even when other characteristics change. (p. 339)

4. **Reversibility** is the logical principle that a transformation process can be reversed to restore the original conditions. (p. 339)

5. **Information-processing theory** models human cognition after the computer, analyzing each component, step by step. (p. 342)

6. **Sensory memory** is the first component of the information-processing system that stores incoming stimuli for a split second, after which it is passed into working memory, or discarded as unimportant; also called the *sensory register.* (p. 342)

7. **Working memory** is the component of the information-processing system that handles current, conscious mental activity; also called *short-term memory.* (p. 343)

8. **Long-term memory** is the component of the information-processing system that stores unlimited amounts of information for days, months, or years. (p. 343)

9. The **knowledge base** is a broad body of knowledge in a particular subject area that has been learned, making it easier to learn new information in that area. (p. 344)

10. **Control processes** (including selective attention, metacognition, and emotional regulation) regulate the analysis and flow of information within the information-processing system. (p. 344)

11. **Metacognition** is the ability to evaluate a cognitive task to determine what to do and to monitor and adjust one's performance on that task. (p. 345)

12. An **English-language learner (ELL)** is a child who is learning English as a second language. (p. 350)

13. A **language shift** is a shift from one language to another, which occurs not only in speaking and writing but also in the brain. (p. 350)

14. **Immersion** is an approach to bilingual education in which the child's instruction occurs entirely in the new language. (p. 351)

15. **Bilingual education** is a strategy in which school subjects are taught in both the learner's original language and the second (majority) language. (p. 351)

16. **ESL (English as a second language)** is an approach to bilingual education in which children are taught separately, and exclusively in English, to prepare them for attending regular classes. (p. 351)

17. **Progress in International Reading Literacy Study (PIRLS)** is a five-year cycle of trend studies of reading ability among fourth-graders around the world. (p. 355)

18. **The TIMSS (Trends in Math and Science Study)** is an international assessment of math and science skills of fourth- and eighth-graders. (p. 355)

19. The **No Child Left Behind Act** is a controversial law, enacted in 2001, that uses multiple assessments and achievement standards to try to improve public education in the United States. (p. 358)

20. The **National Assessment of Educational Progress (NAEP)** is an ongoing program of measurement of children's achievement in reading, mathematics, and other subjects. (p. 358)

21. The **hidden curriculum** is the unofficial, unstated, or implicit rules and priorities that influence the academic curriculum and every other aspect of school learning. (p. 359)

22. The **phonics approach** is a method of teaching reading by having children learn the sounds of letters before they begin to learn words. (p. 361)

23. The **whole-language approach** is a method of teaching reading by encouraging children to develop all their language skills simultaneously. (p. 361)

Cross-Check

ACROSS

3. long-term
5. sensory
7. control
8. stages
9. logic
12. bilingual
13. Piaget
14. identity
15. reversibility

DOWN

1. working
2. myelination
4. metacognition
6. ESL
10. concrete
11. knowledge base

Middle Childhood: Psychosocial Development

Chapter Overview

This chapter brings to a close the unit on middle childhood. We have seen that from ages 7 to 11, the child becomes stronger and more competent, mastering the biosocial and cognitive abilities that are important in his or her culture. Psychosocial accomplishments are equally impressive.

The first section explores the growing social competence of children, as described by Freud and Erikson. The section continues with a discussion of the growth of social cognition and self-understanding and closes with a discussion of the ways in which children cope with stressful situations.

The next section explores the ways in which families influence children, including the experience of living in single-parent, stepparent, and blended families. Although no particular family structure guarantees optimal child development, income, harmony, and stability are important factors in the quality of family functioning.

Children's interactions with peers and others in their ever-widening social world is the subject of the third section. Because middle childhood is also a time of expanding moral reasoning, the final section examines Kohlberg's stage theory of moral development as well as current evaluations of his theory. Although the peer group often is a supportive, positive influence on children, some children are rejected by their peers or become the victims of bullying.

NOTE: Answer guidelines for all Chapter 13 questions begin on page 186.

Chapter Review

When you have finished reading the chapter, work through the material that follows to review it. Complete the sentences and answer the questions. In some cases, Study Tips explain how best to learn a difficult concept, while Think About It and Applica-

tions help you to know how well you understand the material. As you proceed, evaluate your performance for each section by consulting the answers beginning on page 186. Do not continue with the next section until you understand each answer. If you need to, review or reread the appropriate section in the textbook before continuing.

The Nature of the Child (pp. 372–380)

1. According to Erikson, the crisis of middle childhood is _____ _____ _____ .

2. Freud describes middle childhood as the period of _____ , when emotional drives are _____ and unconscious sexual conflicts are _____ .

3. As their self-understanding sharpens, children gradually become _____ (more/less) self-critical, and their self-esteem _____ (rises/dips). One reason is that they more often evaluate themselves through _____ _____ .

4. Self-esteem is that is unrealistically high may reduce the child's _____ _____ , thus lowering _____ . However, the same may occur if _____ is unrealistically low. Self-esteem _____ (is/is not) universally valued; many cultures expect children to be _____ . Self-esteem is prized in countries such as _____ , but not in countries such as _____ .

5. Some children are better able to adapt within the context of adversity; that is, they seem to be more _____ . This trait is a _____ process that represents a _____ adaptation to stress.

6. Difficult daily _____ may build up stress in children.

7. A key aspect of resilience is the child's own ability to develop _____ , _____ , and _____ .

8. Another element that helps children deal with problems is the _____ _____ they receive.

9. During middle childhood, there are typically _____ (fewer/more) sources of social support. This can be obtained from grandparents or siblings, for example, or from _____ and _____ . In addition, _____ can be psychologically protective for children in difficult circumstances.

STUDY TIP: To consolidate your understanding of how stress can affect children during the school years, write a paragraph describing a hypothetical child who remains resilient despite experiencing chronic daily stress. Be sure to describe various protective factors such as social support that promote this child's resistance.

APPLICATIONS:

10. Dr. Ferris believes that skill mastery is particularly important because children develop views of themselves as either competent or incompetent in skills valued by their culture. Dr. Ferris is evidently working from the perspective of _____ .

11. The Australian saying that "tall poppies" are cut down underscores the fact that
   a. older children often ignore their parents and teachers.
   b. culture influences standards of social comparison.
   c. middle childhood is a time of emotional latency.
   d. personal friendships become even more important in middle childhood.

12. Concluding her presentation on resilient children, Brenda notes that
   a. children who are truly resilient are resilient in all situations.
   b. resilience is merely the absence of pathology.
   c. resilience is a stable trait that becomes apparent very early in life.
   d. resilience is a dynamic process that represents a positive adaptation to significant adversity or stress.

13. Of the following children, who is likely to have the lowest overall self-esteem?
   a. Karen, age 5   c. Carl, age 9
   b. David, age 7   d. Cindy, age 10

14. Ten-year-old Benjamin is less optimistic and self-confident than his 5-year-old sister. This may be explained in part by the tendency of older children to
   a. evaluate their abilities by comparing them with their own competencies a year or two earlier.
   b. evaluate their competencies by comparing them with those of others.
   c. be less realistic about their own abilities.
   d. be overly confident about their abilities.

Families and Children (pp. 380–391)

15. No human trait is entirely _____ or entirely _____ .

16. Research demonstrates that _____ (shared/nonshared) influences on most traits are far greater than _____ (shared/nonshared) influences. However, recent research indicates that parents _____ (do/do not) have a significant influence over their children.

17. Family function refers to how well the family _____ _____ .

18. A functional family nurtures school-age children by providing basic _____ , encouraging _____ , fostering the development of _____ , nurturing peer _____ , and ensuring _____ and _____ .

19. (text and Table 13.3) Family structure is defined as the _____ _____ .

Identify each of the following family structures:

a. _____ A family that includes three or more biologically related generations, including parents and children.

b. _____ A family that consists of the father, the mother, and their biological children.

c. _____ A family that consists of one parent with his or her biological children.

d. _____ A family consisting of two parents, at least one with biological children from previous unions and/or of the new couple.

e. _____ In some nations, a family that consists of one man, several wives, and their children.

f. _____ A family that consists of one or more nonbiological children whom adults have legally taken to raise as their own.

g. _____ A family that consists of one or more orphaned, neglected, abused, or delinquent children who are temporarily cared for by an adult to whom they are not biologically related.

h. _____ A family that consists of a parent, his or her biological children, and his or her spouse, who is not biologically related to the children.

i. _____ A family that consists of one or two grandparents and their grandchildren.

j. _____ A family that consists of a homosexual couple and the biological or adopted children of one or both partners.

20. Although the _____ family is still the most common, more than _____ (what percentage?) of all school-age children live in _____-_____ households.

21. Extended families are more common among _____-_____ households. The benefit is that they can share _____ and _____ .

22. Children in polygamous families _____ (do/do not) fare as well because income per child _____ (increases/decreases).

23. Having homosexual parents _____ (seems/does not seem) to have negative effects on children.

24. Whether children thrive in blended families depends largely on the adults' _____ and _____ security. Such families _____ (are/are not necessarily) better for children than single-parent families.

Give several reasons for the benefits of the nuclear family structure.

25. Children in every type of family structure may grow up very well or run into trouble. Thus, family _____ seems more critical than family _____ .

26. Family income _____ (correlates/does not correlate) with optimal child development. Economic distress _____ family functioning. According to the _____-_____ model, economic hardship in a family increases _____ , which often makes adults tense and _____ toward their children.

27. A second factor that has a crucial impact on children is the _____ and _____ that characterizes family interaction. Children are particularly affected when there are multiple _____ .

28. The child's _____ _____ of a negative family situation is crucial in determining the impact of that situation. When children feel responsible for whatever happens in their family, the problem called _____ has occurred.

THINK ABOUT IT: Blended families are extremely common today. To review your understanding of family function, describe a hypothetical blended family that functionally is as effective as a high functioning nuclear family.

_____

APPLICATIONS:

29. Shen's parents have separated. Since then, his grades have dropped, he's moody, and he spends most of his time alone in his room. Research regarding the factors that contribute to problems such as Shen's found the strongest correlation between children's peace of mind and
    a. marital discord.
    b. income.
    c. illness in the family.
    d. feelings of self-blame and vulnerability.

30. Sandra's family consists of her biological mother, her stepfather, and his two daughters from a previous marriage. Sandra's family would be classified as _____ .

31. Kyle and Jessica are as different as two siblings can be, despite growing up in the same nuclear family structure. In explaining these differences, a developmentalist is likely to point to
    a. shared environmental influences.
    b. nonshared environmental influences.
    c. genetic differences and shared environmental influences.
    d. genetic differences and nonshared environmental influences.

The Peer Group (pp. 391–398)

32. Getting along with _____ is especially important during middle childhood. Compared to younger children, school-age children are _____ (more/less) deeply affected by others' acceptance or rejection.

33. Peers create their own _____
    _____ _____ , which

includes the particular rules and rituals that are passed down from slightly older to younger children and that _____ (mirror/do not necessarily mirror) the values of adults.

34. _____ (In some parts of the world/Throughout the world), the culture of children encourages _____ from adults.

35. During the school years, children prefer to play with children _____ (of their own sex/of the opposite sex) because _____ stereotypes become more elaborate. _____ and ethnic prejudice is rejected at this time.

36. Having a personal friend is _____ (more/less) important to children than acceptance by the peer group.

37. Friendships during middle childhood become more _____ and _____ . As a result, older children _____ (change/do not change) friends as often and find it _____ (easier/harder) to make new friends.

38. Middle schoolers tend to choose best friends whose _____ , _____ , and _____ are similar to their own.

39. A research study of social acceptance among schoolchildren revealed that approximately _____ (what proportion?) are popular, approximately _____ are average in popularity, and approximately _____ are unpopular.

40. Children who are not really rejected but not picked as friends are _____ . Children who are actively rejected tend to be either _____ - _____ or _____ - _____ .

Briefly explain why rejected children are disliked.

41. The ability to understand human interactions, called _____ _____ , begins in infancy with _____ _____ , continues in early childhood with _____ _____ _____ , and by middle childhood is well established. As they improve in this area, school children also improve in _____ _____ .

Describe how well-liked children demonstrate their newfound ability to correctly interpret social situations.

42. Bullying is defined as _____ efforts to inflict harm through _____ , _____ , or _____ attacks on a weaker person. A key aspect in the definition of bullying is that harmful attacks are _____ . The three types of bullying are _____ , _____ , and _____ .

43. Most bullies usually _____ (have/do not have) friends who admire them, and they are socially _____ but without _____ .

44. Victims of bullying are often _____ -rejected children. Less often, _____ -rejected children become _____ - _____ .

45. Boys who are bullies are often above average in _____ , whereas girl bullies are often _____ - _____ . Boys who are bullies typically use _____ aggression, whereas girls use _____ aggression.

46. The origins of bullying may lie in a _____ _____ or a _____ predisposition and are then strengthened by _____ _____ , a stressful _____ life, ineffective _____ , hostile _____ , and other problems that intensify _____ impulses.

47. One effective intervention in controlling bullying in Norway involved using an _____ - _____ approach to change the _____ .

APPLICATIONS:

48. Concluding her presentation on bullying, Olivia notes that one factor in the possible development of bullying is
    a. an inborn brain abnormality.
    b. insecure attachment.
    c. the presence of hostile siblings.
    d. any of these factors.

49. Ten-year-old Ramón, who is disliked by many of his peers because of his antagonistic, confrontational nature, would probably be labeled as _____ .

50. In discussing friendship, 9-year-old Melissa, in contrast to a younger child, will
    a. deny that friends are important.
    b. state that she prefers same-sex playmates.
    c. stress the importance of loyalty and similar interests.
    d. be less choosy about who she calls a friend.

51. Eight-year-old Henry is unpopular because he is a very timid and anxious child. Developmentalists would classify Henry as _____ .

52. Of the following children, who is most likely to become a bully?
    a. Karen, who is taller than average
    b. David, who is above average in verbal assertiveness
    c. Carl, who is insecure and lonely
    d. Cindy, who was insecurely attached

53. I am an 8-year-old who frequently is bullied at school. If I am like most victims of bullies, I am probably
    a. obese.
    b. unattractive.
    c. a child who speaks with an accent.
    d. anxious and insecure.

Children's Moral Codes (pp. 398–401)

54. The theorist who has extensively studied moral development by presenting people with stories that pose ethical dilemmas is _____ . According to his theory, the three levels of moral reasoning are _____ , _____ , and _____ .

55. (Table 13.5) In preconventional reasoning, emphasis is on getting _____ and avoiding _____ . "Might makes right" describes stage _____ (1/2), whereas "look out for number one" describes stage _____ (1/2).

56. (Table 13.5) In conventional reasoning, emphasis is on _____ _____ , such as being a dutiful citizen, in stage _____ (3/4), or on winning approval from others, in stage _____ (3/4).

57. (Table 13.5) In postconventional reasoning, emphasis is on _____ _____ , such as _____ _____ (stage 5) and _____ _____ _____ (stage 6).

58. One criticism of Kohlberg's theory is that it does not take _____ or _____ differences into account.

APPLICATION:

59. During a neighborhood game of baseball, Sam insists that Bobby cannot take another swing at the bat following his third strike because, "that's the rule." Sam is evidently thinking about this issue at Kohlberg's _____ stage of moral reasoning.

Progress Test 1

Multiple-Choice Questions

Circle your answers to the following questions and check them with the answers beginning on page 187. If your answer is incorrect, read the explanation for why it is incorrect and then consult the appropriate pages of the text (in parentheses following the correct answer).

1. Between 9 and 11 years of age, children are likely to demonstrate moral reasoning at which of Kohlberg's stages?
   a. preconventional
   b. conventional
   c. postconventional
   d. It is impossible to predict based only on a child's age.

2. Which of the following is NOT among the highest values of middle childhood?
   a. protect your friends
   b. don't tell adults what really goes on
   c. try not to be too different from other children
   d. don't depend on others

3. The best strategy for helping children who are at risk of developing serious psychological problems because of multiple stresses would be to
   a. obtain assistance from a psychiatrist.
   b. increase the child's competencies or social supports.
   c. change the household situation.
   d. reduce the peer group's influence.

4. The culture of children refers to
   a. the specific habits, styles, and values that reflect the rules and rituals of children.
   b. a child's tendency to assess abilities by measuring them against those of peers.
   c. children's ability to understand social interactions.
   d. all of these factors.

5. Girls who are bullies are often above average in _____ , whereas boys who are bullies are often above average in _____ .
   a. size; verbal assertiveness
   b. verbal assertiveness; size
   c. intelligence; aggressiveness
   d. aggressiveness; intelligence

6. A family that consists of two parents, at least one with biological children from a previous union, and any children the two adults have together is called a(n) _____ family.
   a. extended
   b. polygamous
   c. nuclear
   d. blended

7. Compared with average or popular children, rejected children tend to be
   a. brighter and more competitive.
   b. affluent and "stuck-up."
   c. economically disadvantaged.
   d. socially immature.

8. School-age children advance in their awareness of classmates' opinions and accomplishments. These abilities are best described as advances in their
   a. social comparison.
   b. social cognition.
   c. metacognition.
   d. pragmatic intelligence.

9. Resilience is characterized by all but which of the following characteristics?
   a. Resilience is a stable trait that a child carries throughout his or her life.
   b. Resilience represents a positive adaptation to stress.
   c. Resilience is more than the absence of pathology.
   d. Resilience is the capacity to develop optimally despite significant adversity.

10. With their expanding social world and developing cognition, children may be stressed by a variety of disturbing problems. Which of the following is NOT a means by which children can overcome these problems?
    a. school success
    b. healthy diet
    c. religious faith
    d. after-school achievements

11. Bully-victims are typically children who would be categorized as
    a. aggressive-rejected.
    b. withdrawn-rejected.
    c. isolated-rejected.
    d. immature-rejected.

12. Bullying during middle childhood
    a. occurs only in certain cultures.
    b. is more common in rural schools than in urban schools.
    c. seems to be universal.

    d. is rarely a major problem, because other children usually intervene to prevent it from getting out of hand.

13. During the school years, children become _____ selective about their friends, and their friendship groups become _____ .
    a. less; larger
    b. less; smaller
    c. more; larger
    d. more; smaller

14. Erikson's crisis of industry versus inferiority corresponds to which of Freud's psychosexual stages?
    a. genital stage
    b. oral stage
    c. anal stage
    d. period of latency

15. Erikson's crisis of the school years is that of
    a. industry versus inferiority.
    b. acceptance versus rejection.
    c. initiative versus guilt.
    d. male versus female.

True or False Items

Write T (*true*) or F (*false*) on the line in front of each statement.

_____ 1. As they evaluate themselves according to increasingly complex self-theories, school-age children typically experience a rise in self-esteem.

_____ 2. During middle childhood, acceptance by the peer group is valued more than having a close friend.

_____ 3. Children from low-income homes often experience more stress.

_____ 4. Bullies and their victims are usually of the same gender.

_____ 5. Children who are labeled "resilient" demonstrate an ability to adapt positively in all situations.

_____ 6. The way a family functions seems to be a more powerful predictor of children's development than the actual structure of the family.

_____ 7. Withdrawn-rejected and aggressive-rejected children both have problems regulating their emotions.

_____ 8. Most aggressive-rejected children clearly interpret other people's words and behavior.

_____ 9. School-age children are less able than younger children to cope with chronic stresses.

_____ 10. Children's ability to cope with stress may depend as much on their appraisal of events as on the objective nature of the actual events.

_____ 11. Friendship circles become wider as children grow older.

Progress Test 2

Progress Test 2 should be completed during a final chapter review. Answer the following questions after you thoroughly understand the correct answers for the Chapter Review and Progress Test 1.

Multiple-Choice Questions

1. Children who are categorized as _____ are particularly vulnerable to bullying.
   a. aggressive-rejected
   b. passive-aggressive
   c. withdrawn-rejected
   d. passive-rejected

2. Environmental influences on children's traits that result from contact with different teachers and peer groups are classified as
   a. shared influences.
   b. nonshared influences.
   c. epigenetic influences.
   d. nuclear influences.

3. Compared with parents in other family structures, married parents tend to be
   a. wealthier.
   b. better educated.
   c. healthier.
   d. all of these things.

4. More than half of all school-age children live in
   a. one-parent families.
   b. blended families.
   c. extended families.
   d. nuclear families.

5. Typically, children in middle childhood experience a decrease in self-esteem as a result of
   a. a wavering self-theory.
   b. increased awareness of personal shortcomings and failures.
   c. rejection by peers.
   d. difficulties with members of the opposite sex.

6. A 10-year-old's sense of self-esteem is most strongly influenced by his or her
   a. peers.   c. mother.
   b. siblings.   d. father.

7. Which of the following most accurately describes how friendships change during the school years?
   a. Friendships become more casual and less intense.
   b. Older children demand less of their friends.
   c. Older children change friends more often.
   d. Close friendships increasingly involve members of the same sex, ethnicity, and socioeconomic status.

8. Which of the following is an accurate statement about school-age bullies?
   a. They are socially perceptive but not empathic.
   b. They usually have a few admiring friends.
   c. They are adept at being aggressive.
   d. All of these statements are accurate.

9. One effective intervention to prevent bullying in the school is to
   a. change the culture through community-wide and classroom education.
   b. target one victimized child at a time.
   c. target each bully as an individual.
   d. focus on improving the academic skills of all children in the school.

10. Which of the following most accurately describes the relationship between family income and child development?
    a. Adequate family income allows children to own whatever possessions help them to feel accepted.
    b. Because parents need not argue about money, household wealth provides harmony and stability.
    c. The basic family functions are enhanced by adequate family income.
    d. Family income is not correlated with child development.

11. Two factors that most often help the child cope well with multiple stresses are social support and
    a. social comparison.
    b. religious faith.
    c. remedial education.
    d. referral to mental health professionals.

12. An 8-year-old child who measures her achievements by comparing them with those of her friends is engaging in social
    a. cognition.
    b. comparison.
    c. reinforcement.
    d. modeling.

13. In Kohlberg's theory, moral reasoning that is based on seeking rewards and avoiding punishment is called
    a. universal
    b. postconventional
    c. preconventional
    d. conventional

14. According to Freud, the period between ages 7 and 11 when a child's sexual drives are relatively quiet is the
    a. phallic stage.
    b. genital stage.
    c. period of latency.
    d. period of industry versus inferiority.

15. Children who are forced to cope with one serious ongoing stress (for example, poverty or large family size) are
    a. more likely to develop serious psychiatric problems.
    b. no more likely to develop problems.
    c. more likely to develop intense, destructive friendships.
    d. less likely to be accepted by their peer group.

Matching Items

Match each term or concept with its corresponding description or definition.

Terms or Concepts

_____ 1. relational bullying
_____ 2. nuclear family
_____ 3. social comparison
_____ 4. provocative victim
_____ 5. foster family
_____ 6. aggressive-rejected
_____ 7. withdrawn-rejected
_____ 8. physical bullying
_____ 9. effortful control
_____ 10. blended family
_____ 11. extended family

Descriptions or Definitions

a. another term for a bully-victim
b. adults living with their children from previous marriages as well as their own biological children
c. a father, a mother, and the biological children they have together
d. used by boy bullies
e. children who are disliked because of their confrontational nature
f. evaluating one's abilities by measuring them against those of other children
g. three or more generations of biologically related individuals living together
h. children who are disliked because of timid, anxious behavior
i. used by girl bullies
j. a family in which one or more children are temporarily cared for by an adult individual or couple to whom they are not biologically related
k. the ability to regulate one's emotions

Key Terms

Using your own words, write a brief definition or explanation of each of the following terms on a separate piece of paper.

1. industry vs. inferiority
2. latency
3. social comparison
4. effortful control
5. resilience
6. family structure
7. family function
8. nuclear family
9. single-parent family
10. extended family
11. polygamous family
12. blended family
13. culture of children
14. aggressive-rejected
15. withdrawn-rejected
16. social cognition
17. bullying
18. bully-victim
19. preconventional moral reasoning
20. conventional moral reasoning
21. postconventional moral reasoning

Answers

CHAPTER REVIEW

1. industry versus inferiority
2. latency; quiet; submerged
3. more; dips; social comparison
4. effortful control; achievement; self-esteem; is not; modest; the United States; Angola
5. resilient; dynamic; positive
6. routines
7. friends; skills; activities
8. social support
9. more; peers; pets; religion
10. Erik Erikson's theory of development. The question describes what is, for Erikson, the crisis of middle childhood: industry versus inferiority.
11. b. is the answer.
12. d. is the answer.

13. d. is the answer. Self-esteem decreases throughout middle childhood.
14. b. is the answer. Social comparison becomes important for these children as they evaluate their competencies.
15. genetic; environmental
16. nonshared; shared; do
17. works to meet the needs of its members
18. necessities; learning; self-respect; relationships; harmony; stability
19. genetic and legal relationships among related people living in the same household
    a. extended family
    b. nuclear family
    c. one-parent family
    d. blended family
    e. polygamous family
    f. adoptive family
    g. foster family
    h. stepparent family
    i. grandparents alone
    j. homosexual family
20. nuclear; one-fourth; single-parent
21. low-income; expenses; responsibilities
22. do not; decreases
23. does not seem
24. emotional; economic; are not

Parents in a nuclear family tend to be wealthier, better educated, healthier, and less hostile than other parents.

25. function; structure
26. correlates; decreases; family-stress; stress; hostile
27. harmony; stability; transitions
28. cognitive interpretation; parentification
29. d. is the answer. More important than marital discord, income, or illness is the child's interpretation of the situation. If the child blames himself or herself for the problems, psychic and academic problems are more likely to occur.
30. blended. This is a type of stepparent family. It is a particularly difficult structure for school-age children.
31. d. is the answer. Even within the same family, siblings experience nonshared environments.
32. peers; more
33. culture of children; do not necessarily mirror
34. Throughout the world; independence

35. of their own sex; gender; Racial

36. more

37. intense; intimate; do not change; harder

38. interests; values; backgrounds

39. one-third; one-half; one-sixth

40. neglected; aggressive-rejected; withdrawn-rejected

Aggressive-rejected children are disliked because of their antagonistic and confrontational behavior, while withdrawn-rejected children are timid, withdrawn, and anxious. Both types often misinterpret social situations, lack emotional regulation, and are likely to be mistreated at home.

41. social cognition; social referencing; theory of mind; effortful control

Given direct conflict with another child, well-liked children seek compromise in order to maintain the friendship. They assume that social slights are accidental and, in contrast with rejected children, do not respond with fear, self-doubt, or anger. These prosocial impulses and attitudes are a sign of social maturity.

42. systematic; physical, verbal; social; repeated; physical; verbal; relational

43. have; perceptive; empathy

44. withdrawn; aggressive; bully-victims

45. size; sharp-tongued; physical; relational

46. brain abnormality; genetic; insecure attachment; home; discipline; siblings; aggressive

47. dynamic-systems; whole school

48. d. is the answer. Parents can teach young children to restrain their aggressive impulses.

49. aggressive-rejected. Children such as Ramón tend to misread social situations and lack emotional regulation.

50. c. is the answer. In middle childhood, friendship becomes more selective and intimate, and children choose each other because of similar interests, values, and backgrounds.

51. withdrawn-rejected. Withdrawn-rejected children are most likely to become bully-victims. Like aggressive-rejected children, they tend to misread social situations and lack emotional regulation.

52. b. is the answer. Verbal bullying is one of the three major types of bullying (physical and relational are the other two types of bullying).

53. d. is the answer. Surprisingly, children who are different because of obesity or looks, for example, are not necessarily singled out for bullying.

54. Kohlberg; preconventional; conventional; post-conventional

55. rewards; punishments; 1; 2

56. social rules; 4; 3

57. moral principles; social contracts; universal ethical principles

58. cultural; gender

59. conventional. During Stage Four, law and order, being a proper citizen means obeying the rules set down by society.

PROGRESS TEST 1

Multiple-Choice Questions

1. **b.** is the answer. (p. 399)

2. **d.** is the answer. (p. 401)

3. **b.** is the answer. (p. 378)

4. **a.** is the answer. (p. 392)

   b. This is social comparison.

   c. This is social cognition.

5. **b.** is the answer. (p. 396)

6. **d.** is the answer. (pp. 384)

   a. In an extended family, children live with grandparents or other relatives.

   b. In a polygamous family, one man has several wives.

   c. A nuclear family has two parents and their biological children.

7. **d.** is the answer. (p. 395)

8. **b.** is the answer. (p. 395)

   a. Social comparison is the tendency to assess one's abilities by measuring them against those of others, especially those of one's peers.

   c. Metacognition, which is not discussed in this chapter, is the ability to monitor and adjust one's cognitive processes.

   d. This term was not discussed in the chapter.

9. **a.** is the answer. Resilience is a dynamic, not a stable, trait. (p. 377)

10. **b.** is the answer. (pp. 377–378)

11. **a.** is the answer. (p. 396)

    b. Withdrawn-rejected children are often the victims of bullies, but rarely are bullies themselves.

    c. & d. There are no such categories.

12. **c.** is the answer. (p. 395)

    d. In fact, children rarely intervene, unless a best friend is involved.

13. **d.** is the answer. (p. 394)

14. **d.** is the answer. (p. 373)

15. **a.** is the answer. (p. 373)

True or False Items

1. F In fact, just the opposite is true. (p. 375)

2. F In fact, just the opposite is true. (p. 393)

3. T (p. 388)

4. T (p. 396)

5. F A given child is not resilient in all situations. (p. 377)

6. T (p. 388)

7. T (p. 395)

8. F Just the opposite is true: They tend to misinterpret other people's words and behavior. (p. 395)

9. F Because of the coping strategies that many school-age children develop, they are better able than younger children to cope with stress. (p. 378)

10. T (p. 377)

11. F Friendship circles become narrower because friendships become more selective and exclusive. (p. 394)

PROGRESS TEST 2

Multiple-Choice Questions

1. **c.** is the answer. (p. 395)

   a. These are usually bullies.

   b. & d. These are not subcategories of rejected children.

2. **b.** is the answer. (pp. 380–381)

   a. Shared influences are those that occur because children are raised by the same parents in the same home, although children raised in the same home do not necessarily share the same home environment.

   c. & d. There are no such influences.

3. **d.** is the answer. (p. 387)

4. **d.** is the answer. (p. 384)

5. **b.** is the answer. (p. 375)

   a. This tends to promote, rather than reduce, self-esteem.

   c. Only 10 percent of schoolchildren experience this.

   d. This issue becomes more important during adolescence.

6. **a.** is the answer. (p. 374)

7. **d.** is the answer. (p. 394)

   a., b., & c. In fact, just the opposite is true of friendship during the school years.

8. **d.** is the answer. (p. 396)

9. **a.** is the answer. (p. 397)

10. **c.** is the answer. (p. 388)

11. **b.** is the answer. (pp. 378–379)

12. **b.** is the answer. (p. 374)

13. **d.** is the answer. (pp. 399, 400)

14. **c.** is the answer. (p. 373)

15. **b.** is the answer. (pp. 376–377)

   c. & d. The text did not discuss how stress influences friendship or peer acceptance.

Matching Items

1. i (p. 395)
2. c (p. 384)
3. f (p. 374)
4. a (p. 396)
5. j (p. 384)
6. e (p. 395)
7. h (p. 395)
8. d (p. 395)
9. k (p. 375)
10. b (p. 386)
11. g (p. 385)

KEY TERMS

1. According to Erikson, the crisis of middle childhood is **industry vs. inferiority,** in which children try to master many skills and develop views of themselves as either competent and industrious or incompetent and inferior. (p. 373)

2. In Freud's theory, middle childhood is a period of **latency,** during which emotional drives are quieter and unconscious sexual conflicts are submerged. (p. 373)

3. **Social comparison** is the tendency to assess one's abilities, achievements, social status, and other attributes by measuring them against those of others, especially those of one's peers. (p. 374)

4. **Effortful control** is the ability to regulate one's impulses and emotions through effort, not simply through natural inclination. (p. 375)

5. **Resilience** is the capacity to adapt positively despite adversity and to overcome serious stress. (p. 377)

6. **Family structure** refers to the legal and genetic relationships among relatives in the same household. (p. 382)

7. **Family function** refers to the ways families work to foster the development of children by meeting their basic material needs, encouraging them to learn, helping them to develop self-respect, nurturing friendships, and providing harmony and stability. (p. 382)

8. A **nuclear family** consists of two parents and their mutual biological offspring under age 18. (p. 384)

9. A **single-parent family** consists of one parent and his or her biological children under age 18. (p. 385)

10. An **extended family** consists of three or more generations of biologically related individuals living in one household. (p. 385)

11. A **polygamous family** consists of one man with several wives, each bearing his children. (p. 385)

12. A **blended family** consists of two parents, at least one with biological children from a previous union, and any children the adults have together. (p. 386)

13. The **culture of children** refers to the specific habits, styles, and values that reflect the rules and rituals of children. (p. 392)

14. The peer group shuns **aggressive-rejected** children because they are overly confrontational. (p. 395)

15. **Withdrawn-rejected** children are shunned by the peer group because of their timid, withdrawn, and anxious behavior. (p. 395)

16. **Social cognition** is the ability to understand social interactions. (p. 395)

17. **Bullying** is the repeated, systematic effort to inflict harm through physical, verbal, or social attacks on a weaker person. (p. 395)

18. A **bully-victim** is a bully who has also been a victim of bullying; also called provocative victim. (p. 396)

19. **Preconventional moral reasoning** is Kohlberg's first level of moral reasoning, emphasizing rewards and punishments. (p. 399)

20. **Conventional moral reasoning** is Kohlberg's second level of moral reasoning, emphasizing social rules. (p. 399)

21. **Postconventional moral reasoning** is Kohlberg's third level of moral reasoning, emphasizing moral principles. (p. 399)

14

Adolescence: Biosocial Development

Chapter Overview

Between the ages of 11 and 18, young people cross the great divide between childhood and adulthood. This crossing encompasses all three domains of development—biosocial, cognitive, and psychosocial. Chapter 14 focuses on the dramatic changes that occur in the biosocial domain, beginning with puberty and the growth spurt. The biosocial metamorphosis of the adolescent is discussed in detail, with emphasis on factors that affect the age of puberty, sexual maturation, and changes in body rhythms.

Although adolescence is, in many ways, a healthy time of life, the text also addresses two health hazards that too often affect adolescence: sex too early and the use of alcohol, tobacco, and other drugs.

NOTE: Answer guidelines for all Chapter 14 questions begin on page 200.

Chapter Review

When you have finished reading the chapter, work through the material that follows to review it. Complete the sentences and answer the questions. In some cases, Study Tips explain how best to learn a difficult concept, while Think About It and Applications help you to know how well you understand the material. As you proceed, evaluate your performance for each section by consulting the answers beginning on page 200. Do not continue with the next section until you understand each answer. If you need to, review or reread the appropriate section in the textbook before continuing.

Puberty Begins (pp. 407–416)

1. The period of rapid physical growth and sexual maturation that ends childhood and brings the young person to adult size, shape, and sexual potential is called _____ . The physical changes of puberty typically are complete _____ (how long?) after puberty begins. Although puberty begins at various ages, the _____ is almost always the same.

2. The average girl experiences her first menstrual period, called _____ , at age

_____ .

3. The average boy experiences his first ejaculation of seminal fluid, called _____ , at

age _____ .

4. Puberty begins when biochemical signals from the _____ trigger hormone production in the _____

_____ , which in turn triggers increased hormone production by the

_____ _____ . This route is called the _____ _____ .

5. Another route, called the _____

_____ , affects the body's entire shape and functioning. The hormone

_____ causes the gonads, the

_____ in males and the

_____ in females, to dramatically increase their production of sex hormones, especially _____ in girls and

_____ in boys.

6. The increase in the hormone _____ is dramatic in boys and slight in girls, whereas the increase in the hormone _____ is marked in girls and slight in boys. Emotional extremes and sexual urges _____ (usually do/do not usually) increase during

adolescence. This is due in part to the increasingly high levels of hormones such as

_____ and _____ .

7. During puberty, hormones are quite _____ (consistent from child to child/erratic). Hormones induce adolescents to seek _____ activity and momentary _____ .

8. The reverse is also true: Thoughts and emotions _____ hormonal changes. Thus, there is a _____ _____ between hormones and _____ emotions.

9. Normal children begin to notice pubertal changes between the ages of _____ and _____ . Two-thirds of the variation in the age of puberty is caused by _____ . This is demonstrated by the fact that _____ _____ reach puberty at similar ages. Girls are about _____ (how many?) years ahead of boys in height.

10. The amount of _____ _____ affects the onset of puberty. Nations with the highest rates of childhood obesity also have the _____ (earliest/latest) ages of puberty. This is particularly true for _____ (boys/girls).

11. One hormone that has been implicated in the onset of puberty is _____ , which affects appetite.

12. For both sexes, fat is limited by chronic _____ , which therefore delays puberty by several years.

13. The _____ _____ refers to the long-term upward or downward direction of a statistical measurement. An example is the earlier growth of children over the last two centuries as _____ and _____ _____ have improved. This trend _____ (continues/seems to have stopped) in developed nations.

14. Another influence on the age of puberty is _____ .

15. Research from many nations suggests that family stress may _____ (accelerate/delay) the onset of puberty.

16. Stress may cause production of the hormones that cause _____ . Support for this hypothesis comes from a study showing that early puberty was associated with _____ and _____ .

17. An evolutionary explanation of the relationship between stress and puberty is that ancestral females growing up in stressful environments may have increased their _____ _____ by accelerating physical maturation.

18. For girls, _____ (early/late) maturation may be especially troublesome.

Describe several common problems and developmental hazards experienced by early-maturing girls.

19. For boys, _____ (early/late/both early and late) maturation may be difficult. _____ (Early/Late) maturing boys are more _____ , _____-_____ , and alcohol-abusing. _____ (Early/Late) maturing boys tend to be more anxious, depressed, and afraid of sex.

STUDY TIP: To consolidate your understanding of the major physical changes that accompany puberty, list, in order, the major physical changes of puberty.

20. Girls _____

_____

Boys: _____

_____

APPLICATIONS:

21. I am the hormone that causes the gonads to dramatically increase their production of sex hormones. I am _____ .

22. Which of the following students is likely to be the most popular in a sixth-grade class?
  a. Vicki, the most sexually mature girl in the class
  b. Sandra, the tallest girl in the class
  c. Brad, who is at the top of the class scholastically
  d. Dan, the tallest boy in the class

23. Regarding the effects of early and late maturation on boys and girls, which of the following is NOT true?
  a. Late-maturing boys are more likely to rebel against laws.
  b. Early puberty that leads to romantic relationships often leads to stress and depression among both girls and boys.
  c. Early-maturing girls may be drawn into involvement with older boys.
  d. Late puberty is often difficult for boys.

24. Monica is 16 years old. Her parents are divorced and she lives with her mother in a city. It is most likely that she will experience puberty _____ than other teens, perhaps as a result of _____ .
  a. earlier; greater stress
  b. later; greater stress
  c. earlier; poor nutrition
  d. later; poor nutrition

25. I am the sex hormone that is secreted in greater amounts by females than males. I am

_____ .

26. Of the following teenagers, those most likely to be distressed about their physical development are
  a. late-maturing girls.
  b. early-maturing girls.
  c. early-maturing boys.
  d. girls or boys who masturbate.

Nutrition (pp. 416–420)

27. Most teenagers _____ (do/do not) consume the recommended daily dose of iron, calcium, and zinc. There is a direct link between deficient diets and the availability of

_____ _____ in schools.

28. Another reason for dietary deficiencies is concern about _____ _____ , defined as a person's idea of how

_____ .

29. In an attempt to improve body image, many girls _____ _____ or take _____ _____ , and many boys take _____ .

30. Overweight teenagers are more common in _____ (what country?) than in any other nation. Obesity increases the risk of

_____ .

31. The disorder characterized by self-starvation is _____ _____ . This disorder is suspected when a person's _____ _____ _____ is _____ (what number?) or lower, or if the person loses more than _____ (what percent?) of body weight within a month or two.

32. Anorexia nervosa is diagnosed when four symptoms are present
  (a) _____
  (b) _____
  (c) _____
  (d) _____

33. Two precursors of anorexia are _____ and _____ .

34. A more common eating disorder is _____ _____ , which is diagnosed when three symptoms occur
  (a) _____
  (b) _____
  (c) _____

35. One family practice that seems to reduce the risk of adolescent eating disorders is

_____ .

THINK ABOUT IT: To underscore the prevalence of nutritional deficiencies during adolescence, evaluate your own dietary consumption of iron, calcium, and zinc for a few days. How do your results compare with recommended minimum levels of consumption for these minerals?

_____

APPLICATION:

36. Thirteen-year-old Kristin is more likely to
    a. drink too much milk.
    b. eat more than five servings of fruit per day.
    c. choose expensive foods over inexpensive ones.
    d. be iron deficient.

The Transformations of Puberty (pp. 420–427)

37. A major _____ spurt occurs in late childhood and early adolescence, during which growth proceeds from the _____ (core/extremities) to the _____ (core/extremities). At the same time, children begin to _____ (gain/lose) weight at a relatively rapid rate.

38. The amount of weight gain an individual experiences depends on several factors, including _____ , _____ , _____ , and _____ .

39. During the growth spurt, a greater percentage of fat is retained by _____ (males/females).

40. About a year after the height and weight changes occur, a period of _____ increase occurs, causing the pudginess and clumsiness of an earlier age to disappear. In boys, this increase is particularly notable in the _____ .

41. Internal organs also grow during puberty. The _____ increase in size and capacity, the _____ doubles in size, heart rate _____ (increases/decreases), and blood volume _____ (increases/decreases). These changes increase the adolescent's physical _____ .

Explain why the physical demands placed on a teenager, as in athletic training, should not be the same as those for a young adult of similar height and weight.

42. During puberty, one organ system, the _____ system, decreases in size, making teenagers _____ (more/less) susceptible to respiratory ailments.

43. One secondary sex characteristic that is mistakenly considered a sign of manliness is _____ .

44. Changes in _____ _____ involve the sex organs that are directly involved in reproduction. By the end of puberty, reproduction _____ (is/is still not) possible.

45. Sexual features other than those associated with reproduction are referred to as _____ _____ .

Describe the major pubertal changes in the secondary sex characteristics of both sexes.

46. Although sex hormones trigger thoughts about sexual intimacy, sexual behavior among teens reflects _____ and _____ more than biology.

47. All creatures have a daily day–night cycle of biological activity called the _____ _____ . Our daily rhythms, called _____ rhythms, cause, for instance, changes in the level

of the chemical _____ , which
makes people more _____ .
Adolescents typically get too _____
(little/much) sleep. Among adolescents,
_____ (girls/boys) are particularly
likely to be sleep-deprived.

THINK ABOUT IT: At the beginning of puberty,
many young people want to know whether they will
be short or tall like one of their parents or closer in
height to their grandparents. The answer is that their
full adult height will probably fall somewhere in
between that of their parents. One frequently used
rule of thumb is to add the heights of both parents,
divide by two, then add 3 inches for a boy or sub-
tract 3 inches for a girl. The result is said to be correct within 2 inches about 95 percent of the time.
How well does this formula work in your case? _____

APPLICATIONS:

48. Calvin, the class braggart, boasts that because
his beard has begun to grow, he is more virile
than his male classmates. Jacob informs him that
   a. the tendency to grow facial and body hair has
   nothing to do with virility.
   b. beard growth is determined by heredity.
   c. girls also develop some facial hair and more
   noticeable hair on their arms and legs, so it is
   clearly not a sign of masculinity.
   d. all of these statements are true.

49. Eleven-year-old Linda, who has just begun to
experience the first signs of puberty, laments,
"When will the agony of puberty be over?" You
tell her that the major events of puberty typically
end about _____ after the first
visible signs appear.

Health Hazards (pp. 427–436)

50. Approximately _____ percent of
teenagers put their health in serious jeopardy.
Three major health hazards for teens are
_____
_____ .

51. The leading cause of death for people under age
40 is _____ . Young _____
(men/women) are particularly likely to die
violently.

Identify three reasons adolescents have more injuries
than any other age group.

(a) _____
(b) _____
(c) _____

52. A major developmental risk for sexually active
adolescent girls is _____ . If this
happens within a year or two of menarche, girls
are at increased risk of many complications,
including _____
_____ . If the baby of a teen
mother is born healthy, he or she
_____ (is/is not) likely to experience complications later on, including poor
_____ , inadequate
_____ , low _____ , and
_____ at their family, community,
and society.

53. Worldwide, sexually active teens have higher
rates of diseases caused by sexual contact, called
_____ _____
_____ , than any other age group.
One reason is that they do not have the natural
_____ _____ that fully
developed women have. Another reason is that
they are unlikely to seek _____ .

54. Any sexual activity between a juvenile and an
older person is considered _____
_____ _____ .

55. Sexual abuse is more common between the ages
of _____ and _____
than at any other time.

56. _____ (Girls/Boys) are particularly
vulnerable to child sexual abuse.

57. Drug use is _____ (up/down) since
1976, but the number of abused drugs has
_____ (increased/decreased).
Worldwide, _____ (girls/boys)
have higher rates of drug use than
_____ (girls/boys).

58. By impairing digestion, nutrition, and appetite, tobacco can limit the adolescent

_____ _____ .

59. Alcohol impairs _____ and _____ by damaging the brain's _____ and

_____ _____ .

60. Many adolescents fail to notice when they move past experimenting with drugs to harmful _____ and then _____ , defined as needing the drug.

61. The idea that each new generation forgets what the previous generation has learned is referred to as _____ _____ .

APPLICATIONS:

62. Concluding her talk on adolescent alcohol use and brain damage, Maya notes that
    a. studies have shown only that alcohol use is correlated with damage to the prefrontal cortex.
    b. thus far, studies have shown only that alcohol use is correlated with damage to the hippocampus.
    c. animal research studies demonstrate that alcohol use results in slower thinking.
    d. alcohol use causes brain abnormalities only in teens who are genetically vulnerable.

63. Fifteen-year-old Norbert has a drinking problem. If he is typical of adolescents with one problem, it is likely that
    a. he also has several other problems.
    b. the problem is isolated and does not adversely affect other areas of development.
    c. the consequences are temporary and not severe.
    d. their earlier development during childhood was also problematic.

64. Twenty-four-year-old Connie, who has a distorted view of sexuality, has gone from one abusive relationship with a man to another. It is likely that Connie
    a. has been abusing drugs all her life.
    b. was sexually abused as a child.
    c. will eventually become a normal, nurturing mother.
    d. had attention-deficit disorder as a child.

Progress Test 1

Multiple-Choice Questions

Circle your answers to the following questions and check them with the answers on page 202. If your answer is incorrect, read the explanation for why it is incorrect and then consult the appropriate pages of the text (in parentheses following the correct answer).

1. Which of the following most accurately describes the sequence of pubertal development in girls?
   a. breasts and pubic hair; growth spurt in which fat is deposited on hips and buttocks; first menstrual period; ovulation
   b. growth spurt; breasts and pubic hair; first menstrual period; ovulation
   c. first menstrual period; breasts and pubic hair; growth spurt; ovulation
   d. breasts and pubic hair; growth spurt; ovulation; first menstrual period

2. Although both sexes grow rapidly during adolescence, boys typically gain more than girls in their
   a. muscle strength.
   b. body fat.
   c. internal organ growth.
   d. lymphoid system.

3. For girls, the first readily observable sign of the onset of puberty is
   a. the onset of breast growth.
   b. the appearance of facial, body, and pubic hair.
   c. a change in the shape of the eyes.
   d. a lengthening of the torso.

4. More than any other group in the population, adolescent girls are likely to have
   a. asthma.
   b. acne.
   c. anemia.
   d. testosterone deficiency.

5. The HPA axis is the
   a. route followed by many hormones to regulate stress, growth, sleep, and appetite.
   b. pair of sex glands in humans.
   c. cascade of sex hormones in females and males.
   d. area of the brain that regulates the pituitary gland.

6. For males, the secondary sex characteristic that usually occurs last is
   a. breast enlargement.
   b. the appearance of facial hair.
   c. growth of the testes.
   d. the final growth of pubic hair.

7. For girls, the specific event that is taken to indicate fertility is _____ ; for boys, it is _____ .
   a. the growth of breast buds; voice deepening
   b. menarche; spermarche
   c. hip widening; the testosterone surge
   d. the growth spurt; pubic hair

8. The most significant hormonal changes of puberty include an increase of _____ in _____ and an increase of _____ in _____ .
   a. estrogen; boys; estradiol; girls
   b. estradiol; boys; testosterone; girls
   c. androgen; girls; estradiol; boys
   d. estradiol; girls; testosterone; boys

9. A child who is chronically malnourished will likely
   a. begin puberty at a younger-than-average age.
   b. begin puberty later than the normal age range.
   c. never experience menarche.
   d. never experience spermarche.

10. Dr. Ramirez suspects Jennifer may be suffering from anorexia nervosa because her BMI is
    a. lower than 18.
    b. lower than 25.
    c. higher than 25.
    d. higher than 30.

11. Today, adolescence tends to begin _____ and end _____ .
    a. later biologically; later sociologically
    b. earlier biologically; later sociologically
    c. later sociologically; earlier biologically
    d. earlier sociologically; later biologically

12. Early physical growth and sexual maturation
    a. tend to be equally difficult for girls and boys.
    b. tend to be more difficult for boys than for girls.
    c. tend to be more difficult for girls than for boys.
    d. are easier for both girls and boys than late maturation.

13. Pubertal changes in growth and maturation typically are complete how long after puberty begins?
    a. one to two years
    b. two to three years
    c. four years
    d. The variation is too great to generalize.

14. The hypothalamus–pituitary–adrenal axis triggers
    a. puberty.
    b. the growth spurt.
    c. the development of sexual characteristics.
    d. all of these events.

15. One reason adolescents like intensity, excitement, and risk taking is that
    a. the limbic system matures faster than the prefrontal cortex.
    b. the prefrontal cortex matures faster than the limbic system.
    c. brain maturation is synchronous.
    d. puberty is occurring at a younger age today than in the past.

True or False Items

Write T (*true*) or F (*false*) on the line in front of each statement.

_____ 1. The secular trend is as strong today as ever.
_____ 2. During puberty, hormonal bursts lead to quick emotional extremes.
_____ 3. The first indicator of reproductive potential in males is menarche.
_____ 4. Lung capacity, heart size, and total volume of blood increase significantly during adolescence.
_____ 5. Puberty generally begins sometime between ages 8 and 14.
_____ 6. Girls are about two years ahead of boys in height as well as sexually and hormonally.
_____ 7. Each culture and age cohort has its own patterns of drug use and abuse during adolescence.
_____ 8. Only adolescent girls suffer from anemia.
_____ 9. Early-maturing girls tend to have lower self-esteem.
_____ 10. Both the sequence and timing of pubertal events vary greatly from one young person to another.

Progress Test 2

Progress Test 2 should be completed during a final chapter review. Answer the following questions after you thoroughly understand the correct answers for the Chapter Review and Progress Test 1.

Multiple-Choice Questions

1. Which of the following is the correct sequence of pubertal events in boys?
   a. growth spurt, pubic hair, facial hair, first ejaculation, pubic hair, deepening of voice
   b. pubic hair, first ejaculation, growth spurt, deepening of voice, facial hair, pubic hair
   c. deepening of voice, pubic hair, growth spurt, facial hair, first ejaculation, pubic hair
   d. pubic hair, growth spurt, facial hair, deepening of voice, pubic hair, first ejaculation

2. Which of the following statements about adolescent physical development is NOT true?
   a. Hands and feet generally lengthen before arms and legs.
   b. Facial features usually grow before the head itself reaches adult size and shape.
   c. Oil, sweat, and odor glands become more active.
   d. The lymphoid system increases slightly in size, and the heart increases by nearly half.

3. In puberty, a hormone that increases markedly in girls (and only somewhat in boys) is
   a. estradiol.   c. androgen.
   b. testosterone.   d. menarche.

4. Nutritional deficiencies in adolescence are frequently the result of
   a. eating red meat.
   b. poor eating habits.
   c. menstruation.
   d. excessive exercise.

5. In females, puberty is typically marked by a(n)
   a. significant widening of the shoulders.
   b. significant widening of the hips.
   c. enlargement of the torso and upper chest.
   d. decrease in the size of the eyes and nose.

6. Nonreproductive sexual characteristics, such as the deepening of the voice and the development of breasts, are called
   a. gender-typed traits.
   b. primary sex characteristics.
   c. secondary sex characteristics.
   d. pubertal prototypes.

7. Puberty is initiated when hormones are released from the _____ , then from the _____ gland, and then from the adrenal glands and the
   _____ .
   a. hypothalamus; pituitary; gonads
   b. pituitary; gonads; hypothalamus
   c. gonads; pituitary; hypothalamus
   d. pituitary; hypothalamus; gonads

8. If a girl under age 15 becomes pregnant, she is at greater risk for:
   a. a low-birthweight baby.
   b. high blood pressure.
   c. stillbirth.
   d. all of these conditions.

9. Alcohol impairs memory and self-control by damaging the
   a. hippocampus and prefrontal cortex.
   b. pituitary gland.
   c. hypothalamus.
   d. gonads.

10. The HPG axis is the
    a. route followed by many hormones to affect the body's shape and functioning.
    b. pair of sex glands in humans.
    c. cascade of sex hormones in females and males.
    d. area of the brain that regulates the pituitary gland.

11. The number of substantiated victims of sexual abuse is greatest among children ages:
    a. 12 to 15.   c. 16 to 18.
    b. 4 to 7.   d. 8 to 11.

12. An example of the secular trend is the
    a. complex link between pubertal hormones and emotions.
    b. effect of chronic stress on pubertal hormones.
    c. earlier growth of children due to improved nutrition and medical care.
    d. effect of chronic malnutrition on the onset of puberty.

13. Puberty is *most accurately* defined as the period
    a. of rapid physical growth that occurs during adolescence.
    b. during which sexual maturation is attained.
    c. of rapid physical growth and sexual maturation that ends childhood.
    d. during which adolescents establish identities separate from their parents.

14. Which of the following does NOT typically occur during puberty?
    a. The lungs increase in size and capacity.
    b. The heart's size and rate of beating increase.
    c. Blood volume increases.
    d. The lymphoid system decreases in size.

15. Teenagers' susceptibility to respiratory ailments typically _____ during adolescence, due to a(n) _____ in the size of the lymphoid system.
    a. increases; increase
    b. increases; decrease
    c. decreases; increase
    d. decreases; decrease

Matching Items

Match each term or concept with its corresponding description or definition.

Terms or Concepts

_____ 1. puberty
_____ 2. gonadotropin-releasing hormone (GnRH)
_____ 3. testosterone
_____ 4. estradiol
_____ 5. growth spurt
_____ 6. primary sex characteristics
_____ 7. menarche
_____ 8. spermarche
_____ 9. secondary sex characteristics
_____ 10. body image
_____ 11. anorexia nervosa
_____ 12. bulimia nervosa

Descriptions or Definitions

a. onset of menstruation
b. period of rapid physical growth and sexual maturation that ends childhood
c. an affliction characterized by self-starvation
d. hormone that causes the gonads to enlarge and increase their production of sex hormones
e. hormone that increases dramatically in girls during puberty
f. first sign is increased bone length
g. attitude toward one's physical appearance
h. an affliction characterized by binge-purge eating
i. the sex organs involved in reproduction
j. first ejaculation containing sperm
k. hormone that increases dramatically in boys during puberty
l. physical characteristics not involved in reproduction

Key Terms

Writing Definitions

Using your own words, write a brief definition or explanation of each of the following terms on a separate piece of paper.

1. puberty
2. menarche
3. spermarche
4. hormone
5. pituitary
6. adrenal glands
7. HPA axis
8. gonads
9. HPG axis
10. estradiol
11. testosterone
12. leptin
13. secular trend
14. body image
15. anorexia nervosa
16. bulimia nervosa
17. growth spurt
18. primary sex characteristics
19. secondary sex characteristics
20. sexually transmitted infections (STIs)
21. child sexual abuse
22. generational forgetting

Cross-Check

After you have written the definitions of the key terms in this chapter, you should complete the crossword puzzle to ensure that you can reverse the process—recognize the term, given the definition.

ACROSS

1. Glands near the kidneys that are stimulated by the pituitary at the beginning of puberty.
7. The first ejaculation of seminal fluid containing sperm.
12. The first menstrual period.
15. The ovaries in girls and the testes or testicles in boys.
16. Gland that stimulates the adrenal glands and the sex glands in response to a signal from the hypothalamus.
17. Event, which begins with an increase in bone length and includes rapid weight gain and organ growth, that is one of the many observable signs of puberty.

DOWN

1. The period of biological, cognitive, and psychosocial transition from childhood to adulthood.
2. Organ system, which includes the tonsils and adenoids, that decreases in size at adolescence.
3. Area of the brain that sends the hormonal signal that triggers the biological events of puberty.
4. A chemical messenger that travels through the bloodstream to influence body tissues.
5. The _____ axis is the route followed by many hormones to trigger puberty.
6. Widely abused drug that loosens inhibitions and impairs judgment.
8. Body characteristics that are directly involved in reproduction.
9. Body characteristics that are not directly involved in reproduction but that signify sexual development.
10. Main sex hormone in males.
11. Drug that decreases food consumption, the absorption of nutrients, and fertility.
13. Main sex hormone in females.
14. Period of rapid physical growth and sexual maturation that ends childhood and brings the young person to adult size.

Answers

CHAPTER REVIEW

1. puberty; four years; sequence
2. menarche; 12 years, 8 months
3. spermarche; (just under) 13
4. hypothalamus; pituitary gland; adrenal glands; HPA axis
5. HPG axis; GnRH (gonadotropin-releasing hormone); testes; ovaries; estradiol; testosterone
6. testosterone; estradiol; usually do; estradiol; testosterone
7. erratic; sexual; pleasure
8. cause; reciprocal interaction
9. 8; 14; genes; monozygotic twins; two
10. body fat; earliest; girls
11. leptin
12. malnutrition
13. secular trend; nutrition; medical care; seems to have stopped
14. stress
15. accelerate
16. puberty; conflicted relationships within the family; an unrelated man living in the home
17. reproductive success
18. early

Early-maturing girls may be teased about their developing breasts. They tend to have older boyfriends, which may lead to drug and alcohol use; they have lower self-esteem, more depression, and poorer body image than their classmates do; they exercise less; they engage in sexual activity, which may result in teenage parenthood; and they have a greater risk of violent victimization.

19. both early and late; Early; aggressive; law-breaking; Late
20. Girls: onset of breast growth, initial pubic hair, peak growth spurt, widening of the hips, first menstrual period, completion of pubic-hair growth, and final breast development

    Boys: growth of the testes, initial pubic hair, growth of the penis, first ejaculation of seminal fluid, facial hair, peak growth spurt, voice deepening, and completion of pubic-hair growth
21. GnRH
22. d. is the answer. Early-maturing boys benefit more than early-maturing girls or late-maturing boys.
23. a. is the answer. Late-maturing boys tend to be more anxious, depressed, and afraid of sex.
24. a. is the answer. Surprisingly, stress often results in an earlier onset of puberty.
25. estradiol
26. b. is the answer. Early-maturing girls tend to have lower self-esteem, more depression, and poorer body image than late-maturing girls.
27. do not; vending machines
28. body image; his or her body looks
29. eat erratically; diet pills; steroids
30. the United States; diabetes, heart disease, strokes, and premature death
31. anorexia nervosa; body mass index; 18; 10
32. (a) refusal to maintain a body weight that is at least 85 percent of normal for age and height; (b) intense fear of weight gain; (c) disturbed body perception and denial of the problem; (d) absence of menstruation
33. nature (or genes); nurture (or a cultural obsession with thinness)
34. bulimia nervosa; (a) bingeing and purging at least once a week for three months; (b) uncontrollable urges to overeat; (c) distorted perception of body size
35. eating together during childhood
36. d. is the answer. Many teenage girls, and some boys, suffer from anemia (iron deficiency).
37. growth; extremities; core; gain

38. gender; heredity; diet; exercise
39. females
40. muscle; arms
41. lungs; heart; decreases; increases; endurance

The fact that the more visible spurts of weight and height precede the less visible ones of the muscles and organs means that athletic training and weight lifting should match the young person's size of a year earlier.

42. lymphoid; less
43. facial and chest hair
44. primary sex characteristics; is
45. secondary sex characteristics

Males grow taller than females and become wider at the shoulders than at the hips. Females take on more fat all over and become wider at the hips, and their breasts begin to develop. About 65 percent of boys experience some temporary breast enlargement. As the lungs and larynx grow, the adolescent's voice (especially in boys) becomes lower. Head and body hair become coarser and darker in both sexes.

46. culture; cohort
47. circadian rhythm; diurnal; melatonin; sleepy; little; girls
48. a. is the answer.
49. 4 years
50. 20; injury and death, early sexual activity, and drug abuse
51. accidents; men
    (a) Rapid body changes in size, shape, and hormones trigger dangerous, impulsive reactions.
    (b) Immaturity of the cortex and the activity of the limbic system make adolescents overrate pleasure and disregard danger.
    (c) Adolescents who are alienated from adults are at highest risk.
52. pregnancy; spontaneous abortion, high blood pressure, stillbirth, cesarean section, and a low-birthweight baby; is; health; education; intelligence; anger
53. sexually transmitted infections; biological defenses; treatment
54. child sexual abuse
55. 12; 15
56. Girls
57. down; increased; boys; girls
58. growth rate
59. memory; self-control; hippocampus; prefrontal cortex

60. abuse; addiction

61. generational forgetting

62. **c.** is the answer.

63. **a.** is the answer. Each health risk that an adolescent takes makes it more likely that he or she will take others.

64. **b.** is the answer. Young people who are sexually exploited tend to fear sexual relationships and to devalue themselves lifelong.

PROGRESS TEST 1

Multiple-Choice Questions

1. **a.** is the answer. (p. 407)

2. **a.** is the answer. (p. 421)

    b. Girls gain more body fat than boys do.

    c. & d. The text does not indicate that these are different for boys and girls.

3. **a.** is the answer. (p. 407)

4. **c.** is the answer. This is because each menstrual period depletes some iron from the body. (p. 417)

5. **a.** is the answer. (p. 408)

    b. This describes the gonads.

    c. These include estradiol and testosterone.

    d. This is the hypothalamus.

6. **d.** is the answer. (p. 407)

7. **b.** is the answer. (p. 407)

8. **d.** is the answer. (p. 409)

9. **b.** is the answer.

10. **a.** is the answer. (p. 419)

    b. This is a healthy BMI.

    c. & d. These BMIs are associated with being overweight.

11. **b.** is the answer. (p. 413)

12. **c.** is the answer. (p. 415)

13. **c.** is the answer. (p. 407)

14. **d.** is the answer. (p. 409)

15. **a.** is the answer. (p. 428)

    c. Brain maturation is asynchronous.

    d. This may be true, but it doesn't explain why adolescents have always liked intensity and excitement.

True or False Items

1. F (p. 413)

2. T (p. 410)

3. F The first indicator of reproductive potential in males is ejaculation of seminal fluid containing sperm (spermarche). Menarche (the first menstrual period) is the first indication of reproductive potential in females. (p. 407)

4. T (p. 421)

5. T (p. 407)

6. F Hormonally and sexually, girls are ahead by only a few months. (pp. 411–412)

7. T (p. 432–433)

8. F Boys also suffer from anemia, especially if they engage in physical labor or competitive sports. (p. 417)

9. T (p. 415)

10. F Although there is great variation in the timing of pubertal events, the sequence is very similar for all young people. (p. 407)

PROGRESS TEST 2

Multiple-Choice Questions

1. **b.** is the answer. (p. 407)

2. **d.** is the answer. During adolescence, the lymphoid system *decreases* in size and the heart *doubles* in size. (pp. 421, 422)

3. **a.** is the answer. (p. 409)

    b. Testosterone increases markedly in boys.

    c. Testosterone is the best known of the androgens (the general category of male hormones).

    d. Menarche is the first menstrual period.

4. **b.** is the answer. (p. 416)

5. **b.** is the answer. (pp. 407, 422)

    a. The shoulders of males tend to widen during puberty.

    c. The torso typically lengthens during puberty.

    d. The eyes and nose *increase* in size during puberty.

6. **c.** is the answer. (p. 422)

    a. Although not a term used in the textbook, a gender-typed trait is one that is typical of one sex but not of the other.

    b. Primary sex characteristics are those involving the reproductive organs.

    d. This is not a term used by developmental psychologists.

7. **a.** is the answer. (p. 408)

8. **d.** is the answer. (pp. 428–429)

9. **a.** is the answer. (p. 434)

10. **a.** is the answer. (p. 409)

  b. The gonads are the sex glands.

  c. & d. Hormones and brain areas are involved in the HPG axis, which describes the route taken by the hormones.

11. **a.** is the answer. (p. 431)

12. **c.** is the answer. (p. 413)

13. **c.** is the answer. (p. 407)

14. **b.** is the answer. Although the size of the heart increases during puberty, heart rate *decreases*. (p. 421)

15. **d.** is the answer. (p. 422)

Matching Items

1. b (p. 407)	5. f (p. 421)	9. l (p. 419)
2. d (p. 409)	6. i (p. 422)	10. g (p. 417)
3. k (p. 418)	7. a (p. 407)	11. c (p. 409)
4. e (p. 409)	8. j (p. 407)	12. h (p. 422)

KEY TERMS

1. **Puberty** is the period of rapid physical growth and sexual maturation that ends childhood and brings the young person to adult size, shape, and sexual potential. (p. 407)

2. **Menarche,** which refers to the first menstrual period, signals that the adolescent girl has begun ovulation. (p. 407)

3. **Spermarche,** which refers to the first ejaculation of sperm, signals sperm production in adolescent boys. (p. 407)

4. A **hormone** is an organic chemical substance produced by one body tissue that travels via the bloodstream to another to affect some physiological function. (p. 408)

5. The **pituitary** is a gland in the brain that responds to a biochemical signal from the hypothalamus by producing hormones that regulate growth and control other glands. (p. 408)

6. The **adrenal glands** are two glands, located above the kidneys, that secrete epinephrine and norepinephrine, hormones that prepare the body to deal with stress. (p. 408)

7. The **HPA axis** (hypothalamus–pituitary–adrenal) is the route followed by many hormones to trigger puberty and to regulate stress, growth, and other bodily changes. (p. 408)

8. The **gonads** are the paired sex glands in humans—the ovaries in females and the testes, or testicles, in males. (p. 409)

9. The **HPG axis** (hypothalamus–pituitary–gonads) is the route followed by many hormones to affect the body's shape and functioning. (p. 409)

10. **Estradiol** is a sex hormone that is secreted in much greater amounts by females than by males; considered the chief estrogen. (p. 409)

11. **Testosterone** is a sex hormone that is secreted much more by males than by females; considered the best-known androgen. (p. 409)

12. **Leptin** is a hormone that affects appetite and is believed to affect the onset of puberty. (p. 413)

13. The **secular trend** is the long-term upward or downward direction of a certain set of statistical measurements. For example, it is the tendency toward earlier and larger growth that has occurred among adolescents over the past two centuries. (p. 413)

14. **Body image** is a person's concept of his or her body's appearance. (p. 417)

15. **Anorexia nervosa** is an eating disorder characterized by self-starvation. (p. 418)

16. **Bulimia nervosa** is an eating disorder characterized by binge eating and purging. (p. 419)

17. The **growth spurt,** which is the relatively sudden and rapid physical growth of every part of the body, is one of the many observable signs of puberty. (p. 421)

18. During puberty, changes in the **primary sex characteristics** involve those sex organs that are directly involved in reproduction. (p. 422)

19. During puberty, changes in the **secondary sex characteristics** involve parts of the body that are not directly involved in reproduction but that signify sexual development. (p. 422)

20. **Sexually transmitted infections (STIs),** such as syphilis, gonorrhea, genital herpes, chlamydia, and AIDS, are those that are spread by sexual contact. (p. 429)

21. **Child sexual abuse** is any erotic activity that arouses an adult and excites, shames, or confuses a child—even if the abuse does not involve physical contact. (p. 430)

22. **Generational forgetting** is the idea that each generation forgets what earlier generations had already learned. (p. 435)

Cross-Check

ACROSS

1. adrenal
7. spermarche
12. menarche
15. gonads
16. pituitary
17. growth spurt

DOWN

1. adolescence
2. lymphoid
3. hypothalamus
4. hormone
5. HPA
6. alcohol
8. primary
9. secondary
10. testosterone
11. tobacco
13. estradiol
14. puberty

15

Adolescence: Cognitive Development

Chapter Overview

Chapter 15 describes the cognitive advances and limitations of adolescence. With the attainment of formal operational thought, the developing person becomes able to think in an adult way, that is, to be logical, to think in terms of possibilities, and to reason scientifically and abstractly. Neurological development is the basis of these new developments. Although brain areas dedicated to emotional arousal mature before those dedicated to emotional regulation, ongoing myelination enables faster and deeper thinking.

Even those who reach the stage of formal operational thought spend much of their time thinking at less advanced levels. The discussion of adolescent egocentrism supports this generalization in showing that adolescents have difficulty thinking rationally about themselves and their immediate experiences. Adolescent egocentrism makes them see themselves as psychologically unique and more socially significant than they really are.

The next section of the chapter explores teaching and learning in middle school and high school. As adolescents enter secondary school, their grades often suffer and their level of participation decreases. The rigid behavioral demands and intensified competition of most secondary schools do not, unfortunately, provide a supportive learning environment for adolescents.

NOTE: Answer guidelines for all Chapter 15 questions begin on page 213.

Chapter Review

When you have finished reading the chapter, work through the material that follows to review it. Complete the sentences and answer the questions. In some cases, Study Tips explain how best to learn a difficult concept, while Think About It and Applica-

tions help you to know how well you understand the material. As you proceed, evaluate your performance for each section by consulting the answers beginning on page 213. Do not continue with the next section until you understand each answer. If you need to, review or reread the appropriate section in the textbook before continuing.

Neurological Development (pp. 439–442)

1. During adolescence, different parts of the brain grow at _____ (the same/different) rate(s).

2. Many of the hallmarks of adolescent thinking and behavior originate with maturation of the _____ . The brain's limbic system, which controls _____ and _____ _____ , matures _____ (before/after) the prefrontal cortex.

3. Recent discoveries about the adolescent brain reveal that the _____ lobes (the prefrontal cortex) are the last part of the brain to mature. Their functioning depends less on hormones and more on _____ and _____ .

4. Although adolescents are capable of _____ thinking, they do not always do so. Myelination and _____ proceed from inside to the cortex and from back to front.

5. The brain's _____ predominates in quick _____ reactions, whereas the prefrontal cortex coordinates _____ functions, including the capacity for _____ _____ and arousal.

6. One reason adolescents like intensity and excitement is that the maturing _____ system is attuned to these strong sensations, as yet unchecked by the _____ .

State two reasons that the consequences of impulsive adolescent behavior may be especially severe today.

7. Throughout adolescence, reactions become faster because of increased _____ . Also, additional synaptic _____ occurs, while the _____ system becomes active.

8. The brain becomes fully mature at about age _____ .

Adolescent Thinking (pp. 443–454)

9. The characteristic of adolescent thinking that leads young people to think only about themselves is called _____ _____ .

10. The adolescent's belief that he or she is unique is called the _____ _____ . An adolescent's tendency to feel that he or she is somehow immune to the consequences of dangerous or illegal behavior is expressed in the _____ _____ . Recent research studies have found that many adolescents do not feel _____ .

11. Adolescents, who believe that they are under constant scrutiny from nearly everyone, create for themselves an _____ _____ .

12. Piaget's term for the fourth stage of cognitive development is _____ _____ thought. Adolescent thinking

_____ (is/is not) limited by concrete experiences.

13. Piaget devised a number of famous tasks to demonstrate that formal operational adolescents imagine all possible _____ of a problem's solution in order to draw the appropriate _____ .

Briefly describe how children reason differently about the "balance beam" problem at ages 7, 10, and 13.

14. The kind of thinking in which adolescents consider unproven possibilities that are logical but not necessarily real is called _____ thought.

15. Adolescents become more capable of _____ reasoning—that is, they can begin with an abstract idea or _____ and then use _____ to draw specific _____ . This type of reasoning is a hallmark of formal operational thought.

16. This kind of reasoning contrasts with reasoning that progresses from specifics to reach a general conclusion, called _____ reasoning.

17. Most developmentalists _____ (agree/disagree) with Piaget that adolescent thought can be qualitatively different from children's thought. They disagree about whether the change in thinking is _____ (gradual/sudden), whether it results from _____ (sociocultural) or _____ (epigenetic) changes, and whether it occurs in every _____ , as Piaget thought.

18. The fact that adolescents can use

_____-_____ reasoning does not necessarily mean that they do use it.

19. In addition to advances in the formal, logical, _____-_____ thinking described by Piaget, adolescents advance in their _____ cognition. Researchers believe that the adult brain has two distinct pathways, called _____-_____ networks.

20. The first mode of thinking, which begins with a prior _____ , is called _____ . The second mode, Piaget's formal hypothetical-deductive reasoning, is called _____ thought.

21. Although intuitive thinking generally is _____ and _____ , it is also often _____ (right/wrong).

22. The belief that if time, effort, or money has already been invested in something, then more time, effort, or money should be invested is called the _____ _____

_____ . In another common fallacy, decisions are made on an _____ basis despite statistical evidence to the contrary; this is called _____

_____ _____ .

23. With age, thinking becomes more

_____ .

Problem: Returning to campus following spring break, you hear an odd noise coming from under the hood of your car. You are running late, and the noise seems to be getting louder.

24.

Type of Thinking	Examples
Egocentrism	"Why do these catastrophes always happen to me and not to someone else?" (personal fable)
Hypothetical-Deductive	
Intuitive Thought	
Analytic Thought	

APPLICATIONS:

25. An experimenter hides a ball in her hand and says, "The ball in my hand is either red or it is not red." Most preadolescent children say
   a. the statement is true.
   b. the statement is false.
   c. they cannot tell if the statement is true or false.
   d. they do not understand what the experimenter means.

26. Fourteen-year-old Monica is very idealistic and often develops crushes on people she doesn't even know. This reflects her newly developed cognitive ability to
   a. deal simultaneously with two sides of an issue.
   b. take another person's viewpoint.
   c. imagine possible worlds and people.
   d. see herself as others see her.

27. Which of the following is the best example of the sunk cost fallacy?
   a. Adriana imagines that she is destined for a life of fame and fortune.
   b. Ben makes up stories about his experiences to impress his friends.
   c. Kalil continues to work on his old clunker of a car after hours of unsuccessful efforts to get it to run.
   d. Julio believes that every girl he meets is attracted to him.

28. Which of the following is the BEST example of the adolescent's ability to think hypothetically?
    a. Twelve-year-old Stanley feels that people are always watching him.
    b. Fourteen-year-old Mindy engages in many risky behaviors, reasoning that "nothing bad will happen to me."
    c. Fifteen-year-old Philip feels that no one understands his problems.
    d. Thirteen-year-old Josh delights in finding logical flaws in virtually everything his teachers and parents say.

29. Frustrated because of the dating curfew her parents have set, Melinda exclaims, "You just don't know how it feels to be in love!" Melinda's thinking demonstrates
    a. the invincibility fable.
    b. the personal fable.
    c. the imaginary audience.
    d. hypothetical thinking.

30. Compared to her 13-year-old brother, 17-year-old Yolanda is likely to
    a. be more critical about herself.
    b. be more egocentric.
    c. have less confidence in her abilities.
    d. be more capable of reasoning hypothetically.

31. Nathan's fear that his friends will ridicule him because of a pimple that has appeared on his nose reflects a preoccupation with

    _____ .

32. The reasoning behind the conclusion, "if it waddles like a duck and quacks like a duck, then it must be a duck," is called

    _____ .

33. Which of the following is an example of deductive reasoning?
    a. Alonza is too lazy to look up an unfamiliar word he encounters while reading.
    b. Brittany loves to reason from clues to figure out "whodunit" crime mysteries.
    c. Morgan, who has enjoyed unscrambling anagrams for years, prefers to follow his hunches rather than systematically evaluate letter combinations.
    d. When taking multiple-choice tests, Trevor carefully considers every possible answer before choosing one.

Teaching and Learning (pp. 455–468)

34. The period after primary education and before _____ education is called _____ education. With puberty coming _____ (earlier/later) than in years past, many intermediate _____ schools have been established to educate children in grades 6, 7, and 8.

35. During the middle school years, academic achievement often _____ (slows down/speeds up). In addition, behavioral problems become _____ (more/less) common. Some research has found that _____ _____ — treating students as individual learners within each class—advances education in middle schools.

36. The "digital divide" that once separated _____ from _____ and _____ from _____ has been bridged. In the United States today, the greatest divide, in terms of technology use, is _____ .

37. Potential dangers of the use of computers include sexual predators; _____ , which occurs when one person spreads online insults and rumors about someone else; and Web sites devoted to cutting, or _____ .

38. The first year of a new school often correlates with increased _____ , decreased _____ , and the onset of _____ .

39. The curriculum prescribed by a school's educational leaders is called its _____ curriculum. The curriculum that is actually offered is called the _____ curriculum, and the learning that actually occurs is called the _____ curriculum.

40. By high school, curriculum and teaching style are often quite _____ and _____ . Most academic subjects emphasize _____ .

41. Another feature of the high school environment is
_____-_____
testing, so called because the consequences of
failing are so severe. Whenever this type of testing is a requisite for graduation, there is a potential unintended consequence of more

_____ .

42. A second problem with the high school environment involves student persistence, diligence, and
_____ ; many adolescents express
_____ and unhappiness with
school.

43. Adolescents are more likely to be engaged with
school if the school is _____
(small/large). Also, adolescents who are active in
school _____ and _____
are more likely to graduate and go to college.

44. The same practices that foster motivation and
education can also prevent _____ .

THINK ABOUT IT: During adolescence, formal
operational thought—including scientific reasoning,
logical construction of arguments, and critical thinking—becomes possible. Consider the kinds of multiple-choice and essay questions you have been given
as a student. Which kind of question typically gives
you the most trouble? Does this type of question
require thinking at the formal operational level? _____

APPLICATIONS:

45. Summarizing her presentation on the mismatch
between the needs of adolescents and the traditional structure of their schools, Megan notes
that
a. most high schools feature intensified competition.
b. the curriculum of most high schools emphasizes formal operational thinking.
c. the academic standards of most schools do
not reflect adolescents' needs.
d. all of these statements are true.

46. Malcolm, a middle schooler who lately is very
sensitive to the criticism of others, feels significantly less motivated and capable than when he
was in elementary school. Malcolm probably
a. is experiencing a sense of vulnerability that is
common in adolescents.
b. is a lower-track student.

c. is a student in a school that emphasizes rigid
routines.
d. has all of these characteristics.

47. Concluding her presentation on academic
achievement during adolescence, LaToya notes
that the "low ebb" of learning is the
a. last year of primary education.
b. first year of tertiary education.
c. first year of middle school.
d. last year of middle school.

48. The dangers of adolescents' increasing use of
technology include
a. cyberbullying.
b. self-mutilation Web sites.
c. the potential to push them toward violent
sex.
d. all of these dangers.

Progress Test 1

Multiple-Choice Questions

Circle your answers to the following questions and
check them with the answers on page 214. If your
answer is incorrect, read the explanation for why it is
incorrect and then consult the appropriate pages of
the text (in parentheses following the correct answer).

1. Many psychologists consider the distinguishing
feature of adolescent thought to be the ability to
think in terms of
a. moral issues.
b. concrete operations.
c. possibility, not just reality.
d. logical principles.

2. Piaget's last stage of cognitive development is
a. formal operational thought.
b. concrete operational thought.
c. universal ethical principles.
d. symbolic thought.

3. The sunk cost fallacy is the mistaken assumption
that
a. because one has already spent time on something, one should spend more.
b. analytical thinking works in all situations.
c. intuitive thinking is generally best.
d. emotional thinking is sometimes better.

4. The adolescent who takes risks and feels immune to the laws of mortality is showing evidence of the
   a. invincibility fable.
   b. personal fable.
   c. imaginary audience.
   d. death instinct.

5. Imaginary audiences and invincibility fables are expressions of adolescent
   a. morality.
   b. thinking games.
   c. decision making.
   d. egocentrism.

6. The typical adolescent
   a. is tough-minded.
   b. is indifferent to public opinion.
   c. is self-absorbed and hypersensitive to criticism.
   d. has all of these characteristics.

7. When adolescents enter middle school, many
   a. experience a drop in their academic performance.
   b. show increased behavioral problems.
   c. lose connections to teachers.
   d. experience all of these things.

8. The psychologist who first described adolescent egocentrism is
   a. Jean Piaget.
   b. David Elkind.
   c. Lev Vygotsky.
   d. Noam Chomsky.

9. Thinking that begins with a general premise and then draws logical conclusions from it is called
   a. inductive reasoning.
   b. deductive reasoning.
   c. intuitive thinking.
   d. hypothetical reasoning.

10. Serious reflection on important issues is a wrenching process for many adolescents because of their newfound ability to reason
    a. inductively.
    b. deductively.
    c. hypothetically.
    d. symbolically.

11. Hypothetical-deductive thinking is to contextualized thinking as:
    a. rational analysis is to intuitive thought.
    b. intuitive thought is to rational analysis.
    c. experiential thinking is to intuitive reasoning.
    d. intuitive thinking is to analytical reasoning.

12. Many adolescents seem to believe that *their* love-making will not lead to pregnancy. This belief is an expression of the:
    a. sunk cost fallacy.
    b. invincibility fable.
    c. imaginary audience.
    d. "game of thinking."

13. Adolescents' improving ability to plan, reflect, and analyze is partly the result of maturation of the:
    a. hippocampus.
    b. amygdala.
    c. limbic system.
    d. prefrontal cortex.

14. One problem with many high schools is that the formal curriculum ignores the fact that adolescents thrive on:
    a. formal operational thinking.
    b. intellectual challenges that require social interaction.
    c. inductive reasoning.
    d. deductive reasoning.

15. (A View from Science) A recent research study investigating teenage religion found that
    a. most adolescents did not feel close to God.
    b. most adolescents identified with the same tradition as their parents.
    c. few respondents claimed that their beliefs were important to their daily life.
    d. faith was generally not viewed as a personal tool to be used in times of difficulty.

True or False Items

Write T (*true*) or F (*false*) on the line in front of each statement.

_____ 1. The appropriateness of the typical high school's high-stakes testing environment has been questioned.

_____ 2. Adolescents are generally better able than younger children at recognizing the sunk cost fallacy.

_____ 3. Adolescents' egos sometimes seem to overwhelm logic.

_____ 4. When high-stakes tests are a requisite for graduation, there is a potential consequence of more high school dropouts.

_____ 5. Adolescents often create an imaginary audience as they envision how others will react to their appearance and behavior.

_____ 6. Thinking reaches heightened self-consciousness at puberty.

_____ 7. Adolescent egocentrism is always irrational.

_____ 8. Inductive reasoning is a hallmark of formal operational thought.

_____ 9. Academic achievement often slows down during the middle school years.

_____ 10. The brain has two distinct processing networks.

Progress Test 2

Progress Test 2 should be completed during a final chapter review. Answer the following questions after you thoroughly understand the correct answers for the Chapter Review and Progress Test 1.

Multiple-Choice Questions

1. Adolescents who fall prey to the invincibility fable may be more likely to
   a. engage in risky behaviors.
   b. suffer from depression.
   c. have low self-esteem.
   d. drop out of school.

2. Thinking that extrapolates from a specific experience to form a general premise is called
   a. inductive reasoning.
   b. deductive reasoning.
   c. intuitive thinking.
   d. hypothetical reasoning.

3. Education during grades 7 through 12 is generally called
   a. primary education
   b. secondary education
   c. tertiary education.
   d. analytical education.

4. When young people overestimate their significance to others, they are displaying
   a. concrete operational thought.
   b. adolescent egocentrism.
   c. a lack of cognitive growth.
   d. immoral development.

5. The imaginary audience refers to adolescents imagining that:
   a. they are immune to the dangers of risky behaviors.
   b. they are always being scrutinized by others.
   c. their own lives are unique, heroic, or even legendary.
   d. the world revolves around their actions.

6. The typical high school environment
   a. limits social interaction.
   b. does not meet the cognitive needs of the typical adolescent.
   c. emphasizes formal operational thought.
   d. is described by all of these conditions.

7. As compared to elementary schools, most middle schools exhibit all of the following EXCEPT
   a. a more flexible approach to education.
   b. intensified competition.
   c. inappropriate academic standards.
   d. less individualized attention.

8. Which of the following is true regarding experiential thinking?
   a. It does not advance significantly in most people until adulthood.
   b. It is slower than formal operational thinking.
   c. It is quicker and more passionate than formal operational thinking.
   d. It often deteriorates during early adolescence.

9. The brain area that predominates in quick, emotional reactions is the
   a. prefrontal cortex.
   b. amygdala.
   c. dendrite.
   d. axon.

10. Analytic thinking is to _____ thinking as emotional force is to _____ thinking.
    a. intuitive; egocentric
    b. egocentric; intuitive
    c. formal; intuitive
    d. intuitive; formal

11. One of the hallmarks of formal operational thought is
    a. egocentrism.
    b. deductive reasoning.
    c. symbolic thinking.
    d. all of these types of thinking

12. Analytic thinking and experiential thinking
    a. both use the same neural pathways in the brain.
    b. are really the same type of information processing.
    c. both improve during adolescence.
    d. are characterized by all of these conditions.

13. The pathways that form the brain's dual-processing networks involve the
    a. hypothalamus and the amygdala.
    b. cerebellum and the corpus callosum.
    c. prefrontal cortex and the limbic system.
    d. left and right cerebral hemispheres.

14. In the United States, the greatest divide between Internet users and nonusers is now
    a. gender.   c. ethnicity.
    b. age.   d. income.

15. To avoid a mismatch between its formal curriculum and the needs of adolescents, a middle school should:
    a. minimize group interaction.
    b. discourage role-playing in the classroom.
    c. establish the same goals for every student.
    d. treat students as individual learners.

Matching Items

Match each term or concept with its corresponding description or definition.

Terms or Concepts
_____ 1. invincibility fable
_____ 2. imaginary audience
_____ 3. high-stakes test
_____ 4. hypothetical thought
_____ 5. deductive reasoning
_____ 6. inductive reasoning
_____ 7. formal operational thought
_____ 8. sunk cost fallacy
_____ 9. dual-process model
_____ 10. adolescent egocentrism
_____ 11. base rate neglect

Descriptions or Definitions
a. the tendency of adolescents to focus on themselves to the exclusion of others
b. adolescents feel immune to the consequences of dangerous behavior
c. mistaken belief that if a person has already spent time or money on something, he or she should continue to do so
d. the idea held by many adolescents that others are intensely interested in them, especially in their appearance and behavior
e. the idea that there are two thinking networks in the brain
f. reasoning about propositions that may or may not reflect reality
g. the last stage of cognitive development, according to Piaget
h. thinking that moves from premise to conclusion
i. thinking that moves from a specific experience to a general premise
j. an evaluation that is critical in determining success or failure
k. faulty reasoning that ignores the actual frequency of some behavior

Key Terms

Using your own words, write a brief definition or explanation of each of the following terms on a separate piece of paper.

1. adolescent egocentrism
2. personal fable
3. invincibility fable
4. imaginary audience
5. formal operational thought
6. hypothetical thought
7. deductive reasoning
8. inductive reasoning
9. dual-process model
10. intuitive thought
11. analytic thought
12. sunk cost fallacy

13. base rate neglect
14. secondary education
15. middle school
16. digital divide
17. cyberbullying
18. high-stakes test

Answers

CHAPTER REVIEW

1. different
2. brain; fear; emotional impulses; before
3. frontal; age; experience
4. rational; maturation
5. amygdala; emotional; executive; emotional regulation
6. limbic; prefrontal cortex
   (a) Changing economic conditions mean that puberty now precedes employment and marriage by much more time than in the past.
   (b) Guns, drugs, and sex are now more widely available, making momentary lapses of judgment potentially lethal.
7. myelination; pruning; dopamine
8. 25
9. adolescent egocentrism
10. personal fable; invincibility fable; invincible
11. imaginary audience
12. formal operational; is not
13. determinants; conclusions

Three- to five-year-olds have no understanding of how to solve the problem. By age 7, children understand balancing the weights but don't know that distance from the center is also a factor. By age 10, they understand the concepts but are unable to coordinate them. By ages 13 or 14, they are able to solve the problem.

14. hypothetical
15. deductive; premise; logic; conclusions
16. inductive
17. agree; sudden; context; biological; domain
18. hypothetical-deductive
19. hypothetical-deductive; intuitive; dual-processing
20. belief, experience, or assumption; intuitive (or contextualized or experiential); analytic

21. quick; powerful; wrong
22. sunk cost fallacy; emotional; base rate neglect
23. efficient
24. Possible answers follow.

Type of Thinking	Examples
Egocentrism	"Why do these catastrophes always happen to me and not to someone else?" (personal fable)
Hypothetical-Deductive	"I think there's a gremlin in my car and he's letting me know he's there" (thinking about possibilities that may not be real)
Intuitive Thought	"Last time this happened my car broke down. What am I going to do?" (experiential)
Analytic Thought	"I need to get my car to a mechanic as soon as possible." (logical thought)

25. c. is the answer. Although this statement is logically verifiable, preadolescents who lack formal operational thought cannot prove or disprove it.
26. c. is the answer. Monica now has the ability to use hypothetical-deductive reasoning.
27. c. is the answer. a. is an example of a personal fable. The behaviors described in b. and d. are more indicative of a preoccupation with the imaginary audience.
28. d. is the answer. Hypothetical reasoning involves thinking about possibilities. a. is an example of the imaginary audience. b. is an example of the invincibility fable. c. is an example of adolescent egocentrism.
29. b. is the answer. The personal fable is the adolescent's belief that his or her feelings and thoughts are unique.
30. d. is the answer. Adolescents become less critical of themselves and less egocentric as they mature and as the prefrontal cortex matures.
31. an imaginary audience.
32. inductive reasoning. This is reasoning that moves from the specific to reach a general conclusion.
33. b. is the answer. solving mysteries is an example of deductive reasoning.
34. tertiary; secondary; earlier; middle
35. slows down; more; differential learning
36. boys; girls; rich; poor; age
37. cyberbullying; self-mutilation

38. bullying; achievement; depression and eating disorders

39. intended; implemented; attained

40. analytic; abstract; logic

41. high-stakes; dropouts

42. motivation; boredom

43. small; clubs; athletics

44. violence

45. **d.** is the answer.

46. **a.** is the answer. Middle school is a time when academic achievement slows down. Also, adolescents become more self-conscious socially because they are confronted by many new classmates.

47. **c.** is the answer. Some psychologists have proposed that this occurs because students lose close connection to teachers in overly large classes.

48. **d.** is the answer.

PROGRESS TEST 1

Multiple-Choice Questions

1. **c.** is the answer. (p. 448)

   a. Although moral reasoning becomes much deeper during adolescence, it is not limited to this stage of development.

   b. & d. Concrete operational thought, which *is* logical, is the distinguishing feature of childhood thinking.

2. **a.** is the answer. (p. 446)

   b. In Piaget's theory, this stage precedes formal operational thought.

   c. & d. These are not stages in Piaget's theory.

3. **a.** is the answer. (p. 452)

4. **a.** is the answer. (p. 444)

   b. This concept refers to adolescents' tendency to imagine their own lives as unique, heroic, or even legendary.

   c. This refers to adolescents' tendency to fantasize about how others will react to their appearance and behavior.

   d. This is a concept in Freud's theory.

5. **d.** is the answer. These thought processes are manifestations of adolescents' tendency to see themselves as being much more central and important to the social scene than they really are. (p. 444)

6. **c.** is the answer. (p. 446)

7. **d.** is the answer. (p. 456)

8. **b.** is the answer. (p. 443)

9. **b.** is the answer. (p. 449)

   a. Inductive reasoning moves from specific facts to a general conclusion.

   c. By its very nature, intuitive thinking does not move logically either from a general conclusion to specific facts or from specific facts to a general conclusion.

   d. Hypothetical reasoning involves thinking about possibilities rather than facts.

10. **c.** is the answer. (p. 448)

11. **a.** is the answer. (p. 450)

    c. Contextualized thinking is both experiential *and* intuitive.

12. **b.** is the answer. (p. 444)

    a. The sunk cost fallacy is the mistaken belief that, because one has invested time and effort in something, one should continue doing so.

    c. This refers to adolescents' tendency to fantasize about how others will react to their appearance and behavior.

    d. This concept was not discussed in the text.

13. **d.** is the answer. (p. 441)

    a., b., & c. The hippocampus (a) and amygdala (b), which are both part of the limbic system (c), are important in quick emotional reactions.

14. **b.** is the answer. (p. 467)

    a., c., & d. Adolescents are more likely to thrive on *intuitive* thinking.

15. **b.** is the answer. (p. 453)

True or False Items

1. T (p. 464)

2. T (p. 452)

3. T (p. 444)

4. T (p. 464)

5. T (p. 445)

6. T (pp. 443–444)

7. F Adolescents *do* judge each other. (p. 446)

8. F Deductive reasoning is a hallmark of formal operational thought. (p. 449)

9. T (p. 456)

10. T (p. 450)

PROGRESS TEST 2

Multiple-Choice Questions

1. **a.** is the answer. (p. 444)

   b., c., & d. The invincibility fable leads some teens to believe that they are immune to the dangers of risky behaviors; it is not necessarily linked to depression, low self-esteem, or the likelihood that an individual will drop out of school.

2. **a.** is the answer. (p. 449)

   b. Deductive reasoning begins with a general premise and then draws logical conclusions from it.

   c. By its very nature, intuitive thinking does not move logically either from a general conclusion to specific facts or from specific facts to a general conclusion.

   d. Hypothetical reasoning involves thinking about possibilities rather than facts.

3. **b.** is the answer. (p. 455)

4. **b.** is the answer. (pp. 443–444)

5. **b.** is the answer. (p. 445)

   a. This describes the invincibility fable.

   c. This describes the personal fable.

   d. This describes adolescent egocentrism in general.

6. **d.** is the answer. (p. 467)

7. **a.** is the answer. (p. 464)

8. **c.** is the answer. (p. 453)

9. **b.** is the answer. (p. 441)

   a. The prefrontal cortex is responsible for planning, analysis, and emotional regulation.

   c. & d. Dendrites and axons are parts of neurons.

10. **c.** is the answer. (p. 451)

11. **b.** is the answer. (p. 449)

12. **c.** is the answer. (p. 451)

13. **c.** is the answer. (p. 441)

14. **b.** is the answer. (p. 459)

15. **d.** is the answer. (p. 458)

Matching Items

1. b (p. 444)
2. d (p. 445)
3. j (p. 464)
4. f (p. 448)
5. h (p. 449)
6. i (p. 449)
7. g (p. 446)
8. c (p. 452)
9. e (p. 450)
10. a (p. 443)
11. k (p. 452)

KEY TERMS

1. **Adolescent egocentrism** refers to the tendency of young adolescents to focus on themselves to the exclusion of others. (p. 443)

2. The **personal fable** refers to an adolescent's belief that his or her thoughts, feelings, and experiences are unique. (p. 444)

3. Adolescents who experience the **invincibility fable** feel that they are immune to the dangers of risky behaviors. (p. 444)

4. Adolescents often create an **imaginary audience** for themselves, because they assume that others are as intensely interested in them as they themselves are. (p. 445)

5. In Piaget's theory, the last stage of cognitive development, which arises from a combination of maturation and experience, is called **formal operational thought**. A hallmark of formal operational thinking is more systematic logic and the ability to think about abstract ideas. (p. 446)

6. **Hypothetical thought** involves reasoning about propositions and possibilities that may not reflect reality. (p. 448)

7. **Deductive reasoning** is thinking that moves from the general to the specific, or from a premise to a logical conclusion; also called *top-down reasoning*. (p. 449)

8. **Inductive reasoning** is thinking that moves from one or more specific experiences or facts to a general conclusion; also called *bottom-up reasoning*. (p. 449)

9. The **dual-process model** is the idea that there are two thinking networks in the human brain, one for emotional thinking and one for analytical thinking. (p. 450)

10. **Intuitive thought** is that which arises from a hunch or emotion, often triggered by past experiences and cultural assumptions. (p. 450)

11. **Analytic thought** is logical thinking that arises from rational analysis and the systematic evaluation of consequences and possibilities. (p. 450)

12. The **sunk cost fallacy** is the mistaken belief that, because one has already invested money, time, or effort that cannot be recovered, one should continue doing so in an effort to reach the desired goal. (p. 452)

13. **Base rate neglect** is a faulty form of emotional decision making that ignores the actual frequency of a behavior. (p. 452)

14. **Secondary education** is education that follows primary education and precedes tertiary education, usually occurring from about age 12 to 18. (p. 455)

15. **Middle school** refers to the years of school between elementary school and high school. (p. 455)

16. The **digital divide** refers to the gap between people who have access to computers and those who do not. (p. 459)

17. **Cyberbullying** occurs when one person spreads online insults or rumors about someone else. (p. 461)

18. **High-stakes tests** are exams and other forms of evaluation that are critical in determining a person's success or failure. (p. 464)

16

Adolescence: Psychosocial Development

Chapter Overview

Chapter 16 focuses on the adolescent's psychosocial development. The first section explores the paths that lead to the formation of identity, which is required for the attainment of adult status and maturity. The next two sections examine the influences of family and friends on adolescent psychosocial development, including the development of romantic relationships and sexual activity. Depression, self-destruction, and suicide—the most perplexing problems of adolescence—are then explored. The special problems posed by adolescent lawbreaking are discussed, and suggestions for alleviating or treating these problems are given. The chapter concludes with the message that with the help of family and friends, most adolescents make through the teen years unscathed.

NOTE: Answer guidelines for all Chapter 16 questions begin on page 225.

Chapter Review

When you have finished reading the chapter, work through the material that follows to review it. Complete the sentences and answer the questions. In some cases, Study Tips explain how best to learn a difficult concept, while Think About It and Applications help you to know how well you understand the material. As you proceed, evaluate your performance for each section by consulting the answers beginning on page 225. Do not continue with the next section until you understand each answer. If you need to, review or reread the appropriate section in the textbook before continuing.

Identity (pp. 472–477)

1. The momentous changes that occur during the teen years challenge adolescents to find their own

   _____ .

2. According to Erikson, the challenge of adolescence is _____ _____

   _____ .

3. The ultimate goal of adolescence is to establish a new identity that involves both rejection and acceptance of childhood values; this is called

   _____ _____ .

4. The young person who has few commitments to goals or values and is apathetic about defining his or her identity is experiencing

   _____ _____ .

5. The young person who prematurely accepts earlier roles and parental values without exploring alternatives or truly forging a unique identity is experiencing identity _____ .

6. A time-out period during which a young person experiments with different identities, postponing important choices, is called an identity

   _____ . An obvious institutional example of this in North America is attending

   _____ .

7. Erikson described four aspects of identity:

   _____ , _____ ,

   _____ , and _____ .

8. Today, a person's identification as either male or female is called _____ _____ , which usually leads to a gender

   _____ and a sexual _____ .

9. A person's sexual attraction to people of the same sex, other sex, or both sexes constitutes his or her

   _____ _____ .

10. Since Erikson's time, _____ identity has become more important than _____ identity. The more appropriate term has become _____ _____ .

11. Although parents sometimes discourage their children from following their career path, _____ , social _____ , and _____ _____ propel many adolescents toward their parents' careers.

12. Employment of 20 or more hours during adolescence is likely to weaken _____ formation, _____ relationships, _____ achievement, and _____ success.

STUDY TIP: To keep the differences among the identity statuses of role confusion, foreclosure, and moratorium straight, remember that role confusion is a state in which adolescents seem unfocused and unconcerned about their future. Foreclosure and moratorium represent different strategies for dealing with this state of confusion. You may find it helpful to think of how *foreclosure* is used in financial circumstances. Economic foreclosure occurs when someone who has borrowed money, typically to purchase a home, defaults on the loan. To *foreclose* is to deprive the borrower of the right to ownership. Similarly, adolescents who have foreclosed on their identities have deprived themselves of the healthy practice of thoughtfully questioning and trying out different possible identities before settling on one. In contrast, a moratorium is a time-out during which adolescents postpone their final identity, often by attending college or engaging in other socially acceptable activities that allow them to make a more mature decision.

APPLICATIONS:

13. From childhood, Sharon thought she wanted to follow in her mother's footsteps and be a homemaker. Now, at age 40 with a home and family, she admits to herself that what she really wanted to be was a medical researcher. Erik Erikson would probably say that Sharon
    a. adopted a negative identity when she was a child.
    b. experienced identity foreclosure at an early age.

c. never progressed beyond the obvious identity diffusion she experienced as a child.
d. took a moratorium from identity formation.

14. Jennifer has a well-defined religious identity. This is true because she
    a. self-identifies herself as a religious person.
    b. worships regularly.
    c. reads scripture.
    d. does all of these things.

15. In 1998, 6-year-old Raisel and her parents emigrated from Mexico to the United States. Because her parents hold to the values and customs of their native land, Raisel is likely to
    a. have an easier time achieving her own unique identity.
    b. have a more difficult time forging her identity.
    c. stick with her parents' cultural identity.
    d. a shorter span of time in which to forge her identity.

Relationships with Elders and Peers (pp. 477–485)

16. Adolescence is often characterized as a time of waning adult influence; this _____ (is/is not) necessarily true. An important aspect of healthy development is supportive relationships with _____ adults.

17. Parent–adolescent conflict peaks during _____ _____ and is particularly notable with _____ (mothers/fathers) and their _____ (sons/daughters). This conflict often involves _____ , which refers to repeated, petty arguments about daily habits.

18. By age 18, increased _____ maturity and reduced _____ bring some renewed appreciation for parents.

19. There _____ (are/are not) cultural differences in parent–adolescent relationships. Some cultures value _____ _____ above all else and avoid conflict. Thus, the very idea of adolescent rebellion may be a _____ construction in Western culture.

20. Four other elements of parent–teen relationships that have been heavily researched include

_____ , _____ ,

_____ , and _____ .

21. In terms of family control, a powerful deterrent to drugs and risky sex is _____

_____ . Too much interference, however, may contribute to adolescent

_____ . Particularly harmful to teens are threats to withdraw love and support,

or _____ _____ .

22. Adolescents group themselves into clusters of close friends, called _____ , and larger groups, or_____ , who share common interests. These groups provide social

_____ and social

_____ .

23. Social pressure to conform to peer activities is called _____ _____ .
This pressure is _____ as often as it is _____ . Destructive peer support is called _____ _____ .

24. Two helpful concepts in understanding the influence of peers are _____ , meaning that peers _____ one another; and

_____ , referring to the fact that peers encourage one another to do things that

_____ .

25. Friends play a special role for adolescents whose parents are _____ . They are particularly important in protecting the adolescent's

_____ , especially if the adolescent is of a(n) _____ background.

APPLICATIONS:

26. Bill's parents insist on knowing the whereabouts and activities of their son at all times. Clearly, they are very good at _____ .

27. First-time parents Norma and Norman are worried that, during adolescence, their healthy parental influence will be undone as their children are encouraged by peers to become sexually promiscuous, drug-addicted, or delinquent. Their wise neighbor, who is a developmental psychologist, tells them that

   a. peers are constructive as often as they are destructive.
   b. research suggests that peers provide a negative influence in every major task of adolescence.
   c. only through authoritarian parenting can parents give children the skills they need to resist peer pressure.
   d. unless their children show early signs of learning difficulties or antisocial behavior, parental monitoring is unnecessary.

Sexuality (pp. 485–492)

Briefly outline the four-stage progression of heterosexual involvement.

28. Culture _____ (affects/does not affect) the _____ and

_____ of these stages, but the basic

_____ seems to be based on

_____ factors. In modern developed nations, each stage typically lasts several years.

29. For homosexual adolescents, added complications usually _____ (slow down/speed up) romantic attachments.

30. Adolescents who are _____

_____ and who experience

_____ (early/late) puberty are more likely to become sexually active.

31. Many parents _____ (underestimate/overestimate) their adolescent's need for sexual information. Religion is _____ (more/less) of a factor in determining whether parents talk to their children about sex than

_____ and _____ .

32. Developmentalists agree that high schools
_____ (should/should not) teach
sex education, and that sex also should be part of
_____-_____
conversations.

33. Sex education _____ (varies/does
not vary) from nation to nation. The timing and
content of sex education in the United States
_____ (varies/does not vary) by
state and community.

34. Sexual activity among adolescents _____
(varies/does not vary) from nation to nation. The
teen birth rate is _____ (increas-
ing/decreasing). At the same time, contraceptive
use has _____ (increased/
decreased).

35. In the United Statues, the rate of teen abortions
has _____ (increased/decreased) in
recent years.

THINK ABOUT IT: To help you understand the
role of the peer group during adolescence, think
about your own social experiences as a teenager. Did
you hang out in loosely associated groups of girls
and boys before gradually joining together? Did you
double- or triple-date to avoid the awkwardness of
being alone with someone you "liked"? Did you have
a best friend of the same gender with whom you
shared details of your sexual experiences in order to
confirm that they were normal? _____

APPLICATION:

36. Padma's parents are concerned because their 14-
year-old daughter has formed an early romantic
relationship with a boy. You tell them
   a. not to worry, because boys are more likely to
   say they have a girlfriend than vice versa.
   b. not to worry; healthy romances are a mani-
   festation of good relationships with parents
   and peers.
   c. most romantic relationships last throughout
   high school.
   d. they should do everything they can to break
   up the relationship.

Sadness and Anger (pp. 492–501)

37. Adolescents who have one serious problem
_____ (often have/do not usually
have) others.

38. The situation in which a person has two or more
unrelated illnesses or disorders at the same time
is _____ .

39. From late childhood through adolescence, people
generally feel _____ (more/less)
competent, on average, each year in most areas of
their lives.

40. Clinical depression _____
(increases/decreases) at puberty, especially
among _____ (males/females). One
explanation is that talking about and mentally
replaying past experiences, which is called
_____ , is more common among
_____ (males/females).

41. Thinking about committing suicide, called
_____ _____ , is
_____ (common/relatively rare)
among high school students.

42. Adolescents are _____ (more/less)
likely to kill themselves than adults are.

43. When a town or school sentimentalizes the "trag-
ic end" of a teen suicide, the publicity can trigger
_____ _____ .

44. Most suicide attempts in adolescence
_____ (do/do not) result in death.
A deliberate act of self-destruction that does not
result in death is called a _____ .

45. List four factors that increase a teen's risk of
suicide.
   a. _____
   b. _____
   c. _____
   d. _____

46. The rate of suicide is higher for adolescent
_____ (males/females). The rate of
parasuicide is higher for _____
(males/females).

47. Around the world, cultural differences in the rates of suicidal ideation and completion _____ (are/are not) apparent.

48. Since 1990, rates of adolescent suicide have _____ (risen/fallen), especially among those with more _____ and

_____ .

49. Psychologists influenced by the _____ perspective believe that adolescent rebellion and defiance are normal.

50. Lawbreakers who are under age _____ are called _____

_____ . In terms of the frequency of arrests, _____ (only a few/virtually all) adolescents break the law at least once before age 20.

Briefly describe data on gender and ethnic differences in adolescent arrests.

51. Developmentalists have found that it _____ (is/is not) currently possible to distinguish children who actually will become career criminals.

List several of the childhood factors that correlate with delinquency.

52. Experts find it useful to distinguish _____-_____ offenders, whose criminal activity stops by age 21, from _____-_____-

_____ offenders, who become career criminals.

53. One innovative strategy for helping delinquents is _____ _____

_____ , in which violent youth are assigned to _____ families trained to establish a relationship with this child and his or her teachers.

APPLICATIONS:

54. Carl is a typical 16-year-old adolescent who has no special problems. It is likely that Carl has
   a. contemplated suicide.
   b. engaged in some minor illegal act.
   c. struggled with "who he is."
   d. engaged in all of these behaviors.

55. Statistically, who of the following is most likely to commit suicide?
   a. Elena, a female from South America
   b. Yan, a male from the Eastern United States
   c. James, a male from the Western United States
   d. Alison, a female from western Europe

56. Coming home from work, Rashid hears a radio announcement warning parents to be alert for possible cluster suicide signs in their teenage children. What might have precipitated such an announcement?
   a. government statistics that suicide is on the rise
   b. the highly publicized suicide of a teen from a school in town
   c. the recent crash of an airliner, killing all on board
   d. any of these events

Progress Test 1

Multiple-Choice Questions

Circle your answers to the following questions and check them with the answers on page 226. If your answer is incorrect, read the explanation for why it is incorrect and then consult the appropriate pages of the text (in parentheses following the correct answer).

1. According to Erikson, the primary task of adolescence is that of establishing
   a. basic trust.   c. intimacy.
   b. an identity.   d. integrity.

2. According to developmentalists who study identity formation, foreclosure involves
   a. accepting an identity prematurely, without exploration.
   b. taking time off from school, work, and other commitments.
   c. opposing parental values.
   d. failing to commit oneself to a vocational goal.

3. A large group of adolescents who share common interests is a
   a. clique.   c. crowd.
   b. peer group.   d. cluster.

4. The main sources of social support for most young people who are establishing independence from their parents are
   a. older adolescents of the opposite sex.
   b. older siblings.
   c. teachers.
   d. peer groups.

5. For members of minority ethnic groups, identity achievement may be particularly complicated because
   a. their cultural ideal clashes with the Western emphasis on adolescent self-determination.
   b. peers, themselves torn by similar conflicts, can be very critical.
   c. parents and other relatives tend to emphasize ethnicity and expect teens to honor their roots.
   d. of all of these reasons.

6. In a crime-ridden neighborhood, parents can protect their adolescents by keeping close watch over activities, friends, and so on. This practice is called
   a. a moratorium.   c. peer screening.
   b. foreclosure.   d. parental monitoring.

7. Conflict between adolescent girls and their mothers is most likely to involve
   a. bickering over hair, neatness, and other daily habits.
   b. political, religious, and moral issues.
   c. peer relationships and friendships.
   d. relationships with boys.

8. Destructive peer support in which one adolescent shows another how to rebel against authority is called
   a. peer pressure.
   b. deviancy training.
   c. peer selection.
   d. peer facilitation.

9. In our society, obvious examples of institutionalized moratoria on identity formation are
   a. the Boy Scouts and the Girl Scouts.
   b. college and the military.
   c. marriage and divorce.
   d. bar mitzvahs and baptisms.

10. In a Disney movie, two high school students encourage each other to participate in the school musical. This type of peer influence is called
    a. peer pressure.
    b. deviancy training.
    c. selection.
    d. peer facilitation.

11. Jill, who has cut herself and engaged in other self-destructive acts, is receiving treatment for these acts of
    a. suicidal ideation.
    b. comorbidity.
    c. parasuicide.
    d. rumination.

12. Thirteen-year-old Adam, who never has doubted his faith, identifies himself as an orthodox member of a particular religious group. A developmentalist would probably say that Adam's religious identity is
    a. achieved.
    b. foreclosed.
    c. in moratorium.
    d. oppositional in nature.

13. The early predictors of life-course-persistent offenders include all of the following EXCEPT
    a. short attention span.
    b. hyperactivity.
    c. high intelligence.
    d. neurological impairment.

14. Regarding gender differences in self-destructive acts, the rate of parasuicide is _____ and the rate of suicide is _____ .
    a. higher in males; higher in females
    b. higher in females; higher in males
    c. the same in males and females; higher in males
    d. the same in males and females; higher in females

15. Conflict between parents and adolescent offspring is
    a. most likely to involve fathers and their early-maturing offspring.
    b. more frequent in single-parent homes.

c. more likely between daughters and their mothers.

d. likely in all of these situations.

True or False Items

Write T (*true*) or F (*false*) on the line in front of each statement.

_____ 1. Identity achievement before age 18 is elusive.

_____ 2. Most adolescents have political views and educational values that are markedly different from those of their parents.

_____ 3. Peer pressure is inherently destructive to the adolescent seeking an identity.

_____ 4. For most adolescents, group socializing and dating precede the establishment of true intimacy with one member of the opposite sex.

_____ 5. Worldwide, virtually every adolescent breaks the law at least once before age 20.

_____ 6. Abstinence-only sex education has led to decreased rates of adolescent sex.

_____ 7. Because of their tendency to ruminate, girls are more likely than boys to be clinically depressed.

_____ 8. In finding themselves, teens try to find an identity that is stable, consistent, and mature.

_____ 9. From ages 6 to 18, children feel more competent, on average, each year in most areas of their lives.

_____ 10. Increased accessibility of guns is a factor in the increased rate of youth suicide in the United States.

Progress Test 2

Progress Test 2 should be completed during a final chapter review. Answer the following questions after you thoroughly understand the correct answers for the Chapter Review and Progress Test 1.

Multiple-Choice Questions

1. Which of the following is NOT one of the arenas of identity formation in Erik Erikson's theory?

    a. religious   c. political
    b. sexual   d. social

2. Which of the following is true of gender identity?

    a. It is a person's self-definition as male or female.
    b. It always leads to sexual orientation.

c. It is a person's biological male/female characteristics.

d. It is established at birth.

3. Rodesia repeatedly thinks and talks about past experiences to the extent that her doctor believes it is contributing to her depression. Rodesia's behavior is an example of

    a. comorbidity.
    b. deviancy training.
    c. parasuicide.
    d. rumination.

4. Ray endured severe child abuse, has difficulty controlling his emotions, and exhibits symptoms of autism. These factors would suggest that Ray is at high risk of

    a. becoming an adolescent-limited offender.
    b. becoming a life-course-persistent offender.
    c. developing an antisocial personality.
    d. foreclosing his identity prematurely.

5. Thinking about committing suicide is called

    a. cluster suicide.
    b. parasuicide.
    c. suicidal ideation.
    d. fratracide.

6. Which of the following was NOT noted in the text regarding peer relationships among gay and lesbian adolescents?

    a. Romantic attachments are usually slower to develop.
    b. In homophobic cultures, many gay teens try to conceal their homosexual feelings by becoming heterosexually involved.
    c. Many girls who will later identify themselves as lesbians are oblivious to these sexual urges as teens.
    d. Homosexual men report that they do not become aware of their interests until age 17.

7. The adolescent experiencing role confusion is typically

    a. very apathetic.
    b. experimenting with alternative identities without trying to settle on any one.
    c. willing to accept parental values wholesale, without exploring alternatives.
    d. one who rebels against all forms of authority.

8. Gender identity refers to a person's
   a. identification as being female or male.
   b. attraction toward a person of the same sex, the other sex, or both sexes.
   c. self-definition as a unique individual.
   d. self-definition in each of these areas.

9. Crime statistics show that during adolescence
   a. males and females are equally likely to be arrested.
   b. males are more likely to be arrested than females.
   c. females are more likely to be arrested than males.
   d. males commit more crimes than females but are less likely to be arrested.

10. Which of the following is the most common problem behavior among adolescents?
    a. pregnancy
    b. daily use of illegal drugs
    c. minor lawbreaking
    d. attempts at suicide

11. A time-out period during which a young person experiments with different identities, postponing important choices, is called
    a. foreclosure.
    b. a negative identity.
    c. identity diffusion.
    d. a moratorium.

12. Comorbidity is the situation in which
    a. one adolescent encourages another to participate in a dangerous activity.
    b. feelings of lethargy last two weeks or more.
    c. an overwhelming feeling of sadness disrupts a person's normal routine.
    d. two or more unrelated illnesses occur together at the same time.

13. Which of the following is NOT true regarding the rate of clinical depression among adolescents?
    a. At puberty the rate more than doubles.
    b. It affects a higher proportion of teenage boys than girls.
    c. Genetic vulnerability is a predictor of teenage depression.
    d. The adolescent's school setting is a factor.

14. Parent–teen conflict tends to center on issues related to
    a. politics and religion.
    b. education.
    c. vacations.
    d. daily details, such as musical tastes.

15. Suicidal ideation is
    a. not as common among high school students as it was in the past.
    b. more common among males than females.
    c. more common among females than among males.
    d. more common among high-achieving students.

Matching Items

Match each term or concept with its corresponding description or definition.

Terms or Concepts

_____ 1. identity achievement
_____ 2. foreclosure
_____ 3. clique
_____ 4. role confusion
_____ 5. moratorium
_____ 6. peer selection
_____ 7. peer pressure
_____ 8. parental monitoring
_____ 9. parasuicide
_____ 10. cluster suicide

Descriptions or Definitions

a. premature identity formation
b. a group of suicides that occur in the same community, school, or time period
c. the adolescent has few commitments to goals or values
d. process by which adolescents choose their friends based on shared interests
e. self-destructive act that does not result in death
f. awareness of where children are and what they are doing
g. a time-out period during which adolescents experiment with alternative identities
h. the adolescent establishes his or her own goals and values
i. encouragement to conform with one's friends in behavior, dress, and attitude
j. a cluster of close friends

Key Terms

Using your own words, write a brief definition or explanation of each of the following terms on a separate piece of paper.

1. identity versus role confusion
2. identity achievement
3. role confusion
4. foreclosure
5. moratorium
6. gender identity
7. sexual orientation
8. bickering
9. parental monitoring
10. clique
11. crowd
12. peer pressure
13. deviancy training
14. comorbid
15. clinical depression
16. rumination
17. suicidal ideation
18. cluster suicide
19. parasuicide
20. juvenile delinquent
21. life-course-persistent offender
22. adolescent-limited offender

Answers

CHAPTER REVIEW

1. identity
2. identity versus diffusion
3. identity achievement
4. role confusion (identity diffusion)
5. foreclosure
6. moratorium; college
7. religion; sex (gender); politics; vocation
8. gender identity; role; orientation
9. sexual orientation
10. ethnic; political; identity politics
11. genes; modeling; socioeconomic status
12. identity; family; academic; career

13. **b.** is the answer. Apparently, Sharon never explored alternatives or truly forged a unique personal identity.
14. **d.** is the answer.
15. **b.** is the answer. Ethnic adolescents struggle with finding the right balance between transcending their background and becoming immersed in it.
16. is not; non-parent
17. early adolescence; mothers; daughters; bickering
18. emotional; egocentrism
19. are; family harmony; social
20. communication; support; connectedness; control
21. parental monitoring; depression; psychological control
22. cliques; crowds; control; support
23. peer pressure; constructive; destructive; deviancy training
24. selection; choose; facilitation; none of them would do alone
25. immigrants; self-esteem; Asian
26. parental monitoring
27. **a.** is the answer. Developmentalists recommend authoritative, rather than authoritarian, parenting. And, parental monitoring is important for all adolescents.

The progression begins with groups of same-sex friends. Next, a loose, public association of a girls' group and a boys' group forms. Then, a small, mixed-sex group forms from the more advanced members of the crowd. Finally, more intimate couples peel off.

28. affects; timing; manifestations; sequence; genetic
29. slow down
30. physically attractive; early
31. underestimate; less; gender; age
32. should; parent–child
33. varies; varies
34. varies; decreasing; increased
35. decreased
36. **b.** is the answer. Girls are more likely to say they have a boyfriend than vice versa (a.). **c.** is not true; most teen romantic relationships last about a year. And, there's nothing to indicate that the daughter's boyfriend is a negative influence (d.). The relationship may actually be healthy for their daughter, so they shouldn't arbitrarily break it up.
37. often have
38. comorbidity
39. less

40. increases; females; rumination; females
41. suicidal ideation; common
42. less
43. cluster suicides
44. do not; parasuicide
45. a. the availability of guns
    b. lack of parental supervision
    c. availability of alcohol and other drugs
    d. a culture that condones suicide
46. males; females
47. are
48. fallen; income; education
49. psychoanalytic
50. 18; juvenile delinquents; virtually all

Adolescent males are three times as likely to be arrested as females, and African American youth are three times as likely to be arrested as European Americans, who are three times as likely to be arrested as Asian Americans. However, self-reports find much smaller gender and ethnic differences.

51. is

Among the factors are short attention span, being the victim of severe child abuse, hyperactivity, inadequate emotional regulation, maternal cigarette smoking, slow language development, low intelligence, early and severe malnutrition, and autistic tendencies.

52. adolescent-limited; life-course-persistent
53. therapeutic foster care; foster
54. d. is the answer.
55. c. is the answer. Males are more likely to commit suicide, although parasuicide is more common among females. Suicide rates are higher in eastern Europe and Africa than in western Europe and South America, and in the western United States than in the eastern United States.
56. b. is the answer. Cluster suicides occur when the suicide of a local teen leads others to attempt suicide.

PROGRESS TEST 1

Multiple-Choice Questions

1. b. is the answer. (p. 472)
   a. According to Erikson, this is the crisis of infancy.
   c. & d. In Erikson's theory, these crises occur later in life.
2. a. is the answer. (p. 472)

   b. This describes an identity moratorium.
   c. This describes an oppositional, negative identity.
   d. This describes role confusion (identity diffusion).
3. c. is the answer. (p. 481)
4. d. is the answer. (p. 481)
5. d. is the answer. (pp. 483–485)
6. d. is the answer. (p. 480)
   a. A moratorium is a time-out during which adolescents experiment with different identities.
   b. Foreclosure refers to the premature establishment of identity.
   c. Peer screening is an aspect of parental monitoring, but it was not specifically discussed in the text.
7. a. is the answer. (p. 478)
8. b. is the answer. (p. 482)
9. b. is the answer. (p. 473)
10. d. is the answer. (p. 482)
11. c. is the answer. (p. 494)
12. b. is the answer. Foreclosed members of a religious group have, like Adam, never really doubted. (pp. 472, 473)
    a. Because there is no evidence that Adam has asked the "hard questions" regarding his religious beliefs, a developmentalist would probably say that his religious identity is not achieved.
    c. Adam clearly does have a religious identity.
    d. There is no evidence that Adam's religious identity was formed in opposition to expectations.
13. c. is the answer. Life-course-persistent offenders tend to have low intelligence. (p. 499)
14. b. is the answer. (p. 495)
15. c. is the answer. (p. 478)
    a. In fact, parent–child conflict is more likely to involve mothers and their daughters.
    b. The text did not compare the rate of conflict in two-parent and single-parent homes.

True or False Items

1. T (p. 473)
2. F Parent–teen conflicts center on day-to-day details, not on politics or moral issues. (p. 478)
3. F The opposite is just as likely to be true. (p. 481)
4. T (p. 485)

5. T (p. 498)

6. F Researchers found no significant difference in rates of adolescent sex after abstinence-only sex education. (p. 490)

7. T (p. 493)

8. T (p. 472)

9. F Just the opposite is true. (p. 493)

10. T (p. 495)

PROGRESS TEST 2

Multiple-Choice Questions

1. **d.** is the answer. (p. 473)

2. **a.** is the answer. (p. 474)

3. **d.** is the answer. (p. 493)

4. **b.** is the answer. (p. 499)

5. **c.** is the answer. (p. 493)

6. **d.** is the answer. Homosexual men report that they become aware at age 11, but don't tell anyone until age 17. (p. 487)

7. **a.** is the answer. (p. 472)

    b. This describes an adolescent undergoing an identity moratorium.

    c. This describes identity foreclosure.

    d. This describes an adolescent who is adopting an oppositional, negative identity.

8. **a.** is the answer. (p. 474)

    b. This refers to sexual orientation.

    c. This refers to identity in general.

9. **b.** is the answer. (p. 498)

10. **c.** is the answer. (p. 498)

11. **d.** is the answer. (p. 473)

    a. Identity foreclosure occurs when the adolescent prematurely adopts an identity, without fully exploring alternatives.

    b. Adolescents who adopt an identity that is opposite to the one they are expected to develop have taken on a negative identity.

    c. Identity diffusion occurs when the adolescent is apathetic and has few commitments to goals or values.

12. **d.** is the answer. (p. 492)

13. **b.** is the answer. (p. 493)

14. **d.** is the answer. (p. 478)

    a., b., & c. In fact, on these issues parents and teenagers tend to show substantial *agreement*.

15. **c.** is the answer. (p. 495)

Matching Items

1. h (p. 472)
2. a (p. 472)
3. j (p. 481)
4. c (p. 472)
5. g (p. 479)
6. d (p. 482)
7. i (p. 481)
8. f (p. 480)
9. e (p. 494)
10. b (p. 494)

KEY TERMS

1. Erikson's term for the psychosocial crisis of adolescence, **identity versus role confusion,** refers to adolescents' need to combine their self-understanding and social roles into a coherent identity. (p. 472)

2. In Erikson's theory, **identity achievement** occurs when adolescents attain their new identities by establishing their own goals and values and abandoning some of those set by their parents and culture and accepting others. (p. 472)

3. Adolescents who experience **role confusion,** according to Erikson, have few commitments to goals or values and are often apathetic about trying to find an identity; also called *identity diffusion.* (p. 472)

4. In **foreclosure,** according to Erikson, the adolescent forms an identity prematurely, accepting parents' or society's roles and values wholesale. (p. 472)

5. According to Erikson, in the process of finding a mature identity, many young people seem to declare an identity **moratorium,** a socially acceptable time-out during which they experiment with alternative identities without trying to settle on any one. (p. 473)

6. **Gender identity** is a person's self-identification of being female or male. (p. 474)

7. **Sexual orientation** refers to a person's sexual and romantic attraction toward a person of the other sex, the same sex, or both sexes. (p. 475)

8. **Bickering** refers to the repeated, petty arguing that typically occurs in early adolescence about common, daily life activities. (p. 478)

9. **Parental monitoring** is parental awareness about where their children are, what they are doing, and with whom. (p. 480)

10. A **clique** is a group of adolescents made up of close friends who are loyal to one another while excluding others. (p. 481)

11. A **crowd** is a larger group of adolescents who have something in common but who are not necessarily friends. (p. 481)

12. **Peer pressure** refers to the social pressure to conform with one's friends in behavior, dress, and

attitude. It may be positive or negative in its effects. (p. 481)

13. **Deviancy training** is destructive peer pressure to rebel against authority or social norms. (p. 482)

14. **Comorbid** refers to a situation in which two or more illnesses or disorders occur in a person at the same time. (p. 492)

15. **Clinical depression** describes the syndrome in which feelings of hopelessness, lethargy, and worthlessness last in a person for two weeks or longer. (p. 493)

16. **Rumination** is repeatedly thinking and talking about past experiences to the extent of contributing to depression. (p. 493)

17. **Suicidal ideation** refers to thinking about committing suicide, usually with some serious emotional and intellectual or cognitive overtones. (p. 493)

18. A **cluster suicide** refers to a series of suicides that are precipitated by one initial suicide and that occur in the same community, school, or time period. (p. 494)

19. **Parasuicide** is a deliberate act of self-destruction that does not result in death. (p. 494)

20. A **juvenile delinquent** is a person under 18 years of age who breaks the law. (p. 498)

21. **Life-course-persistent offenders** are adolescent lawbreakers who later become career criminals. (p. 499)

22. **Adolescent-limited offenders** are juvenile delinquents whose criminal activity stops by age 21. (p. 499)

Epilogue

Emerging Adulthood

Epilogue Overview

In the Epilogue we encounter the developing person in the prime of life. During emerging adulthood, overall health is good and fertility is high.

The Epilogue begins with a description of the growth, strength, and health of the individual during emerging adulthood. Sexual-reproductive health, a matter of great concern to young adults, is also discussed, with particular attention paid to trends in sexual activity and sexually transmitted infections. The section concludes with a discussion of how social norms can reduce drug abuse and other types of risk taking in this age group.

The second section examines cognitive development during emerging adulthood, beginning with a description of how the emerging adult's thinking differs from adolescent thinking. The experiences and challenges of adulthood result in a new, adventurous, and more flexible kind of thinking—the dynamic, in-the-world cognitive style that adults typically use to solve the problems of daily life.

The final section is concerned with psychosocial development, which is characterized by plasticity during emerging adulthood. Although personality has biological roots, it is also molded by experience. This section also discusses the importance of intimate relationships during this period. The stresses of this period of life combine with genetic vulnerability in some individuals to trigger substance abuse and the development of anxiety disorders or schizophrenia.

NOTE: Answer guidelines for all Epilogue questions begin on page 237.

Epilogue Review

When you have finished reading the chapter, work through the material that follows to review it. Complete the sentences and answer the questions. In some cases, Study Tips explain how best to learn a difficult concept, while Think About It and Applications help you to know how well you understand the material. As you proceed, evaluate your performance for each section by consulting the answers on page 237. Do not continue with the next section until you understand each answer. If you need to, review or reread the appropriate section in the textbook before continuing.

Introduction and *Biosocial Development*
(pp. 505–513)

1. Advances in _____ ,

   _____ , and _____

   have paved the way for the new developmental

   stage called _____ _____ .

State several defining characteristics of this new stage of development.

2. Emerging adulthood is more evident in
   _____ (developed/developing)
   nations and in families with higher

   _____ .

3. Physical growth usually stops by age

   _____ .

4. The beginning of young adulthood has been considered the best time for _____

   _____

   (three categories). Many chronic conditions are

   now _____ (rare/common) among

young adults. Serious illness during emerging adulthood is also _____ (rare/relatively common).

5. Many diagnostic tests, including

_____ , _____ , and

_____ are not recommended until after age 40.

6. Sex hormones peak in both sexes at about age

_____ .

Briefly describe sexual activity and the health of the sexual-reproductive system in emerging adulthood.

7. Most women in their early 20s today _____ (do/do not) have children.

8. Centuries ago, large families were

_____

(essential for species survival/a luxury only the wealthy could afford). Once the connection between _____ and _____ was recognized, however, the size of the average family _____ (increased/decreased).

9. Today, the average number of actual and projected births per woman, or the _____ _____ , is well below the _____ _____ (number of births required to maintain the population).

10. Declining rates of _____ and higher levels of _____ correlate with _____ development and longer _____ .

11. Japan has one of the lowest _____ rates in the world, the longest _____ _____ , and the highest percent of _____ _____ . To stimulate economic development, the nation of

_____ recently began to require couples to postpone marriage and limit family size.

12. Most emerging adults today _____ (condone/do not condone) premarital sex. Most sexually active adults have _____ (one steady partner/multiple partners) at a time. This pattern of sexual activity is called

_____ _____ .

13. Emerging adulthood is marked by a greater willingness to take _____ , including choosing _____ (activities that involve fear and managing stress). One example is the desire to participate in _____

_____ .

14. One consequence of edgework is that emerging adults take more health risks, including

_____

_____ (three behaviors). Worldwide, _____ deaths now far exceed deaths from _____ among emerging adults.

15. One consequence of sexual patterns among today's young adults is that the incidence of

_____ _____

_____ is higher today than ever before.

16. Among emerging adults, the most commonly abused drugs are _____ and _____ . Young adults _____ (overestimate/underestimate) their peer's intake of alcohol and drugs, which makes them more likely to abuse drugs. The _____ _____ approach to reducing drug abuse focuses on providing emerging adults with more accurate information regarding the prevalence of drug use among their peers.

An important theme running through the Epilogue is that development is multidirectional, multicontextual, and plastic. To ensure your understanding of how these themes manifest themselves during emerging adulthood, consider each of the following statements. For each statement, indicate which developmental theme(s) is illustrated. Note that this applies to the entire Epilogue.

17.

   a. Globally, emerging adults are having few babies but more sex. _____

   b. The freedom of edgework also means that emerging adults take more health risks.

   _____

   c. An effective method of reducing drug use among emerging adults is to make them aware that most of their peers are not excessive drug users. _____

   d. Brains adapt to new experiences.

   _____

   e. Personality is not fixed by age 20.

   _____

APPLICATIONS:

18. Summarizing her presentation on sexual attitudes among emerging adults, Carla notes that most
   a. believe that physical relationships need not involve emotional connections.
   b. condone premarital sex.
   c. no longer believe that marriage is a desirable commitment.
   d. believe the primary purpose of sex is reproduction.

19. Elderly Mr. Wilson believes that young adults today have too many sexual partners. Fueling his belief is the fact that
   a. sexually transmitted infections were almost unknown in his day.
   b. half of all emerging adults in the United States have had at least one sexually transmitted infection.
   c. most sexually active adults have several partners at a time.
   d. all of these statements are true.

20. Michael is a college freshman who enjoys weekend "booze parties." He has just learned that a survey regarding drinking on campus found that most of his classmates avoid binge drinking. Michael is most likely to
   a. continue drinking on the weekends.
   b. follow this social norm.
   c. increase his drinking to prove he's not like everyone else.
   d. become more secretive about his drinking.

Cognitive Development (pp. 513–516)

21. Because their brain's _____ systems develop before their _____ _____ matures, adolescents more often switch between _____ thinking and _____ thinking.

22. During emerging adulthood, experiences sculpt brain connections, forming new _____ , while unused _____ disappear.

23. One research study found that the largest shift in how participants described themselves occurred between _____ and _____ _____ .

24. Worldwide, the number of students who receive higher education _____ (has increased/has not increased) since the first half of the twentieth century.

25. Collegiate populations have become _____ (more/less) diverse in recent years. College majors also are changing, with fewer students concentrating on the _____ _____ and more on _____ and the _____ .

26. One cognitive impact of higher education is that students become more _____ thinkers.

27. High school graduates who go to work rather than attending college tend to achieve _____ (less/about the same/more) and are _____ (less/about the same/more) satisfied.

APPLICATIONS:

28. In concluding her presentation on "The College Student of Today," Coretta states that
    a. "The number of students in higher education has increased significantly in virtually every country worldwide."
    b. "Students today are more likely to major in the professions than in liberal arts."
    c. "There are more women in college than ever before."
    d. all of these statements are true.

Psychosocial Development (pp. 516–522)

29. During emerging adulthood, the postponement of permanent _____ and _____ choices, together with the years of _____ and _____ , provide a perfect context for _____ .

30. One of the most enduring aspects of each individual is _____ .

31. The origins of personality are _____ , _____-_____ , and _____ . Over time, personality is characterized by both _____ and _____ .

32. One example of discontinuity in personality development is the tendency toward decreased _____ and increased _____ during adulthood.

33. In Erikson's theory, the identity crisis of adolescence is followed in emerging adulthood by the crisis of _____ _____ .

34. As a buffer against stress and as a source of positive feelings, _____ are particularly important.

35. Traditionally, men's friendships have been based on _____ _____ , whereas friendships between women tended to be more _____ and _____ . Gender differences in friendship are _____ (less/more) apparent among contemporary emerging adults.

36. Cross-sex friendships are _____ (more/less) common today than in the past.

37. Worldwide, couples today marry _____ (earlier/later) than earlier cohorts did.

38. Increasingly common among young adults in many countries is the living pattern called _____ , in which two unrelated adults live together in a committed sexual relationship.

39. Cohabitation _____ (does/does not) seem to benefit the participants. Domestic violence and excessive drinking are _____ (more/less) likely to occur among young adults who cohabit. Married adults who lived together before marriage are _____ (more/less) likely to divorce.

40. Members of families have _____ lives, meaning that experiences and needs of members at one stage are affected by those at other stages. Although emerging adults strive for independence, family support in the form of _____ aid and gifts of time are important. Family dependence _____ (varies/does not vary) from nation to nation.

41. For emerging adults, self-esteem _____ (increases/decreases) over the years. Average well-being _____ (increases/decreases) in emerging adulthood, but so does the incidence of _____ .

42. According to the _____-_____ model, disorders such as schizophrenia are produced by the interaction of _____ with _____ , or an underlying genetic vulnerability.

43. Another major problem is _____ disorders, which are suffered by _____ (what proportion?) of young adults in the United States. These disorders include _____-_____ _____ _____ , _____-_____ _____ , and _____ .

44. In Japan, a new disorder called *hikikomori* is related to anxiety about the _____ and _____ pressures of high school and college.

45. Schizophrenia is experienced by about _____ percent of all adults. This disorder is partly the result of _____, and partly the result of vulnerabilities such as _____ when the brain is developing and extensive _____ pressure. Symptoms of this disorder typically begin in _____ .

STUDY TIP: According to the diathesis-stress model, psychopathology is the result of an environmental stressor interacting with an underlying biological, psychosocial, or sociocultural predisposition.

46. To help solidify your understanding of this concept, for each of the following cases, identify the psychological disorder, and a potential stressor or predisposition that may have contributed to its development.

   a. A 20-year-old Japanese student is so anxious about the pressures of college that he stays in his room almost all of the time.

   Psychological disorder _____

   _____

   Stressor or predisposition _____

   _____

   b. Eighteen-year-old Colin is overwhelmed by the same types of disorganized and bizarre thoughts his mother experienced before she was hospitalized.

   Psychological disorder _____

   _____

   Stressor or predisposition _____

   _____

   c. Returning home from the battlefield, 20-five-year-old Shaleen has recurrent nightmares and flashbacks.

   Psychological disorder _____

   _____

   Stressor or predisposition _____

   _____

APPLICATIONS:

47. I am 25 years old. It is most likely that I
   a. am married.
   b. am divorced.
   c. have never been married.
   d. am divorced and remarried.

48. If asked to explain the high failure rate of marriages between young adults, Erik Erikson would most likely say that
   a. achievement goals are often more important than intimacy in emerging adulthood.
   b. intimacy is difficult to establish until identity is formed.
   c. divorce has almost become an expected stage in development.
   d. today's cohort of young adults has higher expectations of marriage than did previous cohorts.

49. Our friendships are more intimate and emotional, and we tend to share secrets. Who are we?
   a. women
   b. men
   c. adolescents
   d. emerging adults

Progress Test 1

Multiple-Choice Questions

Circle your answers to the following questions and check them with the answers beginning on page 237. If your answer is incorrect, read the explanation for why it is incorrect and then consult the appropriate pages of the text (in parentheses following the correct answer).

1. The new stage proposed to describe development between 18 and 25 years of age is called
   a. late adolescence.
   b. young adulthood.
   c. post-puberty.
   d. emerging adulthood.

2. The majority of emerging adults rate their own health as
   a. very good or excellent.
   b. average or fair.
   c. poor.
   d. worse than it was during adolescence.

3. Diagnostic tests such as mammograms and colonoscopy are not recommended until after age
   a. 25   c. 40
   b. 30   d. 50

4. According to Erik Erikson, the first basic task of adulthood is to establish
   a. a residence apart from parents.
   b. intimacy with others.
   c. generativity through work or parenthood.
   d. a career commitment.

5. According to Erikson, the failure to achieve intimacy during emerging adulthood is most likely to result in
   a. generativity.   c. role diffusion.
   b. stagnation.   d. isolation.

6. Friendships are important for emerging adults because
   a. friendship ties are voluntary.
   b. they defend against the many stresses of this age.
   c. young adults are likely to postpone marriage.
   d. of all these reasons.

7. An arrangement in which two unrelated, unmarried adults live together in a romantic partnership is called
   a. cross-sex friendship.
   b. a passive-congenial pattern.
   c. cohabitation.
   d. affiliation.

8. Which of the following is true of brain maturation during early adulthood?
   a. The limbic system begins to mature.
   b. The prefrontal cortex, which matured during adolescence, begins to contract.
   c. New dendrites form while unused neurons disappear.
   d. The emerging adult's brain is virtually the same as it was in adolescence.

9. Whereas men's friendships tend to be based on _____ , friendships between women tend to be based on _____ .
   a. shared confidences; shared interests
   b. cooperation; competition
   c. shared interests; shared confidences
   d. finding support for personal problems; discussion of practical issues

10. Research on cohabitation suggests that
    a. there is little variation in why couples cohabit.
    b. most emerging adults in the United States, Canada, and England cohabit at some point.
    c. adults who cohabit tend to be happier and healthier than married people.
    d. cohabitation leads to a stronger marriage.

11. Compared to married adults, cohabiting adults tend
    a. to be younger.
    b. are more likely to drink excessively.
    c. are more likely to end the relationship.
    d. to do all of these things.

12. Today, male–female relationships
    a. are more common than in the past.
    b. are not usually preludes to romance.
    c. can last a lifetime.
    d. have all of these characteristics.

13. The idea that psychopathology is the consequence of the interaction of a genetic vulnerability with challenging life events is expressed in
    a. the social exchange theory.
    b. the diathesis-stress model.
    c. the social norms approach.
    d. Erikson's psychosocial theory.

14. The disorder characterized by disorganized thoughts, delusions, and hallucinations is
    a. post-traumatic stress disorder.
    b. anxiety disorder.
    c. schizophrenia.
    d. obsessive-compulsive disorder.

15. Which of the following is true of colleges today?
    a. They are larger.
    b. They are more career oriented.
    c. They have a more diverse student body.
    d. They have all of these characteristics.

True or False Items

Write T (*true*) or F (*false*) on the line in front of each statement.

_____ 1. Extreme sports such as motocross have existed since the 1950s.

_____ 2. Emerging adults have higher rates of heavy drinking than adolescents.

_____ 3. Most sexually active young adults have several sexual partners at a time.

_____ 4. According to Erikson, the adult experiences a crisis of intimacy versus isolation after achieving identity.

_____ 5. Emerging adults are more flexible in their thinking than adolescents.

_____ 6. Cross-sex friendships are rarer today than in the past.

_____ 7. Cohabitation solves all the problems that might arise after marriage.

_____ 8. Domestic violence is more common among cohabiting couples than among married couples.

_____ 9. A general trend during adulthood is to develop whatever traits are valued within an individual's culture.

_____ 10. In many nations, the replacement rate is below the fertility rate.

Progress Test 2

Progress Test 2 should be completed during a final chapter review. Answer the following questions after you thoroughly understand the correct answers for the Chapter Review and Progress Test 1.

Multiple-Choice Questions

1. The early 20s are the peak years for
   a. hard physical work.
   b. problem-free reproduction.
   c. athletic performance.
   d. all of these things.

2. Serial monogamy refers to the practice among sexually active adults of
   a. having more than one partner at a time.
   b. having one steady partner at a time.
   c. engaging in premarital sex.
   d. engaging in extramarital sex.

3. During emerging adulthood, people follow patterns of development and behavior that vary by
   a. age.
   b. culture.
   c. cohort.
   d. all of these factors.

4. Which of the following is true of gender differences in relation to higher education?
   a. More girls than boys plan on professional careers.
   b. More boys than girls attend college.
   c. More boys than girls are focusing on financial security.
   d. There are no gender differences in relation to higher education.

5. The social norms approach refers to
   a. the particular settings of an individual's various homeostatic processes.
   b. an approach to prevention that increases young adults' awareness of social norms for risky behaviors.
   c. the ratio between a person's weight and height.
   d. the average age at which certain behaviors and events occur

6. Occupations or activities that require a degree of risk or danger are referred to as
   a. senescence.
   b. edgework.
   c. homeostasis.
   d. delay discounting.

7. Which of the following is NOT true today regarding marriage?
   a. Couples are divorcing more often.
   b. Couples are marrying earlier.
   c. Cohabitation before marriage is increasingly common in many nations.
   d. In North America and Europe, more than half of those age 18 to 25 have never married.

8. Which of the following is NOT true of the sexual-reproductive system during emerging adulthood?
   a. Infertility is rare.
   b. Birth is easier.
   c. Gains in this system result primarily from cultural influences.
   d. Orgasm is frequent.

9. Emerging adulthood is distinguished by each of the following EXCEPT
   a. postponement of marriage.
   b. early parenthood.
   c. attainment of education.
   d. vocational uncertainty.

10. Which of the following characterizes physical development by age 20?
    a. the immune system has not yet reached full strength.
    b. blood pressure is often above normal.
    c. lung capacity has reached its maximum.
    d. most emerging adults develop their first cavities.

11. Which of the following most accurately describes sex and reproduction during emerging adulthood?
    a. Emerging adults are having fewer babies but more sex.
    b. Emerging adults are having fewer babies and less sex.
    c. Emerging adults have fewer babies and fewer sexual partners.
    d. Emerging adults are having more babies and more sex.

12. Which of the following is one result of serial monogamy?
    a. There has been an increase in one-parent families.
    b. STIs have spread to a larger population.
    c. Emerging adults are marrying earlier.
    d. Divorce is less likely among emerging adults.

13. "Relatavizing" refers to emerging adults' ability to
    a. set priorities.
    b. consider the perspectives of many people.
    c. combine intuition and logic.
    d. do all of these things.

14. In many nations today, the
    a. fertility rate is well below the replacement rate.
    b. replacement rate is well below the fertility rate.
    c. fertility rate is increasing dramatically.
    d. replacement rate is increasing dramatically.

15. During adulthood, personality tends to become
    a. less neurotic and more conscientious.
    b. less neurotic and less conscientious.
    c. more neurotic and more conscientious.
    d. more neurotic and less conscientious.

Matching Items

Match each definition or description with its corresponding term.

Terms

_____ 1. diathesis-stress
_____ 2. cohabitation
_____ 3. emerging adult
_____ 4. fertility rate
_____ 5. edgework
_____ 6. social norms approach
_____ 7. linked lives
_____ 8. intimacy versus isolation
_____ 9. neuroticism
_____ 10. conscientiousness
_____ 11. extreme sports

Definitions or Descriptions

a. a person between the ages of 18 and 25
b. living together without being married
c. recreation that includes apparent risk of injury or death
d. the notion that family members are affected by each other's lives
e. the sixth of Erikson's eight stages of development
f. a method of reducing risky behavior among emerging adults
g. the average number of actual and projected births per woman
h. personality trait that tends to decrease during adulthood
i. risky occupations or recreational activities
j. personality trait that tends to increase during adulthood
k. genetic vulnerability and environmental factor that combine to trigger a disorder

Key Terms

Using your own words, write a brief definition or explanation of each of the following terms on a separate piece of paper.

1. emerging adult
2. fertility rate
3. edgework
4. extreme sports
5. social norms approach
6. intimacy versus isolation
7. cohabitation
8. linked lives
9. diathesis-stress model

Answers

CHAPTER REVIEW

1. globalization; technology; medicine; emerging adulthood

Emerging adulthood is distinguished by postponement of marriage and parenthood, higher education, financial and vocational uncertainty, and a new freedom to explore possibilities.

2. developed; SES
3. 18
4. hard physical work, child-bearing, and athletic achievement; rare; rare
5. PSA; mammograms; colonoscopy
6. 20

The sexual-reproductive system is at its strongest during emerging adulthood. Young adults have a strong sex drive, fertility is greater and miscarriage is less common, orgasm is more frequent, birth is easier, and sex hormones peak in both men and women.

7. do not
8. essential for species survival; overpopulation; poverty; decreased
9. fertility rate; replacement rate
10. birth; education; economic; life
11. fertility; life expectancy; college graduates; China
12. condone; one steady partner; serial monogamy
13. risks; edgework; extreme sports
14. driving without a seat belt, carrying a loaded gun, and abusing drugs; violent; illness
15. sexually transmitted infections (STIs)
16. alcohol; tobacco; overestimate; social norms
17. a. multidirectional
    b. multidirectional
    c. multicontextual
    d. plasticity
    e. plasticity
18. b. is the answer. Although many emerging adults are either not marrying or marrying later, they do not necessarily believe marriage is wrong.
19. b. is the answer. STIs have always been known. Most emerging adults practice serial monogamy.
20. b. is the answer. The problem with heavy drinking is that most young adults overestimate the amount of drinking their friends do.
21. limbic; prefrontal cortex; intuitive; logical
22. dendrites; neurons
23. adolescence; emerging adulthood
24. has increased
25. more; liberal arts; business; professions
26. flexible
27. less; less
28. d. is the answer.

29. family; vocational; education; exploration; plasticity
30. personality
31. biological; brain-based; genetic; continuity; discontinuity
32. neuroticism; conscientiousness
33. intimacy versus isolation
34. friends
35. shared activities; intimate; emotional; less
36. more
37. later
38. cohabitation
39. does not; more; more
40. linked; economic; varies
41. increases; increases; psychopathology
42. diathesis-stress; stress; diathesis
43. anxiety; one-fourth; post-traumatic stress disorder; obsessive-compulsive disorder; panic attacks
44. social; academic
45. 1; genes; malnutrition; social; adolescence
46. a. The disorder is hikikomori and the stressor is academic pressure.
    b. The disorder is schizophrenia and the predisposition is genetic.
    c. The disorder is post-traumatic stress disorder (PTSD) and the stressor is battlefield action.
47. c. is the answer.
48. b. is the answer. In Erikson's theory of psychosocial development, the alternative to intimacy is isolation.
49. a. is the answer.

PROGRESS TEST 1

Multiple-Choice Questions

1. d. is the answer. (p. 505)
2. a. is the answer. (p. 506)
3. c. is the answer. (p. 506)
4. b. is the answer. (p. 518)
5. d. is the answer. (p. 518)
   a. Generativity is a characteristic of the crisis following the intimacy crisis.
   b. Stagnation occurs when generativity needs are not met.
   c. Erikson's theory does not address this issue.
6. d. is the answer. (p. 518)
7. c. is the answer. (p. 518)
8. c. is the answer. (p. 513)
9. c. is the answer. (p. 518)
10. b. is the answer. (p. 519)
    a. No such finding was reported in the text.

c. In fact, a large study of adults found that cohabitants were much less happy and healthy than married people.

d. In fact, couples who cohabit are more likely to divorce.

11. **d.** is the answer. (p. 519)
12. **d.** is the answer. (p. 518)
13. **b.** is the answer. (p. 522)
14. **c.** is the answer. (p. 522)
15. **d.** is the answer. (pp. 514–515)

True or False Items

1. **F** Extreme sports did not exist before two 20-year-olds invented it in the 1990s. (pp. 510–511)
2. **T** (p. 512)
3. **F** Most sexually active adults have one steady partner at a time. (p. 509)
4. **T** (p. 518)
5. **T** (p. 515)
6. **F** Just the reverse is true. (p. 518)
7. **F** Cohabitation does not solve the problems of marriage. (p. 519)
8. **T** (p. 519)
9. **T** (p. 516)
10. **F** In fact, the fertility rate is well below the replacement rate. (p. 508)

PROGRESS TEST 2

Multiple-Choice Questions

1. **d.** is the answer. (p. 506)
2. **b.** is the answer. (p. 509)
3. **d.** is the answer. (p. 513)
4. **a.** is the answer. (p. 515)
5. **b.** is the answer. (p. 513)
   c. This is the body mass index.
6. **b.** is the answer. (p. 510)
7. **b.** is the answer. In fact, couples are marrying later. (p. 518)
8. **c.** is the answer. (p. 507)
9. **b.** is the answer. A hallmark of emerging adulthood is the postponement of marriage. (p. 505)
10. **c.** is the answer. (p. 506)
11. **a.** is the answer. (p. 509)

12. **b.** is the answer. (p. 511)
13. **d.** is the answer. (p. 513)
14. **a.** is the answer. (p. 508)
15. **a.** is the answer. (p. 516)

Matching Items

1. k (p. 522)
2. b (p. 518)
3. a (p. 505)
4. g (p. 508)
5. i (p. 510)
6. f (p. 513)
7. d (p. 520)
8. e (p. 518)
9. h (p. 516)
10. j (p. 516)
11. c (p. 510)

KEY TERMS

1. An **emerging adult** is a person between the ages of 18 and 25. (p. 505)
2. The **fertility rate** is the average number of actual and projected births per woman in a population. (p. 508)
3. **Edgework** refers to recreational activities and jobs that entail some risk or danger. (p. 510)
4. **Extreme sports** are forms of recreation that include apparent risk of injury or death and that are attractive and thrilling as a result. (p. 510)
5. The **social norms approach** to reducing risky behaviors uses survey data regarding the prevalence of risky behaviors to make emerging adults more aware of social norms. (p. 513)
6. According to Erik Erikson, the first crisis of adulthood is **intimacy versus isolation,** which involves the need to share one's personal life with someone else or risk profound loneliness and isolation. (p. 518)
7. Increasingly common among young adults in all industrialized countries is the living pattern called **cohabitation,** in which two unrelated, unmarried adults live together in a committed sexual relationship. (p. 518)
8. Members of a family have **linked lives** in that the experiences and needs of one generation in a family are connected to those of another generation. (p. 520)
9. The **diathesis-stress model** is the view that psychological disorders are caused by the interaction of a genetic vulnerability with environmental factors and stressful life events. (p. 522)

Appendix B

More About Research Methods

Appendix B Overview

The first section describes two ways of gathering information about development: library research and using the Internet. The second section discusses the various ways in which developmentalists ensure that their studies are valid.

NOTE: Answer guidelines for all Appendix B questions begin on page 240.

Appendix B Review

When you have finished reading Appendix B, work through the material that follows to review it. Complete the sentences and answer the questions. As you proceed, evaluate your performance for each section by consulting the answers on page 240. Do not continue with the next section until you understand each answer. If you need to, review or reread the appropriate section in the textbook before continuing.

Make It Personal (p. B-1)

1. Before asking questions as part of a research assignment, remember that observing _____ _____ comes first.

2. Before interviewing someone, you should _____ the person of your purpose and assure him or her of _____ .

3. Research studies that may be published require that you inform the college's _____ _____ _____ .

Read the Research (pp. B-1–B-3)

4. Four journals that cover development in all three domains are _____ , _____ , _____ , and _____ .

5. The best journals are _____-_____ , which means that scientists other than an article's authors decide if it is worthy of publication.

6. A good handbook in development is _____ _____ .

7. The major advantage of using the Internet to learn about development is that _____ _____ .

8. Two disadvantages of using the Internet are
   a. _____
   b. _____

9. To help you select appropriate information, use general topic lists, called _____ , and _____ _____ , which give you all the sites that use a particular word or words.

Additional Terms and Concepts (pp. B-3–B-4)

10. To make statements about people in general, called a _____ , scientists study a group of research _____ , called a _____ .

11. When a sample is typical of the group under study—in gender, ethnic background, and other important variables—the sample is called a(n) _____ _____ .

12. Ideally, a group of research participants constitute a _____ _____ , which means that everyone in the population is equally likely to be selected. To avoid _____ _____ , some samples are _____ , and trace development of some particular characteristic in an entire cluster.

13. In a _____ study, researchers begin with a group of participants that already share a particular characteristic and then look "backward" to discover other characteristics of the group.

14. Every researcher begins by formulating a _____ .

15. When the person carrying out research is unaware of the purpose of the research, that person is said to be _____ to the hypothesized outcome.

16. Researchers use _____ _____ to define variables in terms of specific, observable behavior that can be measured precisely.

17. Journal articles that summarize past research are called _____ .

18. A study that combines the findings of many studies to present an overall conclusion is a _____ .

19. Researchers often report quantitative analyses that measure _____ _____ , which indicates whether or not a particular result could have occurred by chance.

20. The statistic that indicates how much of an impact the independent variable had on the dependent variable is _____ _____ .

Progress Test

Circle your answers to the following questions and check them with the answers on page 240. If your answer is incorrect, read the explanation for why it is incorrect and then consult the appropriate pages of the text (in parentheses following the correct answer).

1. A journal article that summarizes past research is
   a. a retrospective.
   b. *Child Development Abstracts and Bibliography*.
   c. *Developmental Psychology*.
   d. a review article.

2. Which of the following is NOT one of the journals that publish research on all three domains of development ?
   a. *The Developmentalist*
   b. *Developmental Psychology*
   c. *Human Development*
   d. *Child Development*

3. Which of the following is a disadvantage of conducing Internet research?
   a. You can spend hours sifting through information that turns out to be useless.
   b. Anybody can put anything on the Internet.
   c. There is no evaluation of bias on Internet sites.
   d. Each of these is a disadvantage of Internet research.

4. To say that the study of development is a science means that developmentalists
   a. use many methods to make their research more objective and more valid.
   b. take steps to ensure that a few extreme cases do not distort the overall statistical picture.
   c. recognize the importance of establishing operational definitions.
   d. do all of these things.

5. The entire group of people about whom a scientist wants to learn is called the
   a. reference group.
   b. sample.
   c. representative sample.
   d. population.

6. A researcher's conclusions after conducting a study are not valid because a few extreme cases distorted the results. In designing this study, the researcher evidently failed to pay attention to the importance of
   a. sample size.
   b. "blindness."
   c. representativeness.
   d. all of these factors.

7. Rachel made a study of students' opinions about different psychology professors. She took great care to survey equal numbers of male and female students, students who received high grades and students who received low grades, and members of various minorities. Clearly, Rachel wished to ensure that data were obtained from a
   a. population.
   b. "blind" sample.
   c. representative sample.
   d. comparison group.

8. A person who gathers data in a state of "blindness" is one who
   a. is unaware of the purpose of the research.
   b. is allowing his or her personal beliefs to influence the results.
   c. has failed to establish operational definitions for the variables under investigation.
   d. is basing the study on an unrepresentative sample of the population.

9. Which of the following is an example of a good operational definition of a dependent variable?
   a. walking
   b. aggression
   c. 30 minutes of daily exercise
   d. taking steps without support

10. The technique of combining the results of many studies to come to an overall conclusion is
    a. meta-analysis.
    b. effect size.
    c. a prospective study.
    d. a retrospective study.

11. For a psychologist's generalizations to be valid, the sample must be representative of the population under study. The results must also be
    a. statistically significant.
    b. derived from participants who are all the same age.
    c. large enough.
    d. none of these answers.

12. The particular individuals who are studied in a specific research project are called the
    a. independent variables.
    b. dependent variables.
    c. participants.
    d. population.

13. A research study that begins with participants who share a certain characteristic and then "looks backward" is a
    a. prospective study.
    b. retrospective study.
    c. meta-analysis.
    d. representative sample.

14 A research study that begins with participants who share a certain characteristic and then "looks forward" is a
    a. prospective study.
    b. retrospective study.
    c. meta-analysis.
    d. representative sample.

15. Summarizing the results of his research study, Professor Schulman notes that "the effect size was zero." By this she means that the:
    a. independent variable had no impact on the dependent variable.
    b. independent variable had a large impact on the dependent variable.
    c. dependent variable had no impact on the independent variable.
    d. dependent variable had a large impact on the independent variable

Key Terms

Using your own words, write a brief definition or explanation of each of the following terms on a separate piece of paper.

1. population
2. participants
3. sample
4. representative sample
5. blind
6. operational definition
7. meta-analysis
8. effect size

Answers

APPENDIX B REVIEW

1. ethical standards
2. inform; confidentiality
3. Institutional Review Board (IRB)
4. *Developmental Psychology; Child Development; Developmental Review; Human Development*
5. peer-reviewed
6. *Handbook of Child Psychology*
7. virtually everything you might want to know is on the Internet.
8. **a.** There is so much information available on the Internet that it is easy to waste time.

   b. Anybody can put anything on the Internet.
9. directories; search engines
10. population; participants; sample
11. representative sample
12. random sample, selection bias; prospective
13. retrospective
14. hypothesis
15. blind
16. operational definitions
17. reviews
18. meta-analysis
19. statistical significance
20. effect size

PROGRESS TEST

1. **d.** is the answer. (p. B-4)
2. **a.** is the answer. (p. B-1)
3. **d.** is the answer. (p. B-2)
4. **d.** is the answer. (pp. B-3–B-4)
5. **d.** is the answer. (p. B-3)
6. **a.** is the answer. (p. B-3)

   b. "Blindness" has no relevance here.

   c. Although it is true that a distorted sample is unrepresentative, the issue concerns the small number of extreme cases—a dead giveaway to sample size.
7. **c.** is the answer. Rachel has gone to great lengths to make sure that her student sample is typical of the entire population of students who takes psychology courses. (p. B-3)
8. **a.** is the answer. (p. B-4)
9. **d.** is the answer. (p. B-4)

a., b., & c. Each of these definitions is too ambiguous to qualify as an operational definition.

10. **a.** is the answer. (p. B-4)
11. **a.** is the answer. (p. B-4)
12. **c.** is the answer. (p. B-3)

    a. These are the factors that a researcher manipulates in an experiment.

    b. These are the outcomes that a researcher measures in an experiment.

    d. It is almost always impossible to include every member of a population in an experiment.
13. **b.** is the answer. (p. B-4)
14. **a.** is the answer. (p. B-4)
15. **a.** is the answer. (p. B-4)

    b. In this case, the effect size would be a number close to 1.0.

    c. & d. Independent variables impact dependent variables, and not vice versa.

KEY TERMS

1. The **population** is the entire group of individuals who are of particular concern in a scientific study. (p. B-3)
2. **Participants** are the people who are studied in a research project. (p. B-3)
3. A **sample** is a subset of individuals who are drawn from a specific population. (p. B-3)
4. A **representative sample** is a group of research subjects who accurately reflect key characteristics of the population being studied. (p. B-3)
5. **Blind** is the situation in which data gatherers and sometimes their research participants are deliberately kept unaware of the purpose of the study in order to avoid unintentionally biasing the results. (p. B-4)
6. An **operational definition** is a precise description of a behavior or variable being studied so that another person will know whether it occurred, and how it is measured. (p. B-4)
7. **Meta-analysis** is a research technique in which the results of many studies are combined to produce one overall result (p. B-4)
8. **Effect size** is a statistical measure of how much impact an independent variable had on a dependent variable in a research study. (p. B-4)